1st   1990

925 — SCTB8/7

31098

Pittsburgh Ser

JAMES DICKEY

James Dickey

A DESCRIPTIVE BIBLIOGRAPHY

Matthew J. Bruccoli and
Judith S. Baughman

UNIVERSITY OF
PITTSBURGH PRESS
1990

Published by the University of Pittsburgh Press, Pittsburgh, Pa., 15260
Copyright © 1990, University of Pittsburgh Press
All rights reserved
Baker & Taylor International, London
Manufactured in the United States of America

Library of Congress Cataloging in Publication Data

Bruccoli, Matthew Joseph, 1931–
   James Dickey : a descriptive bibliography / Matthew J. Bruccoli
   and Judith S. Baughman.
      p.   cm.—(Pittsburgh series in bibliography)
    ISBN 0-8229-3629-1
    1. Dickey, James—Bibliography.   I. Baughman, Judith.   II. Title.
III. Series.
Z8230.2.B78   1990
[PS3554.I32]
016.811′54—dc20   89-16585
                                                            CIP

For Deborah
and
for Ron and Elizabeth

Contents

Foreword

WHEN YOU LOOK at all those names—names attached to poems, books of poems, novels, essays in literary criticism, other sorts of essays, screenplays, correspondence, addresses, convocations, reviews, translations, experimental writings (mostly unsuccessful), and other and more unclassifiable bits and pieces composed of words—you are at first bemused at the patience and perhaps doggedness, not to say what may even pass for devotion, of the scholars who have put together such a list. And then the shock-wave hits you, carrying first astonishment and then terror, dread and resignation, for there is, of all these names, only one: one inescapable name, and it is your own. This is due process; no mistake. When you glance back over some of the items, and even read them, you find first that some of them are hostile witnesses. And as you read further you discover that all of them are. Kafka is pointing his finger: "*You* did it. Whether you know it or not, whether you remember it, forgot it, dreamed it, fantasized it, loved it, hated it or disowned it, you did it!"

Yet . . . yet . . . ? Categories? Surely it would be instructive to have a look.

Yes, we have them. First there is poetry. There are many poems in magazines, lots of dead periodicals—as they say—and some alive and much changed. And the poems? Have *they* changed? What did that younger fellow write? Dreadful stuff, mostly: derivative and would-be, trying-for-it third-rate period-style stuff. And all based on the wrong models! How in the world could George Barker be important, be influential on anyone except the untalented and anxious-to-be-flashy? Right! You admit that you were one of those, and there are items in the great List—the Bibliography—to prove it. Too bad, but you go on; you *did* go on. After the bad beginnings, what? Something is beginning to struggle free of "I tear my guts out on the platform or rummage in my stomach with bloody hands." Barker fades, and something *other* appears in thin gleams of words, an image here and there. "The blue-eyed floating of the soul" comes out of nowhere; and this, too, is documented. And you become more and more aware of the others—other than George Barker, who was after all the beginning-place, and so a true ancestor. Was it not Hölderlin who said, "Was bleibet aber, stiften die Dichter"? You, yourself, had begun, though lamely and haltingly, to name the gods, and you had begun to know where they were, and what their names would have to be—no; what they *might* be, or what they might adapt to being, because of you. "The poet speaks the essential word," or so says Heidegger. So? How can one be sure? Something on the inside, you say, and go on. The something becomes larger, more daring, and more problematical. "I want, I want," says Saul Bellow's Gene Henderson, and his voice, his need, is the poet's. And that, too, is part of the retrospective, the canon, the unknown master plan, the black-magic Bibliography. Little did those faithful scholars know!

Novels? At first a spin-off from the poetry, and then that and something else. With characters and the telling of a story over an extended length, new elements come in, and new possibilities. You feel a back-connection with the caves, and maybe even with the trees, where ancestors hung shivering above the cave-bear's fumbling at the trunk that sustained them as they waited, were waiting for the next episode, the "what happened then."

With luck—or with unluck—movies follow from the novels, and you read through what you did when this particular millennium descended on your stories. The writer—reduced to ashes but still with a live coal or two—got onto the screen in some manner, and can still watch the results without turning away. Greatness of spectacle? Tragedy? Well, no. But a moment or two, perhaps, that but for you would not have existed. At least not in the publicly visualizing world. This, too, is on record; is in *these* records.

Essays, literary and other? Contrary to public opinion, you believe that the essay is a great form of writing, and since the review is a form of essay, attention should be paid to your connection with the great in attempting it. You conclude that mostly you have paid such attention, and though some of your judgments are astonishingly wrong, it is your own fault, and not the fault of the great. You were just not great enough. And that's the truth, too. All down here in black and white. And by name, too, as the impresario Carl Denham says in *King Kong,* "right here on this little map."

Of translations, what? Not many. The foreign language-sense is not good, and there has never been time to learn. But you can truly say that you have experienced the real language-exhilaration, and that when a poet does this, when he learns a new word, encounters another poet in *his* element, his language that can be learned, at least learned-*at*, new things in the second poet take place. You have tried for some of these, and take great joy and comfort in realizing that the opportunities are still endless, the personal possibilities infinite. There are many languages, many poets, much refueling of the imagination from as yet unknown resources, the "forms of things unknown."

But there is not time, any longer. The black type, the work of the scholars, rests on the page, and will rest. The name is the same, and will rest, too. Does the writing, does the *name*, add up to anything? Maybe. Though the same name, it will vary with time, and with the people (things unknown) who encounter it. The prosecution rests, as does the defense.

James Dickey

Acknowledgments

ALL GOOD BIBLIOGRAPHIES are collaborations. We are indebted to the following: Craig Anderson, Strand Book Store; Shaye Areheart, Doubleday; Susanna Stratmann Bäckman; Priscilla Barlow and Thomas Rosenthal, André Deutsch; Ronald Baughman, University of South Carolina; Edward N. Beachum, the Darlington School; Karen Buxton, University of Idaho; Suzanne Campbell, State Library of Tasmania; Richard W. Carlson, Voice of America; Paul Carlton; R. V. Cassill, Brown University; Jo Chanaud, Georgia Institute of Technology Library; Elaine Cheng, Marshall University Library; Paul Christensen, Texas A&M University; William Cohen and Alice C. Fountain, United States Information Agency; Robert C. Covel, *James Dickey Newsletter;* Jeanne R. Creighton, Litton Industries; Deborah Dickey; Jim Elledge, *Poetry;* Sara Evans and Hilary Hale, Macmillan—London; Sheila Fitzgibbon, *Medical Economics;* Julie Freeman and Marcia Modugno, Harcourt Brace Jovanovich; John Graham, University of Virginia; Donald J. Greiner, University of South Carolina; Samuel Hazo, International Poetry Forum; Josie Hilliger, Australian Consolidated Press; James W. Hipp; Ida Holland, Washington University Libraries; Peter Howard, Serendipity Books; Susan Jaranowski, *Friends;* Dean Keller, Kent State University Library; Judy Kelly, University of Georgia Libraries; Walter Kent, Southern Illinois University Press; Margaret Klumpp and Daria Papalia, Wesleyan University Press; James G. Lesniak, Gale Research Company; John Logue and Tom Angelillo, Oxmoor House; Carla Long, University of Arizona Library; Stephanie Lovett, Lovett & Lovett; David W. McCullough, Book-of-the-Month Club; Kathleen McNulty, Oradell, N.J., Public Library; Margaret M. Mills, American Academy and Institute of Arts and Letters; John Monk, *Charlotte Observer;* Linda H. Poe, Tulane University Library; Teresa Price; Theron Raines, Raines & Raines; Paul B. Ranslow, Pitzer College; G. E. Rayner, University of Tasmania Library; Anthony Rota, Bertram Rota Ltd.; Julie Sheppard, National Library of Australia; Christopher Sinclair-Stevenson, Hamish Hamilton; William W. Starr, *The*

State, Columbia, S.C.; R. F. Stewart; Roger Stoddard, Houghton Library, Harvard University; Saundra Taylor, Lilly Library; Sam Tindall, Duquesne University; A. Gordon Van Ness III; Jim Varn; Bruce Weigl, Pennsylvania State University; Richard L. Wentworth, University of Illinois Press; and Alissa Wiener, Minnesota Historical Society.

The Library of Congress, the United States Copyright Office, and the British Library are always good places to work. The following staff of the Library of Congress were particularly helpful: William J. Matheson, Dana J. Pratt, Robert R. Shields, and Peter VanWingen.

The libraries and librarians at the University of South Carolina were essential. We thank Allen H. Stokes, Laura Costello, Henry Fulmer, Herb Hartsook, Thelma Hayes, James Hills, and Eleanor Richardson, South Caroliniana Library; Dennis Isbell, Marcia Martin, Roger Mortimer, and Carol Tobin, Thomas Cooper Library. Our greatest obligation is to the long-suffering Interlibrary Loan staff at the Cooper Library: Daniel Boice, Yvonne Andrews, and Cathie Gottlieb.

The University of South Carolina makes it possible for us to get our work done; and we are extremely grateful to Professor Joel Myerson, Chairman of the Department of English, for his support.

Joseph M. Bruccoli did the photographic work.

The working draft was vetted by William Cagle, Charles Mann, and Joel Myerson. We are grateful to Jane Flanders of the University of Pittsburgh Press for giving the setting copy its final editing. Frederick A. Hetzel, Director of the Press, has made this series possible.

Introduction

A DESCRIPTIVE BIBLIOGRAPHY serves many parishioners: collectors, dealers, librarians, bibliographers, editors, literary historians, and biographers. These categories overlap, but certain kinds of information will be required only by some users. Collectors, dealers, and librarians will be mainly interested in identifying the first printings of books and their states or issues. The traditional list for First Book Appearances—Section B here—is of primary utility to collectors and dealers. Bibliographers and editors will be interested in the transmission of the texts. Other scholars will make use of the evidence bearing on the development of the author's career and reputation.

The chief purpose of a primary bibliography is to establish the author's canon: to identify the first appearance in print of everything he wrote. Since printed texts may be revised, corrected, or inadvertently corrupted in subsequent editions, a descriptive bibliography should establish the pedigree of the editions.

The full description of a book must enable the user to determine whether the copy he is examining is identical to the copy described in the bibliography. But description for the sake of description is harmless drudgery. Accordingly, this volume adheres to the degressive principle: the quantity of information provided for reprintings and later editions is sufficient for their identification.

FORMAT

Section A lists chronologically all separately published books and pamphlets wholly or substantially by James Dickey—including all editions published in Britain—as well as posters or broadsides of *previously unpublished* material by Dickey.

At the end of this section there is an AA supplement for broadsides, posters, and keepsakes (privately printed items not intended for sale) that *do not print previously unpublished material* by Dickey; AA also includes publishers' promotional items with material by Dickey.

The numbering system for *Section A* indicates the edition and printing for each entry. Thus A 2.1.a indicates that *Drowning With Others* is the second separately published work by Dickey (A 2) and that the entry is for the first edition (1) and first printing (a). Issues are designated by subscript numbers : A $3.1.a_2$ is the second issue (English issue) of the first printing of the first edition of *Helmets*.

Section B lists chronologically all titles in which material by Dickey first appears in a book or pamphlet written or edited by someone else—whether or not the item previously appeared in a magazine or newspaper. (There can be only one first book appearance for an item.) Previously unpublished items are identified.

Section C lists chronologically the first publication in journals or newspapers of material by Dickey. Blurbs by Dickey have been omitted.

Section D lists chronologically interviews with Dickey and articles containing previously unpublished statements by him.

Section E describes later collections of Dickey's previously collected poems.

Appendix 1: Compilers' notes.

Appendix 2: Major works about Dickey.

TERMS AND METHODS

Edition: All the copies of a book printed from a single setting of type—including all reprintings from standing type, from plates, or by offset. (The term *first edition* as carelessly applied actually refers to the first printing of the first edition.)

Printing: All the copies of a book printed at one time (during a single press run) without removing the type or plates from the press. Printings occur only within editions. (*Impression* is the same as *printing,* but *printing* is used here for consistency.)

Issue: Issues are created by an alteration in the sheets of *some copies* within a particular printing—*affecting the conditions of publication or sale* (usually a title-page change). There cannot be a first issue without a second issue; but simultaneous issues are possible. See the trade and limited issues of *Night Hurdling* (A 43). The increasingly common "join-in" or "run-on" procedure whereby a British publisher agrees to take part of an American publisher's printing with altered title page and copyright page creates issues of that printing. See *Helmets* (A 3.1.a$_2$) and *Poems 1957–1967* (A 9.1.a$_2$).

State: States are created by an alteration in the sheets of *some copies* within a particular printing (usually a stop-press correction or cancellation of leaves).[1] There cannot be a first state without a second state. No states have been identified in Dickey's books.

The terms *issue* and *state* apply only to the sheets of the volume within a single printing. Binding and dust-jacket variants have no bearing on these terms. Such variants are described in this bibliography; but no attempt has been made to classify them as issues or states. They are treated as binding or jacket variants. However, it is not possible to be so inflexible for nineteenth-century publishing practice when parts of a single printing were simultaneously marketed in different formats with different series titles. In such cases, it is tempting to regard the different bindings as creating issues because they represent deliberate attempts to alter the circumstances of sale or distribution. In recent years the simultaneous publication of unaltered sheets from a single press run as clothbound books and as "quality" or trade paperbacks creates a nomenclature problem: see the *Deliverance* screenplay (A 37). Because only the binding is affected, these copies have been treated here as binding variants—not as issues.

Much bibliographical confusion has resulted from the ignorant, inconsistent, and promiscuous misuse of *edition, printing, issue,* and *state.* Accordingly, these terms have been applied conservatively in this volume. It may be that new terms are necessitated by developments in modern printing; but it is reckless to promulgate new terms until the standard ones have been mastered.

Dust jackets for Section A first editions have been described in detail because they were part of the original publication effort. There is, of course, no certainty that a jacket now on a copy was originally on it; collectors and dealers frequently improve copies by transferring dust jackets.

Signature collations indicate how the book is gathered and sewn. Thus the formula $[1-20]^8$ means that the book consists of twenty

---

1. The general rule that *issues* result from postpublication alterations and that *states* result from prepublication alterations must be applied with caution. It is often impossible to determine whether an alteration was made before or after initial distribution of copies.

unsigned gatherings of eight leaves or sixteen pages each; brackets signify unsigned gatherings. [A]^6 B–I^8 means that the first unsigned gathering of six leaves is followed by eight signed gatherings of eight leaves each.[2]

The term *perfect binding* refers to books in which the gatherings are not sewn, but the leaves are held together with adhesive or glue—that is, most paperbacks. *Notch binding* (also known as *book-lock binding*) refers to the process whereby the backs of the gatherings are perforated or cross-hatched and then glue is forced into the notches; these books are not sewn.

The pagination formula indicates unnumbered pages by brackets. Thus [i–viii] [1–2] 3–168 [169–170] 171–312 means that the first eight pages are unnumbered and have been designated i–viii; the next two pages are also unnumbered but are 1 and 2 because they precede the page numbered 3; the pages are numbered through 168; two unnumbered pages follow page 168; pages 171–312 are so numbered.

The transcriptions of type record large capitals, small capitals, and lower-case letters; but no attempt is made to indicate point size or type face—other than italic, roman, or script. The type is roman unless otherwise specified. Line endings are indicated by vertical lines. Since any quasi-facsimile transcription is imprecise, all important title pages and copyright pages have been reproduced.

For binding-cloth designations we have used the method proposed by G. Thomas Tanselle;[3] most of these cloth grains are illustrated in *The Bibliography of American Literature,* ed. Jacob Blanck and Michael Winship (New Haven, Conn.: Yale University Press, 1955–). All editions and printings are clothbound unless otherwise described.

In the transcriptions of title pages, bindings, and dust jackets, the color of the lettering is always black unless otherwise stipulated. A color holds for subsequent lines unless a change is specified.

---

2. A note for neophytes: A signed gathering is one in which a digit or letter (the signature) is printed at the bottom of the first page of the first leaf. To check signature collations in sewn books, look for the threads that appear in the middle of each gathering. In a normal gathering there must be the same number of leaves before and after the threads. For formula problems created by canceled or inserted leaves, see Fredson Bowers, *Principles of Bibliographical Description* (Princeton, N.J.: Princeton University Press, 1949), and M. J. Pearce, *A Workbook of Analytical & Descriptive Bibliography* (Hamden, Conn.: Archon Books, 1970).

3. "The Specifications of Binding Cloth," *The Library*, 21 (September 1966), 246–247.

The spines of bindings and dust jackets are printed horizontally unless otherwise stipulated.

Since there is no case in which paper thickness differentiates concealed printings of Dickey's books, these measurements have not been included.

The number of lines per page has not been stipulated in books of verse with irregular lineation.

Dates provided in brackets do not appear on the title pages. Usually—but not invariably—they are taken from the copyright pages.

The locations rubric does not cite every copy examined.[4] After the first printings in Section A, only books of particular significance or extreme scarcity are located. The deposit-stamp dates are supplied for copies at the Library of Congress and the British Library. Locations are provided in the National Union Catalog symbols—with these exceptions:

BL:	British Library, London
Caroliniana:	South Caroliniana Library, University of South Carolina
JD:	James Dickey Deposit, South Caroliniana Library
JRB:	Collection of Judith and Ronald Baughman
LC:	Library of Congress
Lilly:	Lilly Library, Indiana University
MJB:	Collection of Matthew J. Bruccoli

For paperbacks, the serial number provided is that on the first printing. Publishers normally change these numbers in subsequent printings.

Freak copies—such as books with gatherings out of order—are without bibliographical significance and have been ignored.

It is desirable to ban end-of-line hyphens in bibliographical transcriptions; but it is not always feasible to meet this requirement. End-of-line hyphens have been avoided whenever possible and always when a hyphen would create ambiguity.

The policy for cross-referencing has been conservative because this bibliography has a full index. Cross-references are provided when titles are changed or when supplementary information about a work is contained in another section. In Section A, titles that previously appeared

---

4. The Lilly Library and Pennsylvania State University Library locations have been provided by William Cagle and Charles Mann.

in B entries are identified; in Sections C and D, the republication of individual items in Section A collections is noted.

A bibliography is outdated the day it is published. Addenda and corrigenda are earnestly solicited.

M.J.B.
J.S.B.
The University of South Carolina
21 August 1988

A. Separate Publications

All books, pamphlets, and broadsides wholly or substantially by Dickey—including all printings of all editions in English, arranged chronologically. Broadsides, posters, and keepsakes that do *not* print previously unpublished material by Dickey are listed in the AA Supplement.

A 1.1

First edition, only printing (1960)

POETS OF TODAY
VII

JAMES DICKEY
Into the Stone and Other Poems

PARIS LEARY
Views of the Oxford Colleges and Other Poems

JON SWAN
Journeys and Return: Poems

INTRODUCTORY ESSAY: SOME THOUGHTS
ON POETRY
BY JOHN HALL WHEELOCK

New York

CHARLES SCRIBNER'S SONS

A 1.1: 5¹⁵⁄₁₆″ × 8¼″

[1–12] 13–32 [33–36] 37–51 [52–54] 55–64 [65–66] 67–78 [79–80] 81–92 [93–96] 97–109 [110–112] 113–134 [135–136] 137–160 [161–164] 165–172 [173–174] 175–178 [179–180] 181–189 [190–192] 193–206 [207–208]

[1–5]^{16} [6]^{8} [7]^{16}

Contents: p. 1: half title; p. 2: series list; p. 3: title; p. 4: copyright; p. 5: acknowledgments; p. 6: blank; pp. 7–10: contents; p. 11: section title; p. 12: blank; pp. 13–32: "Some Thoughts on Poetry" by John Hall Wheelock; p. 33: 'INTO THE STONE | AND | OTHER POEMS | By JAMES DICKEY | Copyright © 1960 James Dickey'; p. 34: 'For my wife'; p. 35: 'FAMILY'; p. 36: blank; pp. 37–92: Dickey text; pp. 93–206: Leary and Swan text; pp. 207–208: blank.

24 Dickey poems: *Family:* "Sleeping Out at Easter," "The Signs," "The Call," "The Underground Stream," "The String," "The Game," "The Vegetable King"; *War:* "The Enclosure," "The Jewel," "The Performance," "The Wedding," "Mindoro, 1944"; *Death, and Others:* "Uncle," "Poem," "The Sprinter's Sleep," "The Other," "Trees and Cattle," "Walking on Water"; *Love:* "Awaiting the Swimmer," "Orpheus Before Hades," "On the Hill Below the Lighthouse," "Near Darien," "Into the Stone," "The Landfall." All previously published.

Typography and paper: 5⅞" (6⅞"). No running heads. Wove paper.

Binding: Black V cloth (smooth). Front: '[light green 9-pointed decoration] [gold, vertically up] POETS OF TODAY [gold, horizontally] DICKEY LEARY SWAN'. Spine: '[gold] POETS | [light green quadrangle] [gold] OF | TODAY | [light green] VII | [gold, vertically] DICKEY LEARY SWAN | [gold, horizontally] Scribners'. White endpapers. All edges trimmed. Top edge stained gray. Gold and light green headbands and footbands.

Dust jacket: Front and spine lettered on black, red, white, and green panels. Front: '[white] Poets of Today | VII | Presenting | [black] JAMES DICKEY: Into the Stone and Other Poems | PARIS LEARY: Views of the Oxford Colleges and Other Poems | JON SWAN: Journeys and Return: Poems | Selected and Edited, with an Introductory Essay: | "Some Thoughts on Poetry," by JOHN HALL WHEELOCK | [vertically, white] *Ronald Clyne*'. Spine: '[vertically, white] Poets of Today [black] VII | [horizontally] DICKEY | LEARY | SWAN | [vertically] Scribners'. Back lists volumes in series. Front flap has series description. Back flap has biographical notes on Dickey, Leary, and Swan.

Publication: Unknown number of copies. Published 23 August 1960. $3.95. Copyright #A497961.

Production: Vail-Ballou Press, Binghamton, N.Y.

Locations: Lilly (dj); MJB (dj); ScU (dj).

Poets of Today
VII

Presenting

Poets of Today VII

Poets of Today

Presenting

DICKEY   JAMES DICKEY: Into the Stone and Other Poems

LEARY   PARIS LEARY: Views of the Oxford Colleges and Other Poems

SWAN   JON SWAN: Journeys and Return: Poems

Selected and Edited, with an Introductory Essay:
"Some Thoughts On Poetry," by JOHN HALL WHEELOCK

Scribners

Poets of Today VII

Presenting

Into the Stone and Other Poems
by JAMES DICKEY

Views of the Oxford Colleges and Other Poems
by PARIS LEARY

Journeys and Return: Poems   by JON SWAN

SELECTED AND EDITED WITH
An Introductory Essay "Some Thoughts On Poetry"
by JOHN HALL WHEELOCK

CHARLES SCRIBNER'S SONS present

Poets of Today I
HARRY DUNCAN   Poems and Translations
MURRAY HOSS   Samuel and Sappase Poems
MAY SWENSON   Another Animal: Poems

Poets of Today II
NORMA FARBER   The Hatch: Poems
ROBERT PACK   The Irony of Joy: Poems
LOUIS SIMPSON   Good News of Death and Other Poems

Poets of Today III
LEE ANDERSON   The Floating World and Other Poems
SPENCER BROWN   My Father's Business and Other Poems
JOSEPH LANGLAND   The Green Town: Poems

Poets of Today IV
GEORGE GARRETT   The Reverend Ghost and Other Poems
THEODORE HOLMES   The Harvest and the Scythe: Poems
ROBERT WALLACE   This Various World and Other Poems

Poets of Today V
O. B. HARDISON, JR.   Lyrics and Elegies
KENNETH PITCHFORD   The Blizzard Ape: Poems
SHELLY PRITCHARD   In Reinventor Evening: Poems

Poets of Today VI
GENE BARO   Northwind and Other Poems
DONALD FINKEL   This Clothing's New Emperor and Other Poems
WALTER STONE   Poems, 1952—1958

Poets of Today VII
JAMES DICKEY   Into the Stone and Other Poems
PARIS LEARY   Views of the Oxford Colleges and Other Poems
JON SWAN   Journeys and Return: Poems

JAMES DICKEY

PARIS LEARY

JON SWAN

Dust jacket for A 1.1

A 2 DROWNING WITH OTHERS

A 2.1.a

First edition, first printing (1962)

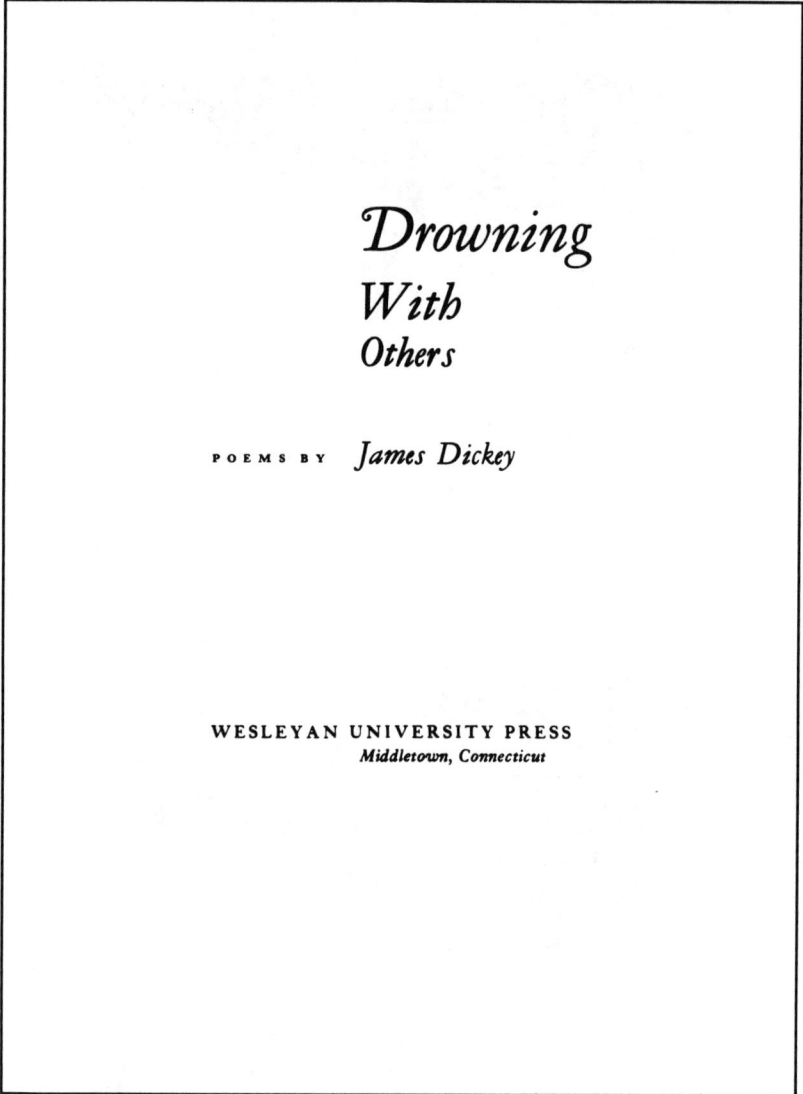

Drowning
With
Others

POEMS BY   *James Dickey*

WESLEYAN UNIVERSITY PRESS
Middletown, Connecticut

A 2.1.a: 5^{15}⁄$_{16}$″ × 7^{15}⁄$_{16}$″

[1–10] 11–40 [41–42] 43–54 [55–56] 57–76 [77–78] 79–96

[1–6]^8

Contents: p. 1: half title; p. 2: blank; p. 3: title; p. 4: copyright and acknowledgments; p. 5: '*To Maxine, Christopher, and Kevin*'; pp. 6–7: contents; p. 8: blank; p. 9: '*Section I*'; p. 10: blank; pp. 11–96: text.

36 poems: "The Lifeguard," "Listening to Foxhounds," "A Dog Sleeping on My Feet," "The Movement of Fish," "The Heaven of Animals," "A Birth," "Fog Envelops the Animals," "The Summons," "In the Tree House at Night," "For the Nightly Ascent of the Hunter Orion over a Forest Clearing," "The Rib,"* "The Owl King" ("The Call," "The Owl King," "The Blind Child's Story"), "Between Two Prisoners," "Armor," "In the Lupanar at Pompeii," "Drowning With Others," "A View of Fujiyama After the War," "The Island," "Dover: Believing in Kings," "To His Children in Darkness,"* "A Screened Porch in the Country,"* "The Dream Flood,"* "The Scratch," "Hunting Civil War Relics at Nimblewill Creek," "The Twin Falls," "The Hospital Window," "The Magus," "Antipolis," "The Change," "Autumn," "Snow on a Southern State,"* "To Landrum Guy, Beginning to Write at Sixty," "Facing Africa," "Inside the River," "The Salt Marsh," "In the Mountain Tent." Asterisks indicate previously unpublished poems.

Drowning With Others was republished in *The Early Motion* (see E 3).

Publication of "Between Two Prisoners" and "Listening to Foxhounds" in *Best Poems of 1960* (Palo Alto, Calif.: Pacific Books, 1962) was subsequent to *Drowning With Others;* publication of "The Lifeguard" and "The Summons" in *Best Poems of 1961* (Palo Alto, Calif.: Pacific Books, 1962) was subsequent to *Drowning With Others.*

Typography and paper: 5^{15}/₁₆″ (6⅜″). 39 lines per page. No running heads. Wove paper; watermarked 'WARREN'S | OLDE STYLE'.

poems by JAMES DICKEY

drowning with others

James Dickey DROWNING WITH OTHERS   Wesleyan

$3.50

JAMES DICKEY
speaks of his work as follows:

"Since my subject matter is inevitably my own life, my own obsessions, possessions and renunciation, I stay fairly close to a few subjects. I want to go in and into these subjects as far as I can, rather than skirting or skimming them. My principal aim is to take myself and my reader beyond the point where the writing is thought of as literature to where it will become a part of experience.

"This, I suppose, is what all writers tend to attempt, and my only difference from others is in my consciousness of the fact and in the means I employ. My feeling is that in every individual the imaginative faculty is completely unique, and that each person is unmatchable and priceless. This irreplaceable value of personal and inimitable response is the quality I am most interested in preserving in my own work, and that which I look for in the work of others. In these poems I have tried to come into that place in myself which is mine."

DROWNING WITH OTHERS

JAMES DICKEY

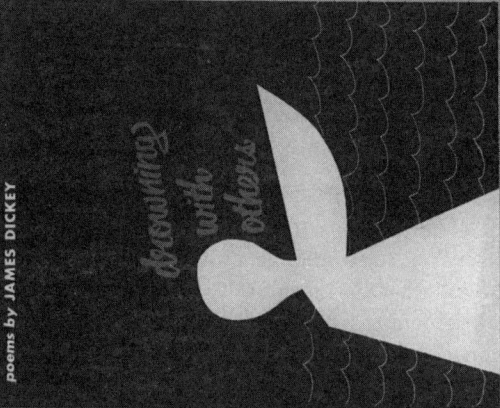

THE world of James Dickey is founded in great and basic realities—the human ties of family and history, the world of nonhuman nature, the inhuman world of war. He sees these things, and their surfaces, as still new and close. But so that general view he adds the special quality of dream, of a constant play back and forth between what is easily evident and the half-glimpsed revelation that lies masked beneath it. Whether it is a bound running fence at night, or the horizon of Pompeii fixed in crude paint on the walls of their chambers, or the memory of dead kings brooding over the cliffs of Dover, all that he sees is given a fresh interpretation and a special meaning that say at once deeply private and broadly universal. To read Mr. Dickey's poems is a rewarding experience indeed.

James Dickey, poet, advertising man, sportsman, and soldier, is a native of Atlanta, which is still his official home. He is a veteran of Air Force service in both World War II and the Korean struggle, with nearly a hundred combat missions and three military decorations. Educated at Clemson and at Vanderbilt, he has taught at Rice Institute and at the University of Florida. Following a year in France under a fellowship from the Sewanee Review, he spent nearly six years with advertising agencies in New York and Atlanta. He quit this field in the autumn of 1961 to enter on a year's work abroad under a Guggenheim Fellowship. Mr. Dickey's poems have appeared regularly in many leading magazines. His first book, *Into the Stone*, was published in 1960.

WESLEYAN UNIVERSITY PRESS
Middletown, Connecticut

POETRY from Wesleyan University Press

"The most exciting poetry list in current American publishing."—*Sewanee Review*

Alan Ansen: DISORDERLY HOUSES

John Ashbery: THE TENNIS COURT OATH

Robert Bagg: MADONNA OF THE CELLO

Donald Davie: NEW AND SELECTED POEMS

David Ferry: ON THE WAY TO THE ISLAND

Robert Francis: THE ORB WEAVER

Barbara Howes: LIGHT AND DARK

David Ignatow: SAY PARDON

Donald Justice: THE SUMMER ANNIVERSARIES

Vassar Miller: WAGE WAR ON SILENCE

Hyam Plutzik: APPLES FROM SHINAR

Louis Simpson: A DREAM OF GOVERNORS

James Wright: SAINT JUDAS

Each $3.50 cloth, $1.25 paper
WESLEYAN UNIVERSITY PRESS
Middletown, Connecticut

Dust jacket for A 2.1.a

Binding: Cloth: Medium gray V cloth (smooth). Spine stamped vertically: '[black] JAMES DICKEY [purplish blue] DROWNING WITH OTHERS [horizontal black seal]'. White endpapers. All edges trimmed. Dark gray and white headbands and footbands.

Dust jacket: Front lettered against blue: '[white] *poems by* JAMES DICKEY | [red script] drowning | with | others | [white figure against waves]'. Back has description of book and note on Dickey. Spine lettered vertically on white: '[black] James Dickey [blue] DROWNING WITH OTHERS [red] Wesleyan'. Front flap has statement by Dickey. Back flap lists 13 poetry volumes published by Wesleyan University Press.

Wrappers: Front, back, and spine same as dust jacket; price added to back.

Publication: 500 clothbound and 1,750 wrappers. Published simultaneously 15 February 1962. Cloth: $3.50; wrappers: $1.25. Copyright #A569271.

Production: Plimpton Press, Norwood, Mass.; Halliday Lithograph, West Hanover, Mass.

Locations: JRB (cloth—dj); LC (MAR 28 1962—cloth); Lilly (cloth—dj); MJB (cloth—dj); MJB (wrappers); ScU (cloth—dj); ScU (wrappers).

A 2.1.b

Second printing: Middletown, Conn.: Wesleyan University Press, [1963].

Copyright page: '*First printing, February, 1962; second printing, November, 1963.*' Noted in cloth. $3.50.

A 2.1.c

Third printing: Middletown, Conn.: Wesleyan University Press, [1965].

Copyright page: ' . . . *third printing, November, 1965.*' Wrappers. 1,000 copies. $1.85.

A 2.1.d

Fourth printing: Middletown, Conn.: Wesleyan University Press, [1966].

500 cloth and 1,500 wrappers. October 1966. Not seen.

A. 2.1.e

Fifth printing: Middletown, Conn.: Wesleyan University Press, [1967].

Copyright page: ' . . . *fifth printing December 1967*'. 1,000 cloth (not seen) and 3,000 wrappers ($2.00).

A 2.1.f

Sixth printing: Middletown, Conn.: Wesleyan University Press, [1972].

Copyright page: '. . . sixth printing March 1972'. Wrappers. 1,500 copies. $2.45.

A3 HELMETS

A3.1.a$_1$

First edition, first printing, American issue (1964)

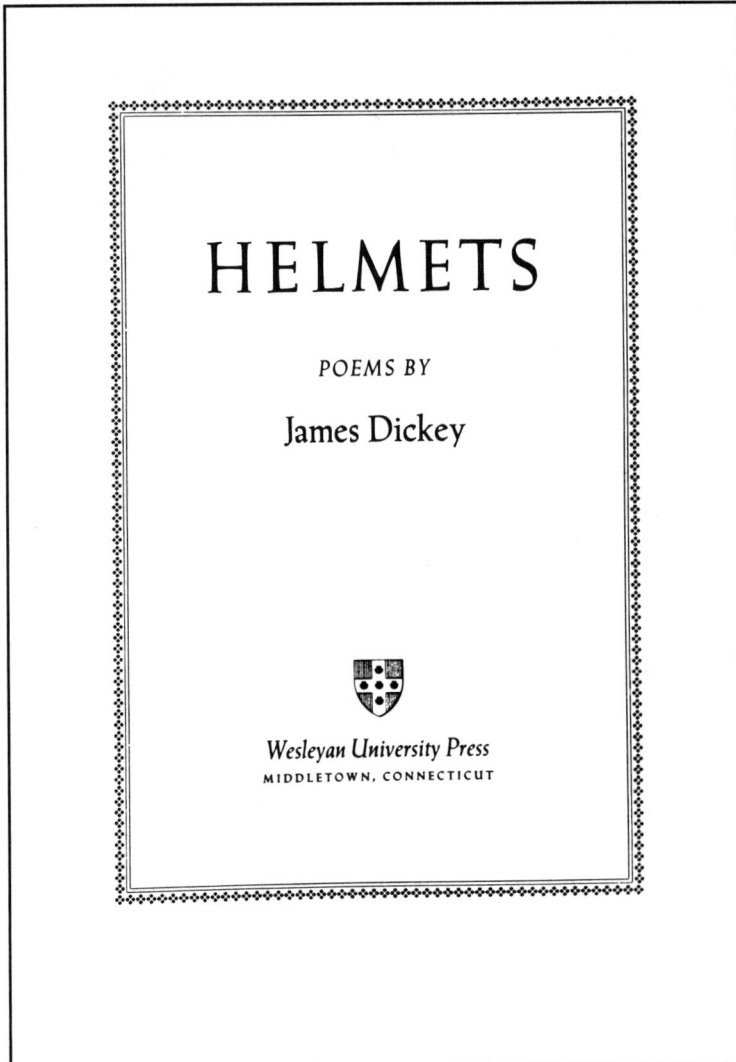

HELMETS

POEMS BY

James Dickey

Wesleyan University Press
MIDDLETOWN, CONNECTICUT

A 3.1.a$_1$: 5$^{15}/_{16}''$ × 7$^{15}/_{16}''$

Copyright © 1962, 1963, 1964 by James Dickey

Most of these poems have been previously published elsewhere. For permission to reprint them in this volume, the author is grateful to the editors of *Hudson Review; Paris Review; Poetry; Sewanee Review; The Virginia Quarterly Review; Yale Review;* and *The New Yorker,* in which the following poems first appeared: "At Darien Brid e," "The Beholders," "Breath," "Bums, on Waking," "Cherrylog Road," "The Drive ," "The Dusk of Horses," "Fence Wire," "Goodbye to Serpents," "The Ice Skin," "Kudzu," "In the Marble Quarry," "The Poisoned Man," "The Scarred Girl," and Part I of "On the Coosawattee."

I should like to thank the editors of *The Virginia Quarterly Review* for the Emily Balch Prize awarded to "Springer Mountain," and the directors of the John Simon Guggenheim Memorial Foundation for the fellowship on which these poems were written.

Library of Congress Catalog Card Number : 64-13610
Manufactured in the United States of America
First Edition

[1–8] 9–93 [94–96]

$[1-6]^8$

Contents: p. 1: half title in decorated frame; p. 2: blank; p. 3: title; p. 4: copyright; p. 5: 'To Maxine | *light and warmth*'; pp. 6–7: contents; p. 8: blank; pp. 9–93: text; p. 94: blank; p. 95: list of series titles; p. 96: blank.

24 poems: "The Dusk of Horses" (see B 4), "Fence Wire," "At Darien Bridge," "Chenille,"* "On the Coosawattee" ("By Canoe Through the Fir Forest"—see B 4, "Below Ellijay," "The Inundation"), "Winter Trout," "Springer Mountain," "Cherrylog Road," "The Scarred Girl," "Kudzu," "The Beholders," "The Poisoned Man," "In the Marble Quarry," "A Folk Singer of the Thirties," "The Being," "Breath," "The Ice Skin," "Bums, on Waking," "Goodbye to Serpents," "In the Child's Night," "Approaching Prayer,"* "The Driver," "Horses and Prisoners," "Drinking from a Helmet." Asterisks indicate previously unpublished poems.

Helmets was republished in *The Early Motion* (see E 3).

Publication of "Bums, on Waking" and "The Driver" in *Best Poems of 1963* (Palo Alto, Calif.: Pacific Books, 1964) was subsequent to *Helmets*.

Typography and paper: 5¾″ (6″). No running heads. Wove paper; watermarked 'WARREN'S | OLDE STYLE'.

Binding: Medium gray V cloth (smooth). Spine stamped vertically: '[black] JAMES DICKEY [green] HELMETS [horizontal black Wesleyan seal]'. White endpapers. All edges trimmed. Black and white headbands and footbands.

Dust jacket: Front: lettered against aerial photograph of forest: '[medium brown] *poems by* JAMES DICKEY | [reddish orange helmet] | [white] HELMETS | [vertically in white] Rich'. Spine lettered vertically against continuation of forest photo: '[black] James Dickey [orange] HELMETS | [white] Wesleyan'. Back has note on *Helmets* and biographical note; printed in reddish

orange and black. Front flap quotes critical comments on Dickey. Back flap lists volumes in the Wesleyan Poetry Program.

Wrappers: Front, spine, and back same as dust jacket; price added to back.

Publication: 1,000 cloth and 2,000 wrappers. Published simultaneously 27 February 1964. Cloth: $4.00; wrappers: $1.85. Copyright #A703842.

Production: Finn Typographic Service, Riverside, Conn.; Halliday Lithograph, West Hanover, Mass.; Plimpton Press, Norwood, Mass.

Locations: JRB (wrappers); LC (cloth); Lilly (wrappers); MJB (cloth—dj); MJB (wrappers); ScU (cloth—dj).

$4.00

poems by JAMES DICKEY

HELMETS

Wesleyan

James Dickey HELMETS

HELMETS

JAMES DICKEY

"WE CAN no longer doubt that we are in the presence of a major talent, a true art."

So said the *Hudson Review* of James Dickey's previous book, *Drowning With Others*. This new collection, presenting his best work of the past three years, shows the poet at the height of his powers, his vision deepened and extended, his individual voice even more certain and more powerful. Here is the world of James Dickey in its fullest expression: a world where the flow of a river, the still-armed aura of a dead man, the wild lunge of a hunted buck through a laurel slick, each carries its particular revelation and adds its own dimension to our view of man and the universe in which he lives, *Helmets* is truly an outstanding work.

James Dickey, poet, sportsman and soldier, moved from his Atlanta home in 1963 to become poet-in-residence at Reed College, Portland, Oregon.

Of the poems brought together in this volume, the great majority have previously been printed in periodicals: *Poetry, Virginia Quarterly Review, Yale Review, Sewanee Review, Hudson Review, Paris Review*, and especially *The New Yorker*, in which not less than fifteen of them first appeared.

WESLEYAN UNIVERSITY PRESS
Middletown, Connecticut

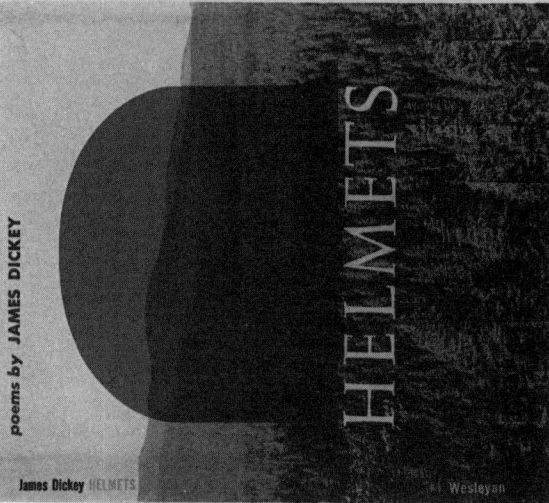

Dust jacket for A 3.1.a₁

A 3.1.a₂

First edition, first printing, English issue (1964)

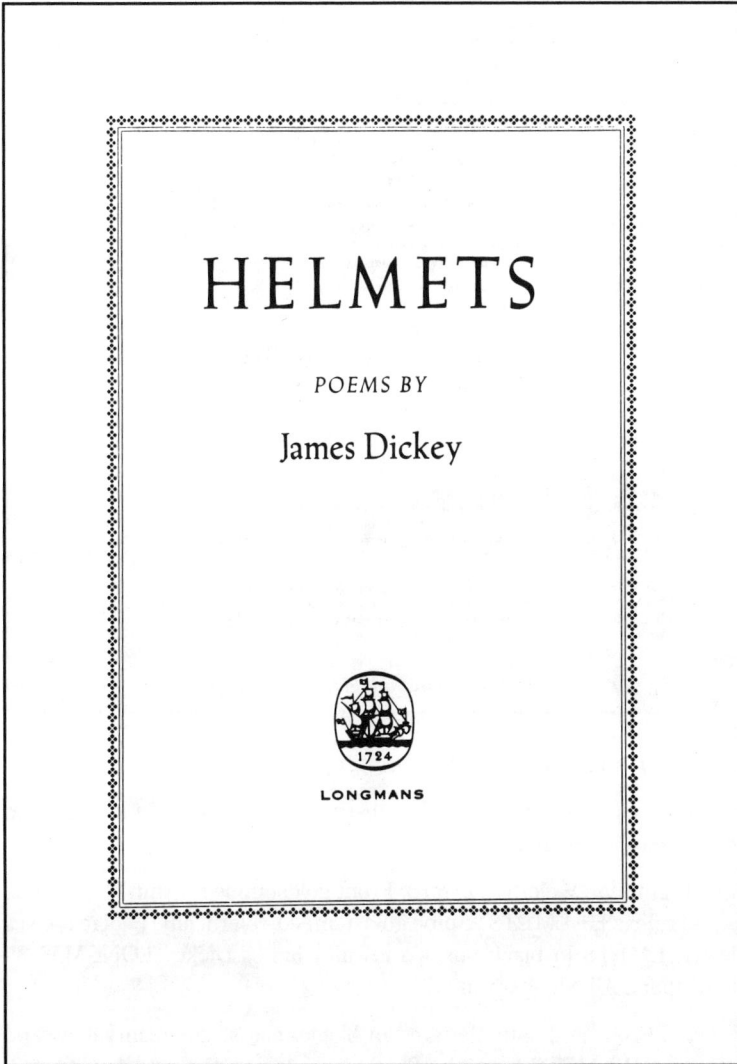

HELMETS

POEMS BY

James Dickey

1724

LONGMANS

A 3.1.a₂: 5¹⁵⁄₁₆″ × 7¹⁵⁄₁₆″

LONGMANS, GREEN AND CO LTD
48 Grosvenor Street, London W1
Railway Crescent, Croydon, Victoria. Australia
Auckland, Kingston (Jamaica). Lahore, Nairobi
LONGMANS SOUTHERN AFRICA (PTY) LTD
THIBAULT HOUSE, THIBAULT SQUARE, CAPE TOWN
LONGMANS OF NIGERIA LTD
W. R. INDUSTRIAL ESTATE, IKEJA
LONGMANS OF GHANA LTD
INDUSTRIAL ESTATE, RING ROAD SOUTH, ACCRA
LONGMANS GREEN (FAR EAST) LTD
443 LOCKHART ROAD, HONG KONG
LONGMANS OF MALAYA LTD
44 JALAN AMPANG, KUALA LUMPUR
ORIENT LONGMANS LTD
CALCUTTA, BOMBAY, MADRAS
DELHI, HYDERABAD, DACCA
LONGMANS CANADA LTD
137 BOND STREET, TORONTO 2

Same pagination and collation as first printing.

Contents same as first printing with substitution of English title page and copyright page; p. 95 blank.

Binding: Light blue V cloth (smooth). Front goldstamped within black frame of boxes and rules: 'HELMETS'. Spine goldstamped: '[vertically] [3 black boxes and rule] HELMETS [3 black boxes and rule] James Dickey LONGMANS'. White endpapers. All edges trimmed.

Dust jacket: Front and spine lettered in black against greenish yellow and white. Front: 'HELMETS | [rule] | *Poems by* | James Dickey | Longmans'. Spine: '[vertically] HELMETS [rule] James Dickey Longmans'. Back lists 8 Longmans titles. Front flap has comment on *Helmets.* Back flap has biographical note on Dickey.

Publication: 1,000 copies. Published 27 July 1964. 18 s.

Production: American sheets with Longmans title leaf; bound in England.

Locations: BL (6 AUG 64); JRB (dj); MJB (dj); ScU (dj).

HELMETS

Poems by
James Dickey

Longmans

HELMETS

James Dickey

Longmans

18s
net

Helmets is James Dickey's third volume of poetry, and introduces to this country the work of one of the most remarkable poets now writing in America—perhaps, since the death of Theodore Roethke, the only one with that peculiar, and very rare, gift of joy, praise and affirmation. A visionary poet, with an extraordinary capacity for responding to a wide range of experience, James Dickey has a feeling for nature—for animals, trees and landscape—which has almost vanished from the poetry of our time. He is an excellent craftsman, with his own unmistakable cadences, who avoids every kind of slickness and merely fashionable cleverness. A lyrical poet, whose forms are entirely organic, James Dickey has a powerful imagination and a superb command of his craft.

Also from Longmans

LAWRENCE SPINGARN
Letters from Exile

STEVIE SMITH
Selected Poems

CHRISTOPHER HASSALL
Bell Harry and Other Poems

JAMES WRIGHT
The Branch will not Break

JAMES BALDWIN
Death on a Live Wire

MICHAEL HAMBURGER
Weather and Season

BRIAN HIGGINS
Notes While Travelling

KEITH BAINES
Goldensheep

James Dickey, poet, advertising man, sportsman, and soldier, is a native of Atlanta, which is still his official home. He is a veteran of Air Force service in both World War II and the Korean struggle, with nearly a hundred combat missions and three military decorations. Following a year in France under a fellowship from the *Sewanee Review*, he spent nearly six years, until 1961, with advertising agencies in New York and Atlanta. His first book, *Into the Stone*, was published in 1960; his second, *Drowning with Others*, was published in 1962. *Helmets* is his third. Mr Dickey's poems have appeared regularly in many leading magazines in the United States.

Dust jacket for A 3.1.a₂

A3.1.b

Second printing: Middletown, Conn.: Wesleyan University Press, [1966].

Copyright page: '. . . *second printing January 1966*'. Cloth and wrappers.

A3.1.c

Third printing: Middletown, Conn.: Wesleyan University Press, [1966].

Copyright page: '. . . *third printing October 1966*'. Cloth. $4.00.

A3.1.d

Fourth printing: Middletown, Conn.: Wesleyan University Press, [1967].

Copyright page: '. . . *fourth printing December 1967*'. Wrappers. $2.00.

A3.1.e

Fifth printing: Middletown, Conn.: Wesleyan University Press, [1971].

Copyright page: '. . . *fifth printing May 1971*'. Wrappers. $2.45.

A4 TWO POEMS OF THE AIR

A4.1

First edition, only printing (1964)

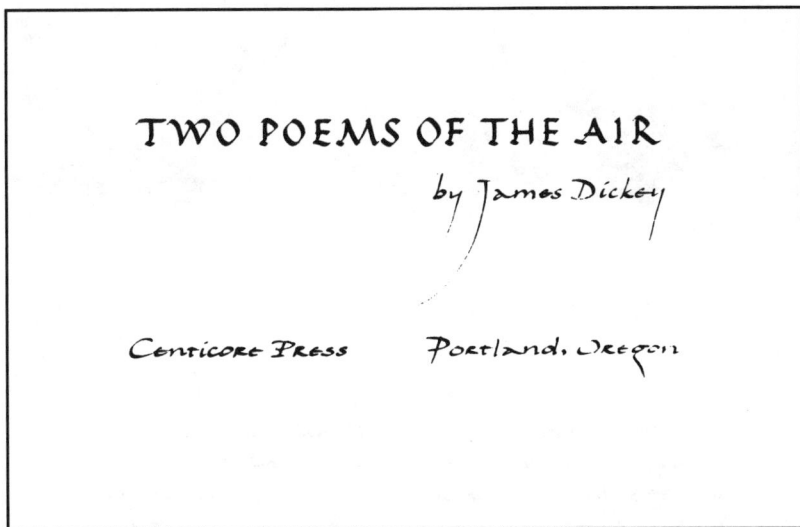

TWO POEMS OF THE AIR

by James Dickey

Centicore Press   Portland, Oregon

A 4.1: 12⅛″ × 6″

Copyright page: '© 1964 by James Dickey'.

[i–viii] 1–37 [38–40] 41–83 [84–88]

Perfect binding.

Contents: pp. i–ii: blank; p. iii: title; p. iv: copyright; p. v: 'To the students of Reed College'; p. vi: blank; p. vii: section title for "The Firebombing" with epigraphs from Günter Eich and the Book of Job; p. viii: blank; pp. 1–84: text; p. 85: blank; p. 86: signatures of Dickey and Monica Moseley Pincus; p. 87: colophon and certificate of limitation; p. 88: blank.

2 poems: "The Firebombing" and "Reincarnation." First publication of "Reincarnation"; collected as "Reincarnation (II)" in *Poems 1957–1967*.

Typography and paper: Entire text in calligraphy by Monica Moseley Pincus. No running heads. Light gray paper. See colophon.

Binding: Light gray and medium gray paper-covered boards with abstract drawing on front and back. Front: '[black] TWO POEMS OF THE AIR | by James Dickey'. Endpapers same as text paper. All edges trimmed.

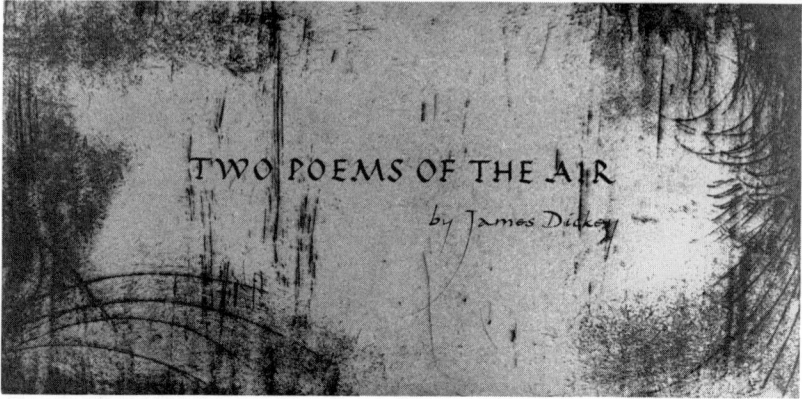

Front cover for A 4.1

This book was written by the hand of Monica Moseley Pincus. The letter forms are basically Carolingian bookhand of the 9th century, chosen for their legibility and adaptability, but written with a distinctly modern rhythm. Reproduction and binding by Abbott, Kerns e Bell Co. of Portland, Oregon by offset from halftone plates. The paper is Simpson Lee's Teton Text, generously contributed by Forest Paper Co. of N.Y.C.

Of three hundred copies printed, this is number 272.

Publication: 300 numbered copies signed by Pincus and Dickey. Published September (?) 1964. $4.95. Copyright #A691907.

Production: See colophon.

Locations: Lilly; MJB; ScU.

A 5 THE SUSPECT IN POETRY

A 5.1

First edition, only printing (1964)

THE SUSPECT
IN
POETRY

by

JAMES DICKEY

1964

THE SIXTIES PRESS

A 5.1: 5¼″ × 8¼″; title, drawing, and rule in red

[1–8] 9–37 [38–39] 40–51 [52–54] 55–99 [100–101] 102–120

$[1-6]^8 [7]^{12}$

Contents: p. 1: half title; p. 2: blank; p. 3: title; p. 4: copyright; p. 5: contents;
p. 6: blank; p. 7: section title; p. 8: blank; pp. 9–120: text.

26 essays: *The Suspect in Poetry:* "The Winters Approach," "Allen Gins-
berg," "Thom Gunn," "Ned O'Gorman," "Robert Mezey," "Charles Olson," "Har-
old Witt," "Anne Sexton," "Philip Booth"; *In the Presence of Anthologies:* "New
Poets of England and America I (1957)," "The Grove Press New American
Poets (1960)"; *The Second Birth:* "The Second Birth," "Theodore Roethke,"
"Kenneth Patchen," "Howard Nemerov," "Hayden Carruth," "Randall Jarrell,"
"E. E. Cummings," "Elder Olson," "Richard Eberhart," "Brother Antoninus";
Toward a Solitary Joy: "Gary Snyder," "Galway Kinnell," "John Logan," "W. S.
Merwin," "William Stafford," "David Ignatow," "Toward a Solitary Joy." All
previously published.

Note 1: "Randall Jarrell" was reprinted in *Randall Jarrell 1914–1965,* ed.
Robert Lowell, Peter Taylor, and Robert Penn Warren (New York: Farrar,
Straus & Giroux, 1967), pp. 33–48.

Typography and paper: 5⅞" (6¼") × 3¹³⁄₁₆". 35 lines per page. No running
heads. Wove paper.

Binding: Blue-gray paper-covered boards. Front stamped in deep red: 'THE |
SUSPECT | IN | POETRY | [horseman]'. Spine: '[vertically in deep red] THE
SUSPECT IN POETRY JAMES DICKEY'. White endpapers. All edges trimmed. Clothbound presentation copies have brownish pink label printed in
black and signed by Dickey on front paste-down endpaper.

Dust jacket: Front: '[deep red] THE | SUSPECT | IN | POETRY | [dragon] |
[black] by | James | Dickey'. Spine: '[vertically in deep red] THE SUSPECT IN
POETRY [black] JAMES DICKEY'. Back lists 9 titles published by Sixties

Press. Front flap has comment on book signed R. B. [Robert Bly]. Back flap describes *The Sixties*. Dust jacket same for clothbound and wrappered copies, except for price change on front flap.

Wrappers: Unprinted white wrappers in dust jacket.

Publication: Unknown number of copies. Published 10 July (?) 1964. Cloth: $2.00; wrappers: $1.00. Copyright #AI-9397.

Production: Printed in the Republic of Ireland.

Locations: Lilly (wrappers—dj); MJB (cloth—review copy with presentation label; wrappers—dj); PSt (wrappers—dj); ScU (cloth—dj).

Page proof: Unbound leaves printed on rectos only. Location: ScU.

Note 2: *British Books in Print* lists a 1964 publication of this title by Mandarin Books, London. No copy with the Mandarin imprint has been seen; and this listing probably refers to imported copies of the Sixties Press edition.

THE SUSPECT IN POETRY

by James Dickey

THE SUSPECT IN POETRY   JAMES DICKEY

We live in an age of poetry, and yet have almost no genuine criticism of it. The older American critics, worshipping the past, write long volumes on Poetry and Original Sin, John Dewey, or their own childhood, and then provide understanding jacket blurbs for all contemporary poets. The chief criticism, bad criticism. The true artist draws the distinction between first and second rate work, and says it out loud. This book is the first in a series the Sixties Press intends to publish, carrying criticism of poetry at the present moment. James Dickey has obviously been one of the best reviewers writing in America in the last few years. He has a temper like a whip, and at the same time a peculiar warmth which nearly to not suspect, and a boisterous affection for it. I admire James Dickey for spending his energy criticizing poetry written last year and this year, and speaking about it seriously, without fear of literary reprisal.

If the distinction between first and second-rate work is not made, freshly, in every generation, poetry suffers: the smaller talents are given more and more poetry disappears down a dead-end road: with-out looking around. Young poets moreover, do not learn in their cradles how to write good poetry: nor can they learn just from reading great poetry. They need active, opinionated criticism. Our volumes imagine Whitman's, and Thoreau's, poems without Emerson's criticism beforehand. The help is made may receive from criticism is incidental. Criticism's greatest value remains in its usefulness to the poets themselves. It lays the foundation for the poetry that is not yet written.

THE SIXTIES PRESS is also the publisher of The Sixties, which is a poetry magazine. The Sixties has two purposes: first to introduce to American readers and writers the work of poets such as Georg Trakl, Pablo Neruda, Antonio Machado, César Vallejo, Blas de Otero and many others from Europe and South America, who write a poetry very different from the poetry written in America in the last decade.

Its second purpose is to publish poems by American poets, and evaluate the poems of the generation of the fifties and sixties. Our work is moving in a direction different from the direction of the old poetry.

Thinking there is no reason to wait until the poet is in his grave, the finances of his work are discussed in each issue, we publish a book review, we publish in each issue an article or two of the poets of the 'fifties and 'sixties whose work seems to us extremely interesting. Articles have appeared or will appear on John Logan, Robert Creeley, James Wright, Denise Levertov, Gary Snyder, Louis Simpson, James Dickey, and others.

The Sixties also publishes, varying on occasion, when we can stand it to be longer. Subscriptions are $3.00 for four issues. Enquiries should go to The Sixties, Odin House, Madison, Minnesota.

Dust jacket for A 5.1

A 6 BUCKDANCER'S CHOICE

A 6.1.a

First edition, first printing (1965)

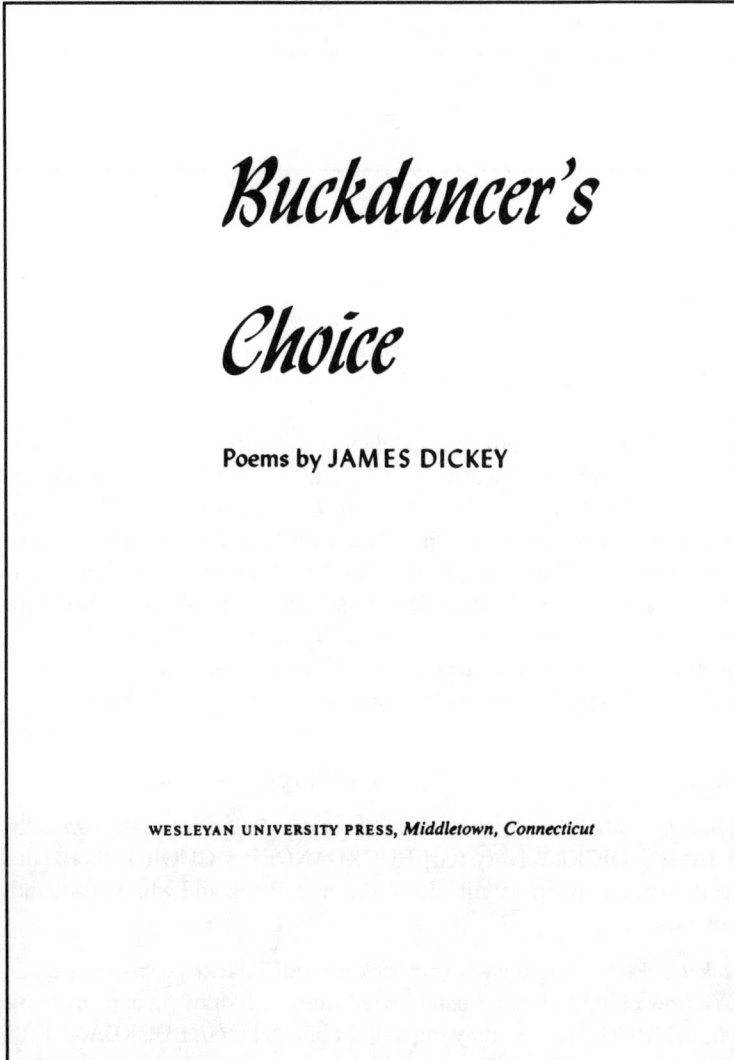

Buckdancer's

Choice

Poems by JAMES DICKEY

WESLEYAN UNIVERSITY PRESS, *Middletown, Connecticut*

A 6.1.a: 5¹⁵⁄₁₆″ × 7¹⁵⁄₁₆″

[1–10] 11–79 [80]

[1–5]^8

Contents: p. 1: half title; p. 2: blank; p. 3: title; p. 4: copyright; p. 5: 'To
Maibelle Swift Dickey | and | Eugene Dickey | *life-givers*'; pp. 6–7: contents;
p. 8: blank; p. 9: half title; p. 10: blank; pp. 11–79: text; p. 80: list of titles in
series.

22 poems: "The Firebombing," "Buckdancer's Choice," "Faces Seen Once,"
"The Common Grave," "Reincarnation," "Them, Crying," "The Celebration,"
"The Escape," "The Shark's Parlor," "Pursuit from Under," "Fox Blood," "Fathers and Sons" ("The Second Sleep," "The Aura"),"Sled Burial, Dream Ceremony," "Gamecock," "The Night Pool," "The War Wound," "Mangham," "Angina," "Dust," "The Fiend," "Slave Quarters." All previously published. "Reincarnation" was collected as "Reincarnation (I)" in *Poems 1957–1967*.

Publication of "Pursuit from Under" and "Them, Crying" in *Best Poems of
1964* (Palo Alto, Calif.: Pacific Books, 1965) was subsequent to *Buckdancer's
Choice*.

Typography and paper: 6¹⁄₁₆″ (6¼″). No running heads. Wove paper.

Cloth binding: Medium gray V cloth (smooth). Spine stamped vertically:
'[black] JAMES DICKEY [very red] BUCKDANCER'S CHOICE [horizontal
black seal]. White endpapers. All edges trimmed. Black and white headbands
and footbands.

Dust jacket: Front: '[against white background] [black] *poems by* JAMES
DICKEY | [row of light bluish green tapered rules with drawing of black banjo
player signed RICH] | [across drawing in light bluish green] BUCKDANCER'S
CHOICE'. Spine: '[vertically in light bluish green] James Dickey: [black]
BUCKDANCER'S CHOICE [medium gray] Wesleyan'. Back has comment on
book and biographical note on Dickey. Front flap quotes statements on *Drowning With Others* and *Helmets*. Back flap lists titles in series.

$4.00

Also by JAMES DICKEY

Drowning With Others

"An astonishingly gifted poet; he has an impeccable ear, a joyous imagination, a unique view of the world around him, and what James Wright has called a 'courageous tenderness.... *Drowning With Others* is a superb poetic achievement."
—GUY OWEN, *Books Abroad*

"We can no longer doubt that we are in the presence of a major talent, a true art.... Dickey's poetry is cosmic."
—*Hudson Review*

Helmets

"His best work of the past three years, Dickey, perhaps more than most of his contemporaries, is a poet of revelation ... illuminating not only himself but his world, which is in the largest sense the world of his readers.

... He is certainly a major poet."
—AUGUST DERLETH

"His best yet. It is rich in the relentless intelligence that has made him, incidentally, the finest of our new critics of poetry."
—X. J. KENNEDY, *New York Times Book Review*

"His subjects, like the steel hat, are rugged, simple, and noble.... The bite of his poems is sudden and sure; through majestic rhythms and disarming simplicity, he unfolds a magnificent depth of feeling and vision.... These are tough poems that insist on the attention of the reader long after the book has been put away."
—*Library Journal*

---

poems by **JAMES DICKEY**

James Dickey: **BUCKDANCER'S CHOICE**

BUCKDANCER'S CHOICE

Wesleyan

JAMES DICKEY

BUCKDANCER'S CHOICE

Whoever looks to a new book by James Dickey for further work in an established mode, or for mere novelty, is going to be disappointed. But those who seek instead a true widening of the horizons of meaning, coupled with a sure-handed mastery of the craft of poetry, will find this latest collection satisfying indeed.

Here is a man who matches superb gifts with a truly subtle imagination, into whose depths he is courageously traveling—pioneering—in exploratory penetrations into areas of life that are too often evaded or denied. "The Firebombing,"

"Slave Quarters," "The Fiend"—these poems, with the others that comprise the present volume, show a mature and original poet at his finest.

James Dickey, born in Atlanta and educated at Vanderbilt, abandoned a successful business career shortly after the publication of his second book. He has been poet-in-residence at Reed College and at San Fernando State College, and has lectured and given readings at many other institutions. His published collections include *Into the Stone* (1960), *Drowning With Others* (1962), and *Helmets* (1964), the two latter in The Wesleyan Poetry Program.

WESLEYAN UNIVERSITY PRESS
Middletown, Connecticut

Dust jacket for A 6.1.a

Wrappers: Front, spine, and back same as dust jacket; price added to back.

Publication: 774 cloth and 1,053 wrappers. Published simultaneously 23 September 1965. Cloth: $4.00; wrappers: $1.85. Copyright #A832183.

Production: Plimpton Press, Norwood, Mass.; Finn Typographic Service, Riverside, Conn.; Halliday Lithograph, West Hanover, Mass.

Locations: LC (NOV 29 1965—cloth); LC (wrappers); Lilly (cloth—dj); MJB (wrappers; cloth—dj); PSt (cloth); ScU (cloth—dj); ScU (wrappers).

Press release: For *Buckdancer's Choice* on Wesleyan University Press letterhead (1965). Includes 162-word statement by Dickey. 8½″ × 11″. Duplicated TS; 1 leaf typed on recto. Location: JD.

Note: Press release statement also appears in flier for Lordly & Dame lecture agency. Location: JD.

Press release: University of Wisconsin News and Publications Service, 15 March 1966. Announcement of Dickey's 1966 National Book Award in poetry for *Buckdancer's Choice*. Quotes Dickey. 8½″ × 11″. Duplicated TS; 3 leaves typed on rectos. Location: JD.

A6.1.b

Second printing: Middletown, Conn.: Wesleyan University Press, [1966].

1,000 cloth and 1,000 wrappers. March 1966. Not seen.

A6.1.c

Third printing: Middletown, Conn.: Wesleyan University Press, [1966].

Copyright page: '. . . *third printing May 1966*.' Wrappers.

A6.1.d

Fourth printing: Middletown, Conn.: Wesleyan University Press, [1966].

Copyright page: '. . . *fourth printing August 1966*.' 1,500 cloth and 1,500 wrappers. Wrappers not seen.

A6.1.e

Fifth printing: Middletown, Conn.: Wesleyan University Press, [1967].

Copyright page: '. . . *fifth printing April 1967*'. Wrappers. 3,000 copies.

A.6.1.f

Sixth printing: Middletown, Conn.: Wesleyan University Press, [1968]. Copyright page: '. . . *sixth printing January 1968*'. Cloth and wrappers.

A6.1.g

Seventh printing: Middletown, Conn.: Wesleyan University Press, [1973]. 500 cloth and 1,500 wrappers. Not seen.

A6.1.h

Eighth printing: Middletown, Conn.: Wesleyan University Press, [1978]. Wrappers. 1,000 copies. Not seen.

A6.1.i

Ninth printing: Middletown, Conn.: Wesleyan University Press, [   ]. Not seen.

A6.1.j

Tenth printing: Middletown, Conn.: Wesleyan University Press, [1982]. Copyright page: '. . . tenth printing, 1982.' Wrappers.

A7 A PRIVATE BRINKSMANSHIP

A7.1

First edition, only printing (1965)

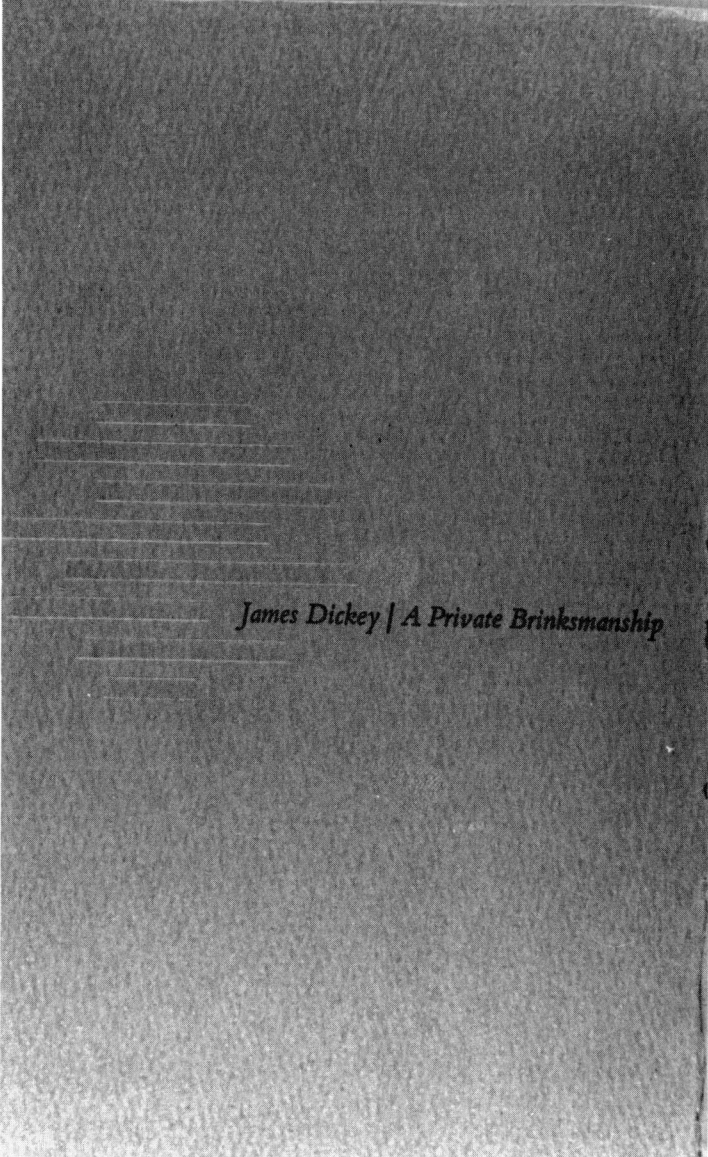

Cover title for A 7.1: 6¹⁄₁₆″ × 9³⁄₁₆″

Pitzer, sixth of the
Claremont Colleges, is a
liberal arts college for
women with curricular
emphasis in the social and
behavioral sciences. It was
founded in February 1963.
VOLUME III, NUMBER 2
NOVEMBER 1965
Published quarterly by
Pitzer College, Claremont,
California. Entered as
second class matter on
November 8, 1963, at the
Post Office at Claremont,
California, under
Act of August 24, 1912.

[1–16]

[1]^8

Contents: p. 1: Pitzer College seal; p. 2: 'Preface | by President John Atherton' and publication information; p. 3: preface; p. 4: 'A | Private | Brinksmanship | An Address by | James Dickey, | Poet-in-Residence, | San Fernando Valley State College | at the First Pitzer College Commencement, | June 6, 1965'; pp. 5–14: address; p. 15: colophon; p. 16: blank. Collected as "Three Girls Outgoing" in *Night Hurdling*. A slightly revised version of "A Private Brinksmanship" appears in *Pitzer Participant* [Pitzer College, Claremont College] (April 1973), 4–7.

Typography and paper: 6⅞₁₆″; ragged right margin. 29 lines per page. No running heads. Laid paper with chainlines 1″ apart.

Binding: Brownish orange paper wrappers with deckle fore-edge. Front: '[8 blindstamped quadrangles] *James Dickey* [slash] *A Private Brinksmanship*'. All edges trimmed. Saddle-stapled.

Publication: 1,000 copies. Identified on p. 2 as vol. III, no. 2 (November 1965). Not for sale.

Production: See colophon.

Locations: Lilly; MJB; ScU.

Note: Dickey's address is excerpted in "Pitzer's Ranks as Most Intimate Commencement: 3 Graduate," *Progress Bulletin* [Claremont, Calif.], 7 June 1965, and in "Commencement 1965: The Generational Conflict," *Time*, 85 (18 June 1965), 32.

1000 copies published by
Mr. William W. Clary for Pitzer College
printed by Grant Dahlstrom / The Castle Press
designed by Thomas Jamieson
Claremont

A 8 NBA ACCEPTANCE SPEECH

A 8.1

First edition, only printing (1966)

JAMES DICKEY

National Book Award in Poetry, 1966

Acceptance Speech

On occasions such as this, writers are not so much invited as summoned, called up. They are called up, surely, in the sense of being called up for jury duty or for military service; but they are also called up in the sense that ghosts and spirits are summoned. Most of you have never seen me before, and very likely you will never see me again. I appear on just this one occasion out of a kind of forest of print, of a never ending rain of words written in the forms -- or no-forms -- of verse and hoping to be poetry. I appear as a result of having had a few such verses printed in a book -- one among thousands -- which you have chosen to honor on this occasion. I have come out of certain lines of print with my name attached to them, and yet I stand here for a moment or two as a man: a man who awoke, if not exactly to find himself famous, at least to find himself slightly notorious among his fellow craftsmen. The main change in my immediate life, however, is merely the addition of a new word to the family vocabulary. Last year's description of the poet -- graciously contributed by my fourteen-year-old son -- was "decadent." This year's, thanks to the National Book Committee and the Poetry Judges, is "insufferable," coming this time not from the son but from the wife, who is certainly in a position to know. And here I am, no ghost yet -- thank God -- but a middle-aged man (<u>early</u> middle-aged, as one continually and a little desperately points out to oneself), and I have this occasion to tell you a couple of things.

It might not be to the purpose here to make any sweeping statements on the nature of poetry; or on that much agitated question, the Place of the Poet in Society; or to dwell on the arduous labor of love that poetry must be in our time. And yet I will generalize, even so. What comes through to me continually as I go on writing poetry is the infinite renewability of the individual human life, both as it is lived and enhanced by the poetry that one knows and reads, and as it is relived in memory. I once read in the

Page [1] for A 8.1: 8½″ × 11″

[1–6]

3 leaves typed on rectos; second and third leaves numbered.

Typography and paper: Duplicated typescript. Wove paper; watermarked 'GOLD LABEL | [rule] | A B DICK | [rule] | BOND'.

Publication: Press release with complete text of Dickey's speech, distributed at National Book Awards ceremony, 15 March 1966.

Location: MJB.

Note 1: Reprinted as "A Poet Is Honored," *Authors Guild Bulletin,* May 1966, 1–2. Collected as "An Acceptance" in *Night Hurdling.*

Note 2: Excerpts from Dickey's NBA acceptance speech have been noted in Seymour Krim, "National Book Awards: A Storm," *New York Herald Tribune,* 16 March 1966, p. 24; Robert R. Kirsch, "Four Winners in National Book Awards Contests," *Los Angeles Times,* 16 March 1966, sec. 5, pp. 1, 12; Geoffrey Wolff, "Schlesinger, 3 Others Receive Book Awards," *Washington Post,* 16 March 1966, p. A3 (revised for *Milwaukee Journal,* 16 March 1966); Ivan Sandrof, "Looks of Books: Poetry Emerges as Cultural Force," *Worcester [Mass.] Evening Gazette,* 22 March 1966, p. 7; Mary Stahlman Douglas, "About New Books: Panels of Newsworthy Authors, Parties, Plays, Museums, Opera Fill National Book Award Week," *Nashville Banner,* 25 March 1966, p. 29; "1966 NBA Awards Ceremonies at Philharmonic Hall," *Publishers Weekly,* 189 (28 March 1966), 35.

A9 POEMS 1957–1967

A9.1.a₁

First edition, first printing, American issue (1967)

James Dickey

POEMS 1957-1967

WESLEYAN UNIVERSITY PRESS

Middletown, Connecticut

A 9.1.a₁: 5⅞″ × 8¹⁵⁄₁₆″

[i–viii] ix–xiii [xiv] xv [xvi] [1–2] 3–13 [14–16] 17–48 [49–50] 51–110 [111–112] 113–178 [179–180] 181–239 [240–242] 243–299 [300–304]

[1–10]¹⁶

Contents: pp. i–ii: blank; p. iii: half title; p. iv: blank; p. v: title; p. vi: copyright; p. vii: 'To Maxine, my wife'; p. viii: blank; pp. ix–xiii: contents; p. xiv: blank; p. xv: 'Acknowledgments'; p. xvi: blank; p. 1: 'Sermon'; p. 2: blank; pp. 3–299: text; pp. 300–304: blank.

107 poems: *Sermon:* "May Day Sermon to the Women of Gilmer County, Georgia, by a Woman Preacher Leaving the Baptist Church"; *Into the Stone:* "Sleeping Out at Easter," "The Underground Stream," "The String," "The Vegetable King," "The Enclosure," "The Jewel," "The Performance," "The Wedding," "The Other," "Trees and Cattle," "Walking on Water," "Awaiting the Swimmer," "On the Hill Below the Lighthouse," "Near Darien," "Into the Stone"; *Drowning With Others:* "The Lifeguard," "Listening to Foxhounds," "A Dog Sleeping on My Feet," "The Movement of Fish," "The Heaven of Animals," "A Birth," "Fog Envelops the Animals," "The Summons," "In the Tree House at Night," "For the Nightly Ascent of the Hunter Orion Over a Forest Clearing," "The Owl King" ("The Call," "The Owl King," "The Blind Child's Story"), "Between Two Prisoners," "Armor," "In the Lupanar at Pompeii," "Drowning With Others," "Dover: Believing in Kings," "To His Children in Darkness," "A Screened Porch in the Country," "Hunting Civil War Relics at Nimblewill Creek," "The Hospital Window," "The Magus," "Facing Africa," "Inside the River," "The Salt Marsh," "In the Mountain Tent"; *Helmets:* "The Dusk of Horses," "Fence Wire," "At Darien Bridge," "Chenille," "On the Coosawattee" ("By Canoe Through the Fir Forest," "Below Ellijay," "The Inundation"), "Winter Trout," "Springer Mountain," "Cherrylog Road," "The Scarred Girl," "Kudzu," "The Beholders," "The Poisoned Man," "In the Marble Quarry," "A Folk Singer of the Thirties," "The Being," "The Ice Skin," "Bums, on Waking," "Goodbye to Serpents," "Approaching Prayer," "The Driver," "Horses and Prisoners," " Drinking from a Helmet"; *Buckdancer's Choice:* "The Firebombing," "Buckdancer's Choice," "Faces Seen Once," "The Common Grave," "Reincarnation (I)" (see A 6.1.a), "Them, Crying," "The Celebration," "The Escape," "The Shark's Parlor," "Pursuit from Under," "Fox Blood," "Fathers and Sons" ("The Second Sleep," "The Aura"), "Sled Burial, Dream Ceremony," "Gamecock," "The Night Pool," "The War Wound,"

"Mangham," "Angina," "Dust," "The Fiend," "Slave Quarters"; *Falling:* "Reincarnation (II)" (see A 4.1), "The Sheep Child," "Sun," "Power and Light," "The Flash," "Adultery," "Hedge Life," "Snakebite," "Bread,"* "Sustainment" (see B 8), "A Letter" (see B 4), "The Head-Aim," "Dark Ones" (see B 14), "Encounter in the Cage Country," "For the Last Wolverine," "The Bee," "Mary Sheffield," "Deer Among Cattle," "The Leap," "Coming Back to America," "The Birthday Dream," "False Youth: Two Seasons" ("False Youth: Summer"—see B 8, "False Youth: Winter"), "Falling." Asterisks indicate previously unpublished poems.

"False Youth: Summer" was subsequently collected as "False Youth: Summer: Porch-Wings" in *False Youth: Four Seasons;* "False Youth: Winter" was subsequently collected as "False Youth: Winter: Thumb-Fire" in *False Youth: Four Seasons.*

"May Day Sermon" and poems in the *"Falling"* section of *Poems 1957–1967* were republished in *Falling, May Day Sermon, and Other Poems* (see E 4).

Typography and paper: 6¹⁵⁄₁₆″ (7⁷⁄₁₆″). Running footlines on rectos: section titles and folios. Wove paper; watermarked 'WARREN'S | OLDE STYLE'.

Binding: Deep yellowish green V cloth (smooth). Spine silverstamped on dark green panel: 'James | Dickey | POEMS | 1957–1967 | [rule] | WESLEYAN | UNIVERSITY | PRESS'. White endpapers. All edges trimmed. White headbands and footbands.

Dust jacket: Front and spine lettered against green forest photo. Front: '[white] JAMES | DICKEY | [olive green] POEMS | 1957–1967'. Spine: '[vertically] [white] JAMES DICKEY [olive green] POEMS 1957–1967 | [horizontally] Wesleyan | University | Press'. Back has excerpts from citation by National Book Award in Poetry judges and comments by Miller Williams and Charles Monaghan. Front and back flaps have description of book and note on Dickey.

Publication: 5,000 copies. Published 24 April 1967. $6.95. Copyright #A932304.

Production: Halliday Lithograph, West Hanover, Mass.; Finn Typographic Service, Riverside, Conn.; Colonial Press, Clinton, Mass.

Locations: JRB (dj); LC (AUG 21 1967); LC (dj—inscribed by Dickey "on April 24th, 1967, the date of publication"); Lilly (dj); MJB (dj); PSt.

Proof copy: Spiral-bound proof in printed light green wrappers. Front: 'JAMES DICKEY | POEMS 1957–1967 | UNCORRECTED PROOF | Wesleyan University Press, Middletown, Connecticut'. Location: MJB.

JAMES DICKEY POEMS 1957-1967

JAMES DICKEY POEMS 1957-1967

This volume presents, under one cover, the major work of the man whom, beyond any other, critics and readers have designated the authentic poet of his American generation.

For this collection, James Dickey has selected from his four published books all those poems that reflect his truest interests and his growth as an artist. And thereto he has added more than a score of new poems—in effect, a new book in themselves—that have not previously been published in volume form.

Specifically, Poems 1957-1967 contains 13 of the 24 poems that were included in his first book, Into the Stone (1957); 23 of the 36 that made up Drowning With Others (1962); 22 of the 24 in Helmets (1964); the entire 22 in the National Book Award winner Buckdancer's Choice (1965); and, under the title Falling, the exciting new poems mentioned above.

Not often can the word "great" be used of the work of a contemporary in any art. But surely it applies to the poems of James Dickey. To test that statement, read this book.

James Dickey, born in Atlanta in 1923, has been called by Life magazine both "the unlikeliest" and "the hottest" of contemporary U.S. poets. And, brash as they are, both those statements are true.

Mr. Dickey's early career was that of a star college athlete (football, hurdles); a night fighter pilot with over 100 missions in World War II and Korea, a hunter and woodsman; and a successful advertising executive in New York and Atlanta.

(continued on back flap)

(continued from front flap)
Whatever his métier, Mr. Dickey at the same time has been an acute and subtle searcher for answers to the ultimate questions; and the medium of his search has been poetry. That quest led him to bachelor's and master's degrees at Vanderbilt; to teaching at Rice and finally, since 1961, to a life wholly dedicated to poetry.

Mr. Dickey's poems have appeared in virtually every American journal of consequence and in four books. He has read and lectured on scores of platforms across the country. His many honors include fellowships from the Sewanee Review and the Guggenheim Foundation; terms as poet-in-residence at Reed, San Fernando Valley State, and Wisconsin; the Melville Cane Award, the National Book Award in Poetry; and for 1966-1967, appointment as Consultant in Poetry to the Library of Congress.

Married and the father of two sons, Mr. Dickey makes his home in Leesburg, Virginia.

About *Buckdancer's Choice* and the work of JAMES DICKEY

"For the clarity, subtlety and passion with which he has used the imagination and the craft of the poet to explore a diverse vision of contemporary experience and extend the resources of poetry."
—Judges' citation,
National Book Award in Poetry, 1966

"These poems are so new, so powerful, and simply so damned good that it's difficult to say much about them.... But I want to talk about greatness. Because that comes to my mind. Greatness comes out of authority; skill; mastery of the craft; sureness, the eye and the ear to see and hear what matters and the hand to understand them. This is part of it. But to see and hear what matters: This is the second germ of greatness: significance. And then blood, passion, concern, love. Whatever it is, they are here. Authority, significance, love. There is not a poem in the book without them. That is an incredible fact.... Surely whatever poetry of our time is remembered, this will be a part of it."—MILLER WILLIAMS, Shenandoah

"*Buckdancer's Choice* is the finest volume of poetry to appear in the sixties.... His poems don't fly, they burn. He uses clear, glistening traps to draw you slowly, pleasantly into his world, as the Venus fly-trap draws the fly. Then suddenly, magically, you are his thrilled victim, and the images are searing you. You are living the poet's agony with him....

Dickey's wonderful ability is to move you greatly, but never with simple rhetoric, never, never with slogans, only with his amused and appointed comprehension of life's energy and complexity. The poet's intelligence, his intensity and ability to communicate combine to stir a moral catharsis in the reader, the product of a very high art indeed."
—CHARLES MONAGHAN, The Commonweal

Wesleyan University Press   MIDDLETOWN, CONNECTICUT

Wesleyan University Press
Middletown, Connecticut

Dust jacket for A 9.1.a₁

Of this "miniature preview
edition," 500 copies have
been printed for complimen-
tary distribution to reviewers, booksellers, and friends
of the author and publisher.
No copies of this edition will
be offered for sale.

Certificate of limitation for A 9.1.a₁
(Miniature Preview Edition)

MINIATURE PREVIEW EDITION: 2″ × 3″.

Contents: p. i: certificate of limitation; p. ii: blank; p. iii: half title; p. iv: blank; p. v: title; p. vi: copyright; p. vii: dedication; p. viii: blank; pp. ix–xiii: contents; p. xiv: blank; p. xv: acknowledgments; p. xvi: blank; p. 1: 'Sermon'; p. 2: blank; pp. 3–13: "May Day Sermon to the Women of Gilmer County, Georgia, by a Woman Preacher Leaving the Baptist Church"; p. 14: blank; p. 15: 'Into the Stone'; pp. 16–112: blank.

Binding and dust jacket: Unprinted tan boards in facsimile of book dust jacket.

Locations: JRB; MJB; ScU.

Note: Wesleyan University Press distributed a "non-erratum" slip typed on yellow paper explaining, "Only the first poem from the regular edition appears in the miniature."

A9.1.a₂

First edition, first printing, English issue (1967)

James Dickey

POEMS 1957-1967

✻

RAPP & CARROLL *London*

A 9.1.a₂: 5⅞″ × 8¹⁵⁄₁₆″

Same pagination and collation as first printing.

Contents same as first printing with substitution of English title page and copyright page.

Binding: Medium olive green paper-covered boards. Spine goldstamped: 'Poems | 1957–1967 | [rosette] | *James* | *Dickey*'. White endpapers. All edges trimmed.

Dust jacket: Front: same as first printing. Spine: same as first printing with omission of publisher. Back has comments on book by Louis Untermeyer, Michael Goldman, Geoffrey A. Wolff, William Meredith, and Miller Williams. Front flap has description of book and note on Dickey. Back flap lists 19 poets published by Rapp & Carroll.

Publication: Unknown number of copies. Published 25 January 1968. 45 s.
  50 copies were signed and numbered in ink on the title page by Dickey. It is not known whether these copies were for sale or for presentation.
  Note: The discrepancy between the 25 October 1967 BL deposit date and the 25 January 1968 publication date specified in *The English Catalogue of Books* probably resulted from the reorganization of Rapp & Carroll as Rapp & Whiting.

Production: American sheets with Rapp & Carroll title leaf; bound in England.

Locations: BL (25 OCT 67); Caroliniana (dj); JRB (dj); LC (dj—#9); Lilly (dj—#8); MJB (dj—#49); ScU (dj—#13 & #28).

See AA 1.

A 9.1.b

Second printing: Middletown, Conn.: Wesleyan University Press, [1967].

Copyright page: '. . . *second printing June, 1967*'. Cloth. 5,000 copies.

A 9.1.c

Third printing: Middletown, Conn.: Wesleyan University Press, [1968].

Copyright page: '. . . *third printing January 1968*'. Cloth. 5,000 copies.

JAMES DICKEY POEMS 1957-1967

JAMES DICKEY POEMS 1957-1967

Rapp & Carroll Limited 128/134 Baker Street London W1

About this Book

'*Poems 1957-1967*) promises the work of a still young, affirmative, and—why laugh at a usually misused adjective?—major poet. . . . For me this is the poetry book of the year, and I have little doubt that it will prove to be the outstanding collection of one man's poems to appear in the decade.'

Leon Uris?, *Saturday Review*

'One of the things we should mean when we call a poet "good" is that his work moves us in the world and not merely to the poet. We do not assimilate good poetry, we become included in its imagination. James Dickey is a good poet, very good.'

Mona? Gitlin?, *The Nation*

'We the fact is that Dickey, more than any other poet writing in English today, is a working poet. That is, there seems to be too experience that does not occasion a poem. He sees everything as metaphor, states everything as verse.'

Guernsey A. Win, *The Washington Post*

'Dickey has defined a poet as "an intensified man". These collected poems of his 46th year are a record of a lot of valid and immediate experience—the intensity of a man intensifying himself honestly and skilfully.'

William Meredith, *The New York Times Book Review*

'Surely whatever poetry of our time is remembered, this will be a part of it.'

Miller Williams, *Shenandoah*

Rapp & Carroll Limited 128/134 Baker Street London W1

Rapp & Carroll POETS

Rafael Alberti
Ingeborg Bachmann
Anna Beresford
Johannes Bobrowski
Paul Claudel
Cid Corman
Jean-Paul de Dadelsen
James Dickey
Gunter Eich
Erich Fried
David Ignatow
Galway Kinnell
Jean L'Anselme
Christopher Logue
Matthew Mead
Howard Nemerov
David Rokeah
Pentti Saarikoski
William Wantling

Rapp & Carroll Limited
128/134 Baker Street London W1

Dust jacket for A 9.1.a₂

A9.1.d

Fourth printing: New York: Collier Books, [1968].

Copyright page: 'First Collier Books Edition 1968'. Wrappers. $1.95.

A9.1.e

Fifth printing: New York: Collier Books, [1968].

Copyright page: 'SECOND PRINTING 1968'. Wrappers. $1.95.

A9.1.f

Sixth printing: New York: Collier Books, [   ].

Not seen.

A9.1.g

Seventh printing: New York: Collier Books, [   ].

Not seen.

A.9.1.h

Eighth printing: New York: Collier Books, [1972].

Copyright page: 'FIFTH PRINTING 1972'. Wrappers.

A9.1.i

Ninth printing: New York: Collier Books, [   ].

Not seen.

A9.1.j

Tenth printing: New York: Collier Books, [   ].

Not seen.

A9.1.k

Eleventh printing: New York: Collier Books, 1978.

Copyright page: 'EIGHTH PRINTING 1978'. Wrappers.

A9.1.l

Twelfth printing: Middletown, Conn.: Wesleyan University Press, [1978].

Copyright page: '*First Wesleyan paperback edition, 1978*'. $5.95; price raised to $9.95 with label.

A9.1.m

Thirteenth printing: Middletown, Conn.: Wesleyan University Press, [1986].

Copyright page: 'First printing, 1967, fourth printing, 1986 | Wesleyan Paperback, 1978; second printing, 1986'. Simultaneously published in cloth and wrappers. Cloth: $17.00; price raised to $18.50 with label.

A 10 SPINNING THE CRYSTAL BALL

A 10.1

First edition, only printing (1967)

SPINNING THE CRYSTAL BALL

Some Guesses at the Future of American Poetry

A Lecture Delivered at the Library of Congress

April 24, 1967

BY JAMES DICKEY

Consultant in Poetry in English at the Library of Congress,

1966–1968

THE LIBRARY OF CONGRESS

Washington : 1967

A 10.1: 5¹³⁄₁₆″ × 9⅛″

```
┌─────────────────────────────────────────────────────────────┐
│                   L. C. Card 68–60008                       │
│  ∿∿∿∿∿∿∿∿∿∿∿∿∿∿∿∿∿∿∿∿∿∿∿∿∿∿∿∿∿∿∿∿∿∿∿∿∿∿∿∿∿∿∿∿∿  │
│  ─────────────────────────────────────────────────────────  │
│   For sale by the Superintendent of Documents, U.S. Government Printing Office │
│            Washington, D.C. 20402 · Price 15 cents           │
│                                                             │
└─────────────────────────────────────────────────────────────┘
```

[i–ii] iii [iv] 1–22 [23–24]

[1]^14

Contents: p. i: title; p. ii: copyright; p. iii: 'ACKNOWLEDGMENTS'; p. iv: blank; pp. 1–22: text; pp. 23–24: blank. Essay; subsequently collected in *Sorties*.

Typography and paper: 6¾6″ (6¹¹⁄₁₆″) × 4″. 37 lines per page. No running heads. Wove paper.

Binding: Yellow-gray wrappers. Front: printed against abstract design in yellow-gray and dark grayish yellow: '[dark grayish yellow] [diagonally down] JAMES DICKEY [diagonally up] SPINNING THE CRYSTAL BALL'. Back: Library of Congress seal in dark grayish yellow. All edges trimmed. Saddle-stapled.

Publication: 2,000 copies. Published 9 February (?) 1968. 15¢. The title page is dated 1967, but this pamphlet was probably not distributed until early February 1968.

Production: p. 22: '☆ U.S. Government Printing Office 1967—o 277-590'.

Locations: JRB; LC (recd FEB 26 1968); Lilly; MJB.

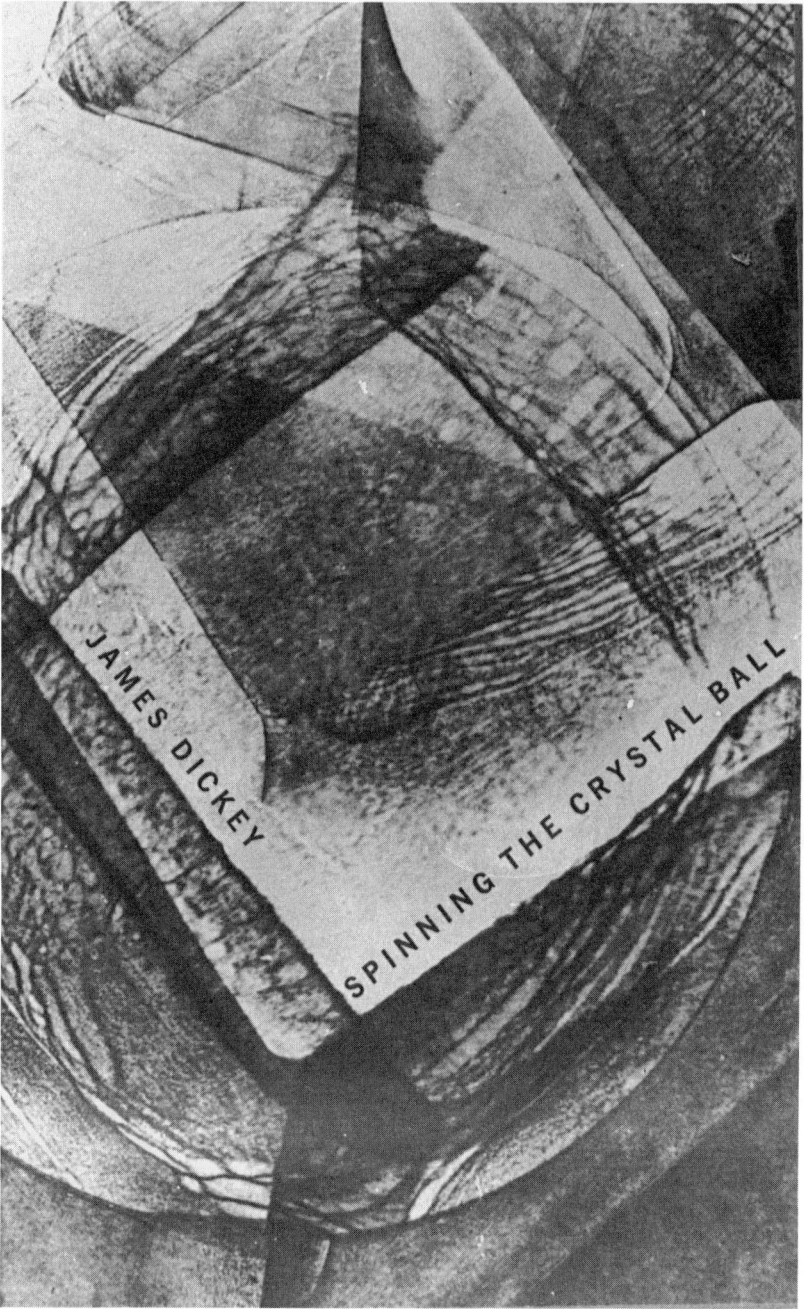

Front wrapper for A 10.1

A 11 BABEL TO BYZANTIUM

A 11.1.a

First edition, first printing (1968)

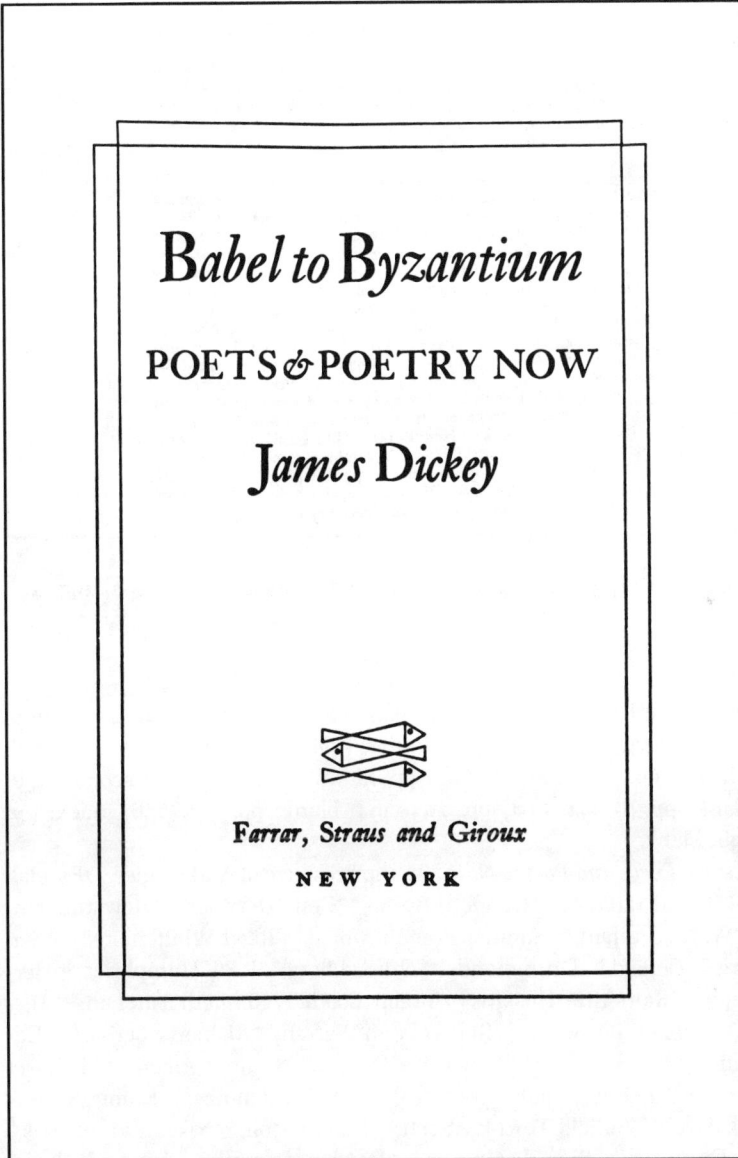

Babel to Byzantium

POETS & POETRY NOW

James Dickey

Farrar, Straus and Giroux

NEW YORK

A 11.1.a: 5½″ × 8″

[i–viii] ix–xiv 1 [2] 3–231 [232] 233–247 [248] 249–292 [293–294] 295–296
[297–298]

[1–7]^{16} [8]^{12} [9–10]^{16}

Contents: p. i: half title; p. ii: blank; p. iii: card page; p. iv: blank; p. v: title;
p. vi: copyright; p. vii: '*to my wife Maxine,* | *the critic's critic, but with love*';
p. viii: blank; pp. ix–x: 'PREFACE'; pp. xi–xiv: contents; p. 1: section title;
p. 2: blank; pp. 3–292: text; pp. 293–294: blank; pp. 295–296: index; pp.
297–298: blank.

76 essays: *Poets and Poetry Now:* "In the Presence of Anthologies," "Randall
Jarrell," "David Ignatow," "Kenneth Burke," "Gene Derwood," "Howard Nem-
erov," "W. S. Graham," "Samuel French Morse," "Reed Whittemore," "Allen
Ginsberg," "Donald F. Drummond," "John Ashbery," "Rolfe Humphries," "Her-
bert Read," "Katherine Hoskins," "Philip Booth," "Kenneth Patchen," "May
Sarton," "William Jay Smith," "Robert Penn Warren," "Richard Eberhart," "Ed-
win Muir," "Ted Hughes," "Lawrence Durrell," "Conrad Aiken," "Margaret
Tongue," "Ellen Kay," "James Merrill," "E. E. Cummings," "Emma Swan,"
"Harold Witt," "Winfield Townley Scott," "Elder Olson," "Nikos Kazantzakis,"
"Thom Gunn," "Brother Antoninus," "Hayden Carruth," "James Kirkup,"

"Anne Sexton," "Galway Kinnell," "Charles Olson," "William Stafford," "Lewis Turco," "W. S. Merwin," "Theodore Weiss," "Josephine Miles," "Theodore Roethke," "Louis MacNeice," "Charles Tomlinson's Versions of Fyodor Tyutchev," "Marianne Moore," "John Logan," "John Frederick Nims," "Richard Wilbur," "Robert Duncan," "Horace Gregory," "I. A. Richards," "Yvor Winters," "Robert Graves," "Robinson Jeffers," "Ralph Hodgson," "Vernon Watkins," "William Carlos Williams," "J. V. Cunningham," "Louis Simpson," "William Meredith," "John Berryman," "Robert Frost," "Edwin Arlington Robinson" (see B 7); *Five Poems:* "Christopher Smart: 'A Song to David' " (see B 10), "Matthew Arnold: 'Dover Beach' " (see B 10), "Gerard Manley Hopkins: 'The Wreck of the Deutschland' " (see B 10), "Francis Thompson: 'The Hound of Heaven' " (see B 10), "William Carlos Williams: 'The Yachts' " (see B 10); *The Poet Turns on Himself:* "Barnstorming for Poetry," "Notes on the Decline of Outrage" (see B 2), "The Poet Turns on Himself" (see B 11). All previously published. "Edwin Arlington Robinson" is different from the essay of the same title in *Sorties.*

Typography and paper: 6″ (6¼″) × 3⅞″. 35 lines per page. Running heads: rectos: chapter title and folio; versos: '[folio] *Babel to Byzantium*'. Wove paper.

Binding: Dark blue V cloth (smooth). Spine: '[gold] *Babel* | *to* | *Byzan-* | *tium* | [metallic light blue] POETS & | POETRY | NOW | [gold] *James* | *Dickey* | [metallic light blue FS&G monogram]'. Deep reddish orange endpapers. All edges trimmed. Top edge stained medium orangish yellow.

Dust jacket: Front and spine have white panel above strong orangish yellow panel with light and medium red decorations. Front: '[medium blue] *Babel to Byzantium* | [medium red] POETS & POETRY NOW | [very dark green] *by James Dickey*'. Spine: '[medium blue] *Babel to* | *Byzan-* | *tium* | [very dark green] *James* | *Dickey* | [vertically between two rows of light and medium red decorations] [medium red] POETS & POETRY NOW | [horizontally] [medium red decoration] | *Farrar,* | *Straus and* | *Giroux* | [row of light and medium red decorations]'. Back has list of Farrar, Straus & Giroux critical books printed in medium red and medium blue on white. Front and back flaps have comments on Dickey; printed in medium blue and medium red.

Wrappers: 5⅜″ × 7¹⁵/₁₆″; perfect bound. Front and spine printed against strong orangish yellow. Front: '*Babel to Byzantium* | [medium red] POETS & POETRY NOW | [black] *by James Dickey* | [at lower right corner of panel with light and medium red decorations] [black] Noonday $2.25'. Spine lettered in black: '*Babel to* | *Byzan-* | *tium* | *James* | *Dickey* | [vertically between two rows of light and medium red decorations] POETS & POETRY NOW | [horizontally] [medium red decoration] | N344 | [row of light and medium red decorations]'. Back printed in black on white; comment on Dickey and blurbs on *Babel to Byzantium* by Thomas Lask and Ralph J. Mills, Jr.

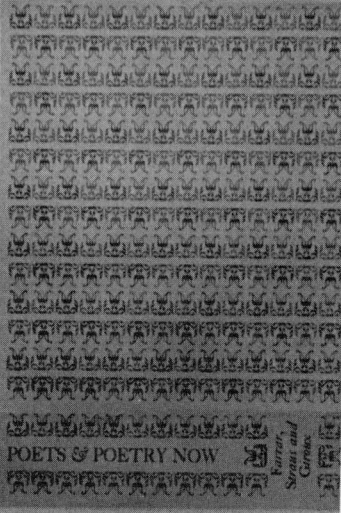

$5.95

Babel to Byzantium
POETS & POETRY NOW
by James Dickey

POETS & POETRY NOW

Farrar, Straus and Giroux

Babel to Byzantium

James Dickey

Distinguished Criticism from
Farrar, Straus & Giroux

F. W. Dupee — The King of the Cats

T. S. Eliot — On Poetry and Poets / To Criticize the Critic

Robert Graves — The White Goddess

Elizabeth Hardwick — A View of My Own

Robert Lowell, Peter Taylor, Robert Penn Warren, editors — Randall Jarrell, 1914–1965

Mary McCarthy — On the Contrary

Alberto Moravia — Man as an End

John Middleton Murry — Jonathan Swift

Norman Podhoretz — Doings and Undoings

Philip Rahv — The Myth and the Powerhouse

Susan Sontag — Against Interpretation

Francis Steegmuller — Flaubert and Madame Bovary

Edmund Wilson — Classics and Commercials / The Bit Between My Teeth / The Shores of Light

---

(continued from front flap)

love of the art of poetry. What makes him more than remarkable—what makes him unique—is the fact that his conception of poetry allows for an art other than his own." Richard Kostelanetz said of *The Suspect in Poetry* (1964), a limited selection of Mr. Dickey's criticism: "In this book James Dickey emerges as unquestionably the finest critic of American poetry today.

. . . He is a model of perception, astuteness, and intelligence . . . an irreplaceable force on the current scene." Nearly all the essays from that influential book are included in *Babel to Byzantium*; they make up about one-quarter of this new, comprehensive collection, which concludes with a brief section of essays in which Mr. Dickey considers his own life and work.

Jacket design by Herbert Johnson

Farrar, Straus & Giroux
19 Union Square West
New York 10003

With the publication of his *Poems 1957–1967*, it became emphatically clear that James Dickey is recognized by both public and critics as a major American poet, one who is valued for his distinctive intensity and intelligence. This recognition had grown with each of the four books he had published previously, from *Into the Stone* (1960) to *Buckdancer's Choice*, for which he received the National Book Award in 1966. That same year he began his two-year appointment as Poetry Consultant to the Library of Congress.

Since 1956 Mr. Dickey has been writing, in addition to his poems, criticism of the poetry of his contemporaries. In *Babel to Byzantium* some sixty poets of our time are discussed, among them Theodore Roethke, Marianne Moore, Randall Jarrell, and Robert Frost, as well as others who are not so well known. Together these essays form a personal chronicle of American and British poetry in the fifties and sixties.

"James Dickey is remarkable among critics," writes Richard Howard. "Yet his criticism is consuming, and even convincing

(continued on back flap)

Dust jacket for A 11.1.a

Publication: 7,500 cloth and wrappers. Cloth: published 1 May 1968; $5.95. Wrappers: published 11 August 1968; $2.25. Copyright #A989588.

Production: H. Wolff Book Manufacturing Co., New York.

Locations: Caroliniana (cloth—dj); JRB (cloth—dj); LC (cloth—MAY 13 1968); Lilly (cloth—dj); MJB (cloth—dj, with review slip); MJB (wrappers); PSt (cloth); ScU (cloth—dj).

Note 1: The Farrar, Straus & Giroux records indicate that 7,500 copies of *Babel to Byzantium* were printed, but it has not been determined how many of these copies were bound in cloth or wrappers. Presumably part of the first printing was stored in sheets and bound in wrappers after the initial cloth-bound publication.

Note 2: Spiral-bound proof copy not seen.

Note 3: A set of uncorrected galleys is at ScU.

A 11.1.b

Second printing: New York: Grosset & Dunlap, [1971].

Grosset's Universal Library UL253. Wrappers. $2.95.

A 11.1.c

Third printing: New York: Octagon, 1973.

Not seen.

A 11.1.d

Fourth printing: New York: Octagon, 1979.

Cloth.

A 11.1.e

Fifth printing: New York: Ecco Press, [1981].

With "Afterword to the New Ecco Edition," pp. 293–298. Wrappers. $7.95. Afterword collected as "Afterword to *Babel to Byzantium*" in *Night Hurdling*.

A 12 METAPHOR AS PURE ADVENTURE

A 12.1

First edition, only printing (1968)

METAPHOR

AS PURE ADVENTURE

A Lecture Delivered at

the Library of Congress

December 4, 1967

by JAMES DICKEY

Consultant in Poetry in English at
the Library of Congress, 1966–68

LIBRARY OF CONGRESS · WASHINGTON   1968

A 12.1: 5⅞″ × 9⅛″

Cover: Reproduction, actual size, of a plate
from *Bizzarie di varie figure,* by Giovanni
Battista Braccelli, printed in Livorno in 1624.
(Lessing J. Rosenwald Collection of the Library
of Congress.)

L.C. Card 68–61809

For sale by the Superintendent of Documents,
U.S. Government Printing Office
Washington, D.C. 20402 - Price 25 cents

[i–ii] 1–20 [21–22]

[1]^{12}

Contents: p. i: title; p. ii: copyright; pp. 1–18: text; pp. 19–20: list of other
Library of Congress publications; pp. 21–22: blank. Essay. Subsequently collected in *Sorties.*

Typography and paper: 6⁹⁄₁₆″ (7⅛″) × 4⅛″. 32 lines per page. No running
heads. Wove paper.

Binding: Off-white paper wrappers. Front: '[grayish brown] *James Dickey:* |
METAPHOR | [illustration] | AS PURE ADVENTURE'. Back cover has gray-
ish brown Library of Congress seal. All edges trimmed. Saddle-stapled.

Publication: 1,500 copies. Published summer 1968. 25¢; price raised to 40¢
in blue ink rubberstamp on copyright page.

Production: U.S. Government Printing Office.

Locations: Caroliniana; JRB; LC (recd DEC 4 1968); Lilly; MJB; PSt.

James Dickey:

METAPHOR

AS PURE ADVENTURE

Front wrapper for A 12.1

A 13 THE EYE-BEATERS ...

A 13.1.a₁

First edition, first printing, trade issue (1970)

THE EYE-BEATERS,
BLOOD, VICTORY,
MADNESS, BUCKHEAD
and
MERCY

James Dickey

1970
DOUBLEDAY AND COMPANY, INC., GARDEN CITY, NEW YORK

A 13.1.a₁: 6⅛″ × 9⅛″

[1–6] 7–26 [27–28] 29–63 [64]

Notch binding; unsewn.

Contents: p. 1: half title; p. 2: card page; p. 3: title; p. 4: '*To Lester Mansfield*'
and copyright matter; p. 5: contents; p. 6: blank; pp. 7–26: text; pp. 27–28:
black leaf; pp. 29–63: text; p. 64: blank.

   21 poems: "Diabetes" ("Sugar," "Under Buzzards"), "Messages" ("Butterflies," "Giving a Son to the Sea"), "Mercy," "Two Poems of Going Home"
("Living There," "Looking for the Buckhead Boys"), "The Place," "Apollo" ("For
the First Manned Moon Orbit," "The Moon Ground"), "The Cancer Match,"
"Venom," "Blood," "In the Pocket,"* "Knock," "Victory," "The Lord in the Air,"
"Pine," "Madness" (see B 19), "The Eye-Beaters," "Turning Away." Asterisks
indicate previously unpublished poems.

   The Eye-Beaters . . . was republished in *The Central Motion* (see E 5).

Typography and paper: 6⅞″ (7⅜″). No running heads. Wove paper.

Binding: Deep red V cloth (smooth). Spine goldstamped vertically: '*James
Dickey* THE EYE-BEATERS, BLOOD, VICTORY, MADNESS, BUCKHEAD
and MERCY *Doubleday*'. Medium yellow endpapers with white versos. All
edges trimmed.

Dust jacket: Front: '[above multicolored smear] The Eye-Beaters, | Blood,
Victory, Madness, | Buckhead and Mercy | James Dickey | NEW POEMS BY
THE AUTHOR OF | "BUCKDANCER'S CHOICE" '. Spine: '[vertically on
white] James Dickey The Eye-Beaters, Blood, Victory, Madness, Buckhead
and Mercy DOUBLEDAY'. Back has photo of Dickey by Christopher Dickey
and statements by Peter Davison, Mark Schorer, John Simon, and Stanley

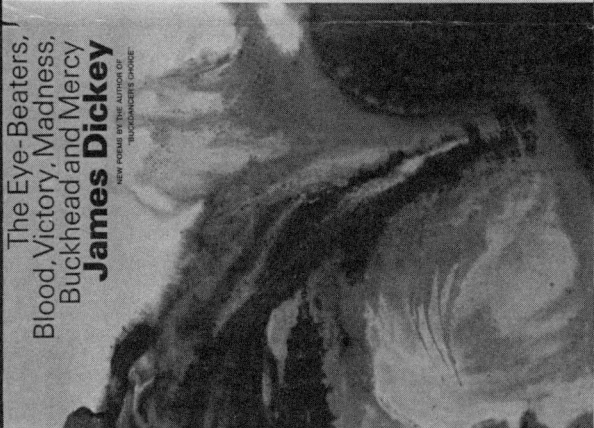

T.E.V.M.B.M.
$4.95

The Eye-Beaters,
Blood, Victory, Madness,
Buckhead and Mercy

NEW POEMS BY THE AUTHOR OF
"BUCKDANCER'S CHOICE"

James Dickey

James Dickey The Eye-Beaters, Blood, Victory, Madness, Buckhead and Mercy   DOUBLEDAY

The Eye-Beaters,
Blood, Victory, Madness, Buckhead
and Mercy
James Dickey

This new collection of poetry displays all the originality and perception, the dramatic power and passion for life that have made James Dickey one of America's foremost modern poets. He writes about the bizarre and the commonplace, about the public and the personal, about the amusing and the tragic. And each subject, from his uniquely poetic perspective, yields its own beauty. Here is poetry that captures the desperate intensity of human experience, poetry that every vital human being can read and feel.

PHOTO BY CHRISTOPHER DICKEY

"If American poetry needs a champion for the new generation, Dickey's power and ambition 'may supply the need.' His archetypal concerns are universal to all languages . . . his sense of urgency is overwhelming."

—Peter Davison, *The Atlantic*

"James Dickey's poetic gift is unique. Perhaps his most striking quality is the way he plunges his reader, with something like aesthetic rudeness, into the heavy stream of experience which is the poem itself. Emerging with a renewed if slightly dazed sense of his own existence, the responsive reader wants only to plunge in again."

—Mark Scherer

"In Dickey's poetry, the country and the city coexist in the most mutually benefiting summer . . . I place Dickey squarely above Lowell."

—John Simon, *Commonweal*

"The Fiend is surely one of the great love poems of our century. Yet even it cannot suggest the range of this poet's achievement: its compassion, immediacy, subtlety, power, its moments of terror, of tenderness; the complex sense of its struggle toward affirmation."

—Stanley Burnshaw

James Dickey was born in Atlanta and educated at Vanderbilt University. After serving in the Air Force during World War II, he began a successful career in advertising. But, following the wide acclaim which greeted his second volume of poetry, he abandoned his business career to devote his full time to writing.

He has been poet-in-residence at Reed College and San Fernando Valley State College and has lectured and read at many other institutions. He has also served as consultant in poetry to the Library of Congress. In 1966, he received the National Book Award in Poetry for *Buckdancer's Choice*; his other collections include *Poems 1957-1967*, *Drowning With Others*, and *Helmets*. In addition, he plans to publish his first novel in 1970.

Mr. Dickey, his wife, and their children now live in Columbia, South Carolina.

JACKET DESIGN BY PATRICIA SAVILLA VERRI.
JACKET PHOTOGRAPH BY URSULA SEHR
Printed in the U.S.A.

Dust jacket for A 13.1.a₁

Burnshaw. Front flap has description of book. Back flap has biographical note on Dickey.

Publication: 7,000 copies. Published 13 February 1970. $4.95. Copyright #A131939. Copyright page: 'FIRST EDITION AFTER A LIMITED EDITION OF 250 COPIES'; but trade and limited issues were published simultaneously. No copies of the first printing bound in wrappers have been located.

Production: Doubleday, Smithsburg, Md.; Westcott & Thompson, Philadelphia; Doubleday, Berryville, Va.

Locations: Caroliniana (dj); JRB (dj); Lilly (dj); MJB (dj); PSt (dj).

Note: "For the First Manned Moon Orbit" was adapted and set to music by Ronald Perera as *Apollo Circling: Four Lyric Songs for High Voice and Piano* (Boston: E. C. Schirmer, [1977]). E.C.S. Facsimile Series, no. 151. Wrappers; cover title. Locations: JRB; MJB.

A 13.1.a$_2$

First edition, first printing, limited issue

Text sheets same as trade issue with limitation leaf on heavier stock tipped in before p. 1: '*This is a limited edition of two hundred and fifty autographed | copies of which this is number* _____.'

Binding: Deep red V cloth (smooth) with very deep red V cloth shelfback. Spine goldstamped same as trade cloth binding. Dark red endpapers. All edges trimmed.

   Slipcase covered with dark red paper. Printed paper label on front: '[white frame; double-rules black frame] [printed against light yellowish brown] *Limited Edition* | THE EYE-BEATERS, | BLOOD, VICTORY, | MADNESS, BUCKHEAD | *and* | MERCY | [rule] | *James Dickey*'.

Publication: See certificate of limitation. Copyright page substitutes 'LIMITED EDITION' for 'FIRST EDITION AFTER A LIMITED EDITION OF 250 COPIES'. $15.00 Published simultaneously with trade issue.

Locations: LC (slipcase—FEB 24 1970); Lilly (slipcase); MJB (slipcase); PSt (slipcase); ScU (slipcase).

A 13.1.b

Second printing: Garden City, N.Y.: Doubleday, 1970.

Wrappers. 5,000? copies. $2.45. This printing has been misidentified as part of the first printing; but the 'FIRST EDITION' slug has been removed from the copyright page.

A 13.1.c

Third printing: Garden City, N.Y.: Doubleday, 1970.

Copyright page: '9 8 7 6 5 4 3 2'. Wrappers. 10,000? copies. $2.45.

E. C. S. Facsimile Series, No. 151

Ronald Perera

Apollo Circling

Four Lyric Songs
for High Voice and Piano

E. C. Schirmer Music Company
112 South Street
Boston, Massachusetts 02111

Front cover for A 13.1.a *Note:* 9″ × 12″

12

A 13.1.d

First edition, first English printing (1971)

THE EYE-BEATERS,
BLOOD, VICTORY,
MADNESS, BUCKHEAD
and
MERCY

James Dickey

HAMISH HAMILTON
LONDON

A 13.1.d: 6⅛″ × 9⅛″

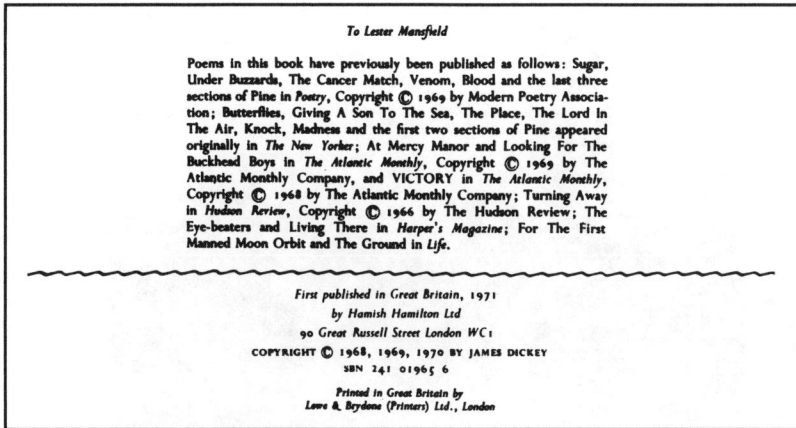

Same pagination as first printing.

[A] B–D^8

Contents: Same as first printing.

Typography and paper: Same typography as first printing with addition of signatures. Wove paper.

Binding: Dark greenish blue paper-covered boards. Spine goldstamped verti-cally: 'james dickey the eye-beaters [above] Hamish [below] Hamilton'. White endpapers. All edges trimmed.

Dust jacket: Front and spine lettered on black: '[olive green incomplete cir-cle] | the eye • beaters | blood | victory | [white] james dickey | [olive green] madness | buckhead | and mercy'. Spine lettered vertically in white: 'james dickey the eye • beaters Hamish Hamilton'. Back has photo of Dickey by Christopher Dickey. Front flap has comment on book, jacket design and photo credits, and price. Back flap has biographical note on Dickey. Flaps partly coated.

Publication: 1,000 copies. Published 28 January 1971. £1.25.

Production: See copyright page.

Locations: BL (1 JAN 1971); JRB (2 copies—dj); LC; Lilly (dj); MJB (2 copies—dj); ScU (dj).

Note: One JRB copy, the LC copy, one MJB copy, and the ScU copy have line 4 in the copyright notice hand-canceled in ink.

£1.25 net

the eye beaters
blood
victory
james dickey
madness
buckhead
and mercy

james dickey   the eye beaters   Hamish Hamilton

SBN 241 01965 6

Dust jacket for A 13.1.d

A 14 DELIVERANCE (PAMPHLET)

A 14.1

First edition, only printing (1970)

Cover title for A 14: 8½″ × 5½″

[1]^{10}

178–187 215–223 [224]

Typography and paper: Reduced facsimile of Dickey's revised typescript pages. Wove paper.

Binding: Wrappers. Front lettered against black: '[blue eye peering through leaves on green background; within green, black, blue, and brown circles] | [outlined in white] DELIVERANCE | [green] A NOVEL BY | [outlined in green] JAMES DICKEY'. Back: [against 1¹⁄₁₆″ vertical black strip at right] [vertically, outlined in white] [above] JAMES [below] DICKEY DELIVER-ANCE | [horizontally in green] HOUGHTON | MIFFLIN | COMPANY'; also mailing permit and coupon for ordering *Deliverance*. Inside front cover: letter beginning 'Dear Bookseller' from Thomas Consolino. Inside back cover: mailing coupon. Saddle-stapled.

Publication: Unknown number of copies distributed prior to publication of *Deliverance*. Not for sale.

Location: JRB; MJB; PSt; ScU.

A 15 DELIVERANCE

A 15.1.a

First edition, first printing (1970)

Deliverance
by James Dickey

HOUGHTON MIFFLIN COMPANY

1970 Boston

A 15.1.a: 5⁷⁄₁₆″ × 8³⁄₁₆″

[i–x] [1–3] 4–22 [23–25] 26–89 [90–93] 94–165 [166–169] 170–240 [241–243] 244–278

[1–9]^{16}

Contents: p. i: half title; p. ii: card page; p. iii: title; p. iv: copyright; p. v: 'To | Edward L. King and | Albert Braselton, | companions | [leaf]'; p. vi: blank; p. vii: epigraphs from Georges Bataille and the Book of Obadiah; p. viii: blank; p. ix: contents; p. x: blank; p. 1: 'Before'; p. 2: blank; pp. 3–278: text. Novel. Excerpts from *Deliverance* were previously published in C 242 and C 245.

Typography and paper: 5⅞″ (6⅛″) × 3¹⁵⁄₁₆″. 30 lines per page. Running heads: rectos: section title and folio; versos: '[folio] *Deliverance*'. Wove paper.

Binding: Yellowish gray V cloth (smooth). Front: '[medium green] Deliverance'. Spine stamped vertically in medium green: '[above] Deliverance [below] James Dickey [at foot] [above] HOUGHTON [middle] MIFFLIN [below] COMPANY'. Dark yellowish green endpapers. All edges trimmed. Top edge stained light bluish green. Dark yellowish green and white headbands and footbands.

Dust jacket: Front and spine lettered against black. Front: '[drawing of blue eye peering through leaves on green background; within black, blue, and green circles] | [green] DELIVERANCE | A NOVEL BY | [green outlined by blue] JAMES DICKEY'. Spine: '[vertically in green] [above] JAMES [below] DICKEY DELIVERANCE [horizontally] HOUGHTON | MIFFLIN | COMPANY'. Back has photo of Dickey by Christopher Dickey and '6-84530'. Front flap has description of novel and '0370'. Back flap has note on Dickey.

Publication: 50,000 copies. Published 23 March 1970. $5.95. Copyright #A128814.

Production: Colonial Press, Clinton, Mass.

Locations: Caroliniana (dj); JRB (dj); LC (FEB 16 1970—rebound); Lilly (dj); MJB (dj); PSt (dj); ScU (dj).

Proof copy: Spiral-bound half-galleys in white wrappers. Front: 'Deliverance | by James Dickey | UNCORRECTED PROOF | HOUGHTON MIFFLIN COMPANY | 1970 Boston'. 7″ × 11″. Location: MJB.

$5.95

DELIVERANCE
JAMES DICKEY

DELIVERANCE
A NOVEL BY
JAMES DICKEY

DELIVERANCE

JAMES DICKEY

JAMES DICKEY

This novel by James Dickey, who is one of America's finest poets, is a heart-stopping tour de force, an overpowering, unforgettable tale of violent adventure and inner discovery.

Four men embark on a three-day canoe trip down a particularly wild section of a river in the heartland of today's South. They are, with one exception, seemingly average suburban Americans: a mutual funds salesman, a supervisor in a soft-drink company, and a successful art director in a consulting firm who is the story's narrator. For them the trip represents a break in the domestic routine, a chance for adventure with few real risks, the last occasion to see a beautiful valley unvisited and free before the river is dammed up. Their leader, an enthusiastic outdoorsman and champion archer, is obsessed by the desire to pit himself against nature.

When, the morning of the second day, two of the group are attacked viciously and perversely by mountaineers, a mildly adventurous canoe trip explodes into a nightmare of horror and murder. Men stalk and are stalked by other men and the treacherous river becomes a graveyard for those without the strength or the luck to survive. The narrator, forced to assume the leadership of his group and to pursue a dangerous multiple deception, must call upon all his resources to try to achieve deliverance.

0370

JAMES DICKEY has been a star college athlete (football at Clemson and track at Vanderbilt), a night fighter pilot with over 100 missions in World War II and Korea, and a successful advertising executive in New York and Atlanta. He became a full-time poet at the age of 38, publishing in virtually every American journal of consequence, and five years later, in 1966, won the National Book Award in Poetry for Buckdancer's Choice. That same year he was appointed Poetry Consultant to the Library of Congress, and in 1967 the publication of his collected volume, Poems 1957–1967, was hailed as one of the literary events of the decade.

Mr. Dickey, who is an avid woodsman, archer, and guitarist, has taught at Reed College, Rice Institute, and the Universities of Florida and Wisconsin, and has lectured on scores of platforms across the country. Married and the father of two sons, he presently lives in Columbia, South Carolina, where he is poet-in-residence at the University of South Carolina. Deliverance, which he began in 1962, is Mr. Dickey's first novel.

Jacket by Paul Bacon Studios, Inc.

HOUGHTON MIFFLIN COMPANY
2 Park Street
Boston, Massachusetts 02107

Photograph by Christopher Dickey

Dust jacket for A 15.1.a

A 15.1.b

First edition, second printing: Boston: Houghton Mifflin, [1970].

Copyright page: '*Second Printing* C'. 10,000 copies. The date was removed from the title page after the first printing.

A 15.1.c

First edition, third printing: Boston: Houghton Mifflin, [1970].

Copyright page: '*Third Printing* C'. 20,000 copies.

A 15.1.d

First edition, later printing: Boston: Houghton Mifflin, [   ].

No printing identification on copyright page. On back cover of dust jacket: '4216'.

A 15.1.e

First edition, pirated printing: Offset reprint of first printing with copyright page in Chinese characters. Probably printed in Taiwan. Location: MJB (dj).

A 15.2

Second edition: Boston: Houghton Mifflin, [1970].

[1–13] 14–32 [33–35] 36–98 [99–101] 102–172 [173–175] 176–246 [247–249] 250–284 [285–286]

On dust jacket front flap: '*Book Club* | 053 *Edition*'. April 1970 Literary Guild selection.

A 15.3.a

Third edition, first English printing (1970)

Deliverance

by

JAMES DICKEY

HAMISH HAMILTON
LONDON

A 15.3.a: 5″ × 7¹¹⁄₁₆″

[i–x] [1–3] 4–21 [22–25] 26–84 [85–87] 88–153 [154–157] 158–223 [224–227] 228–259 [260–262]

$[1–7]^{16} [8]^8 [9]^{16}$

Contents: p. i: half title; p. ii: card page; p. iii: title; p. iv: copyright; p. v: dedication; p. vi: blank; p. vii: epigraphs; pp. viii: blank; p. ix: contents; p. x: blank; p. 1: 'Before'; p. 2: blank; pp. 3–259: text; pp. 260–262: blank.

Typography and paper: 5⅞″ (6⅛″) × 3¹³⁄₁₆″. 33 lines per page. Running heads: rectos: section title and folio; versos: '[folio] *Deliverance*'. Wove paper.

Binding: Strong blue paper-covered boards. Spine goldstamped vertically: 'DELIVERANCE [3 arrowheads] James Dickey [horizontal hh device]'. White endpapers. All edges trimmed. Top edge stained strong red.

Dust jacket: Front and spine printed against black background. Front: '[yellow and red] DELIVERANCE | [white] James Dickey [arrow from top right to bottom left]'. Spine: '[white] James | Dickey | [vertically in yellow and red] DELIVERANCE | [horizontal white hh device]'. Back has photo of Dickey by Christopher Dickey. Front flap has comment on book. Back flap has notes on Dickey and *Deliverance*.

Publication: 7,500 copies. Published 10 September 1970. £1.50.

Production: See copyright page.

Locations: BL (10 AUG 70); JRB (dj); Lilly (dj); MJB (dj); ScU (dj).

Proof copy: Yellow wrappers; front printed in red: '*Deliverance* | *by* | JAMES DICKEY | ADVANCE PROOF. This is an uncorrected | proof and is for your confidential information only. | It is not to be quoted without comparison with the | finally revised text and is in no circumstances to | be offered for sale. | [hh device] | HAMISH HAMILTON | LONDON'. Location: ScU.

DELIVERANCE

James Dickey

SBN 241 01927 3

JAMES DICKEY, one of America's finest poets, has been a star college athlete, a night fighter pilot with over a hundred missions in the Second World War and in Korea, and an advertising executive in New York and Atlanta. He became a full-time poet at the age of thirty-eight and five years later, in 1966, won the American National Book Award in Poetry for *Buckdancer's Choice*. In the same year he was appointed Poetry Consultant to the Library of Congress, and the 1967 publication of his collected volume, *Poems 1957–1967*, was hailed as one of the literary events of the decade. Mr. Dickey is now poet-in-residence at the University of South Carolina.

DELIVERANCE, which is his first novel, has already caused a furore in America. Film rights have been acquired by Warner Brothers; the book has been serialised in the *Atlantic Monthly*; the paperback rights have been sold for a six-figure sum; and it is a Literary Guild Choice.

Four men embark on a canoe-trip down a wild section of river in the heartland of America's South. It is scheduled to last three days. The quartet consists, with one exception, of seemingly average suburban Americans: a mutual funds salesman, a supervisor in a soft-drink company, and a successful art director in a consulting firm who is the book's narrator. For them, the expedition represents a break in the domestic routine, a chance of adventure with few real risks, and the last opportunity to see a beautiful valley, still virtually off the map, before the river coursing through it is dammed up. But the fourth member of the party, the obvious leader, is something different. He is a man obsessed by the desire to pit himself against nature, an expert canoeist and a champion archer.

The trip starts unadventurously enough. But, on the morning of the second day, two men step out of the wood, one of them trailing a shot-gun by the barrel. This is the prelude to a shocking and horrifying attack, and the almost idyllic calm shatters abruptly. The fight for survival becomes paramount. And the odds are appalling for not only are there men intent on murder ever-present just beyond the trees, but the treacherous river suddenly becomes a grave-yard for those without the strength or the luck to defy it. It is the narrator himself, forced to assume the leadership and to pursue a dangerous midnight deception, who must summon up all his resources to try to achieve deliverance.

James Dickey's book is that rare event, a novel of adventure which is superbly written and constructed. He builds up the tension to a nerve-shattering crescendo and invests his characters with tonal and intricate life, as they react to each blood-chilling dilemma and each new catastrophe. *Deliverance* is an overpowering story of violence and inner discovery which is destined to become a classic.

Jacket design by
BERNARD HIGTON
Photograph on back of jacket by
CHRISTOPHER DICKEY

Dust jacket for A 15.3.a

A 15.3.b

Third edition, second printing: London: Hamish Hamilton, [1970].

Cloth. September. Not seen.

A 15.3.c

Third edition, third printing: London: Hamish Hamilton, [1970].

Cloth. October. Not seen.

A 15.4

Fourth edition: New York: Dell, [1971].

Copyright page: 'First Dell printing—April 1971'. Wrappers. $1.25. Dell #1868. 25 printings, 1971–1984. Reprinted in Dell Laurel Series, June 1986.

A 15.5

Fifth edition: London & Sydney: Pan, [1971].

Wrappers. 35 p. ISBN 0 330 026542. 13 printings, 1971–1983.

A 15.6

Sixth edition: Franklin Center, Pa.: Franklin Library, 1981.

Signed by Dickey; no limitation stipulated. With "A special message to subscribers from James Dickey," pp. ix–x. Illustrated by Barron Storey. Leatherbound.

   Published with 22-page booklet in wrappers; cover title: '[rule] | NOTES FROM THE EDITORS | [rule] | JAMES | DICKEY | [rule] | DELIVERANCE | *Signed Limited Editions | from | The Franklin Library*'. Booklet quotes Dickey passim.

A 16 SELF-INTERVIEWS

A 16.1.a.

First edition, first printing (1970)

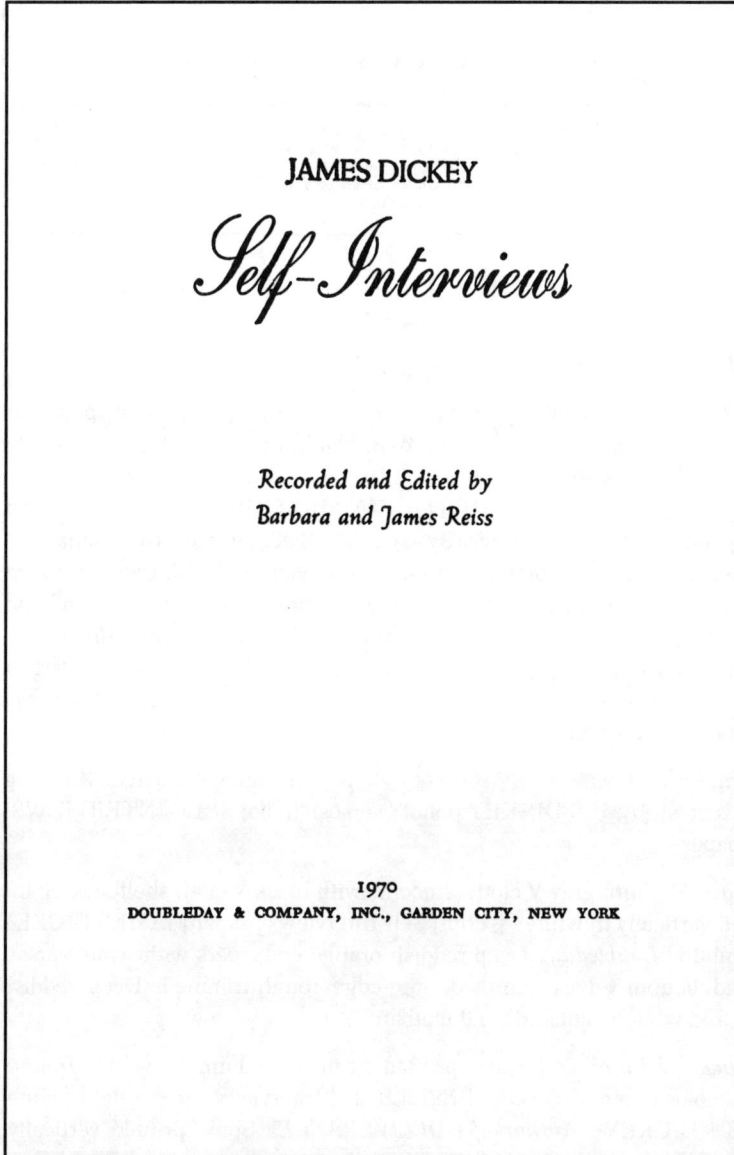

JAMES DICKEY

Self-Interviews

Recorded and Edited by
Barbara and James Reiss

1970
DOUBLEDAY & COMPANY, INC., GARDEN CITY, NEW YORK

A 16.1.a: 5⁷⁄₁₆″ × 8¼″

[1–9] 10–17 [18–23] 24–37 [38–39] 40–50 [51] 52–79 [80–83] 84–121 [122–123] 124–185 [186–187] 188–190 [191–192]

Notch binding; unsewn.

Contents: p. 1: half title; p. 2: blank; p. 3: title; p. 4: copyright; p. 5: '*For Maxine*'; p. 6: blank; p. 7: contents; p. 8: blank; pp. 9–17: '*Introduction*' by Barbara and James Reiss; p. 18: blank; p. 19: half title; p. 20: blank; p. 21: '[script] Part One | [roman] | THE POET IN MID-CAREER'; p. 22: blank; pp. 23–185: text; p. 186: blank; pp. 187–190: 'INDEX'; pp. 191–192: blank.

Essays. 2 parts, 8 chapters: Part One—The Poet in Mid-Career: "Creative Possibilities," "In Medias Res," "Teaching, Writing, Reincarnations, and Rivers"; Part Two—The Poem as Something That Matters: "*Into the Stone*," "*Drowning With Others*," "*Helmets*," "*Buckdancer's Choice*," "*Falling*." Parts of "*Falling*" were previously published in C 249; the rest of this volume was previously unpublished.

Typography and paper: 6¹⁄₁₆″ (6¼″) × 3⅞″. 34 lines per page. Running heads: rectos: 'JAMES DICKEY [folio]'; versos: '[folio] SELF-INTERVIEWS'. Wove paper.

Binding: Medium gray V cloth (smooth) with black V cloth shelfback. Spine stamped vertically in white: '[script] Self-Interviews [roman] JAMES DICKEY [horizontally] *Doubleday*'. Deep reddish orange endpapers with white versos. Top and bottom edges trimmed; fore-edge rough-trimmed. Deep reddish orange and white headbands and footbands.

Dust jacket: Front and spine printed against medium gray background. Front: '[color photo of Dickey] [white] Self- | Interviews | [red rule] | [white] JAMES | DICKEY | *Author of* | *DELIVERANCE*'. Spine printed vertically: '[black] Self-Interviews JAMES DICKEY [horizontally in white] Doubleday'.

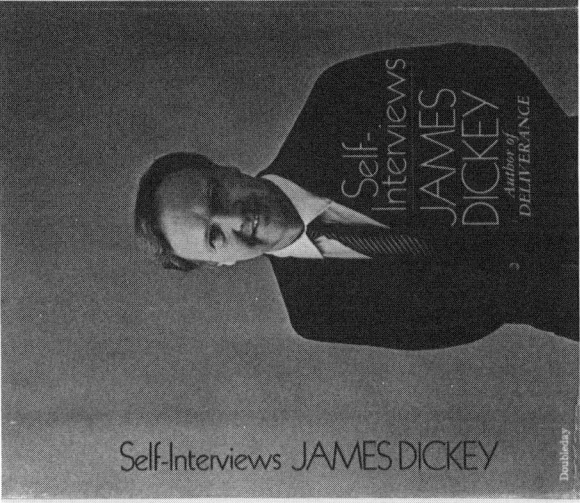

$4.95

Self-Interviews
JAMES DICKEY

The reflections of a poet on his life and work

In this collection of personal reflections, James Dickey talks about those things he knows best—his life and work as a poet. Following an outline prepared by Barbara and James Reiss, Dickey expresses his thoughts in a series of informal tape-recorded monologues that reveal far more than would have been possible in a conventional interview. Printed here, these "self-interviews" constitute an exciting new approach to literary criticism.

Nearly half of the self-interviews are devoted to Dickey's literary career and observations on literary subjects. They describe the young poet's slow self-discovery, his meteoric rise to success since his first book, and his views on a variety of topics from the creative process to politics and poetry in the Saturday Review. In the second section the poet talks about his work, often describing how he came to write a

(continued on back flap)

James Dickey's SELF-INTERVIEWS are about himself—

"I don't have beautiful Mozartian flights of the imagination and write down immortal poems without changing a word. I'm one of those slow, plodding, searching writers. I assume tacitly at the beginning of writing a poem that the first fifty ways I try are going to be wrong. I work by a painful process of elimination in which, after I've tried every possible way I can think of, I finally get maybe not absolutely the right poem but the poem that is less wrong than others."

—and his art—

"In addition to being more human than other people, the poet is also a fiend and a monster. He's got to have that conviction about his work with which nothing can interfere. He's got to have that absolute certainty that what he's doing is really important. No poet has ever been that certain really, because the world may not value him as highly as he values himself. But the poet has to say to himself, 'Whether or not it means that much to other people, it means that much to me.'"

Self-Interviews
JAMES DICKEY

The reflections of a poet on his life and work

Self-Interviews JAMES DICKEY

Self-Interviews
JAMES DICKEY
Author of DELIVERANCE

Doubleday

(continued from front flap)
particular poem or what he intended to convey in it. The result is a fascinating and extremely candid portrait of one of the foremost American poets of our time.

James Dickey was born in Atlanta and educated at Vanderbilt University. After serving in the Air Force in World War II, he began a successful career in advertising. But his rapidly growing reputation as a poet led him to abandon his business career and devote his full time to writing. He has read and lectured widely and served as Consultant in Poetry to the Library of Congress. In 1966 he received the National Book Award in Poetry for his collection Buckdancer's Choice; he has published four other collections, two books of criticism, and a novel, Deliverance.

Barbara and James Reiss graduated from the University of Chicago. Mr. Reiss, a poet, teaches English at Miami University in Ohio. The Reisses conceived the original idea for Self-Interviews; while Mrs. Reiss was working on a Master's thesis about James Dickey.

JACKET TYPOGRAPHY BY PATRICIA SAVILLE VOEHL
JACKET PHOTO OF THE AUTHOR BY ALEX CONTETTE

Printed in the U.S.A.

Dust jacket for A 16.1.a

Back cover has excerpts from book. Front flap has comment on book. Back flap has biographical notes on Dickey and Barbara and James Reiss.

Publication: 6,500 copies. Published 6 November 1970. $5.95. Copyright #A191041.

Production: Doubleday, Berryville, Va.; Doubleday, Smithsburg, Md. P. 190: 'L37'.

Locations: JRB (dj); LC (NOV 13 1970—dj); Lilly (dj); MJB (dj); PSt (dj).

A 16.1.b

Second printing: Garden City, N.Y.: Doubleday, [1971].

2,000 clothbound copies. P. 190: 'M5'.

A 16.1.c

Third printing: Taiwan piracy, [1971?].

Not seen.

A 16.1.d

Fourth printing: [New York: Dell, 1972].

Copyright page: 'First Delta printing—March 1972'. Wrappers. $2.25.

A 16.1.e

Fifth printing: Baton Rouge: Louisiana State University Press, [1984].

Wrappers. $6.95. L-206.

A 17 LORD, LET ME DIE BUT NOT DIE OUT

A 17.1

First edition, only printing (1970)

Self-cover for A 17.1: 8⅜″ × 11″; printed in black and white on yellow

[1–8]

[1]⁴; saddle-stapled.

Contents: Continuity and teaching material from sound film.

Paper: pp. 1–2, 8: yellow; pp. 5, 7: yellow and white. Five holes punched for loose-leaf binding. Wove coated paper.

Publication: Distributed by Encyclopaedia Britannica Educational Corporation in 1970 to accompany sound film, *Lord, Let Me Die But Not Die Out.*

Locations: JRB; MJB.

A 18 EXCHANGES

A 18.1

First edition, only printing (1971)

Exchanges

by James Dickey
being in the form of
a dialogue with
Joseph Trumbull Stickney

A 18.1: 7″ × 8¹³⁄₁₆″

[1–6] 7–15 [16]

[1]^8

Contents: p. 1: half title in gold; p. 2: blank; p. 3: title; p. 4: copyright; p. 5: introductory note by Dickey; p. 6: blank; pp. 7–15: text; p. 16: certificate of limitation and colophon. Poem. Introduction previously unpublished. Poem was previously published in *AS* [Association of Student Chapters/American Institute of Architects] #8 (5 October 1970) as a poster on versos of pp. 5–8; it was subsequently collected in *Strength of Fields*.

Typography and paper: Gold running heads on rectos: 'Exchanges | [rule]'. Off-white paper.

Binding: Black unprinted wrappers. Light olive-brown portfolio paper covers. Front: 'Exchanges | [rule]'. Front flap: '[rule] | [device] | Bloomfield Hills, Michigan | A Bruccoli-Clark Book • 1971'. Deckle fore-edges alternate with trimmed fore-edges. Distributed in white envelope with publisher's name and address printed at top left.

Publication: 200 numbered copies signed by Dickey. Published 14 July 1971. $15.00. Copyright #A277173.

Production: See colophon.

Locations: Caroliniana; JRB; Lilly; MJB; PSt.

Note: Review copies identified by rubber stamp on p. 16. Location: MJB.

Two hundred copies of *Exchanges*, by James Dickey, have been printed by Leonard F. Bahr at his private press, Adagio. The types were set by hand in Palatino Roman and Italic and printed one page at a time on Strathmore Grandee using a C&P Craftsman press. Each copy is signed by the author. This is copy number *35*

James Dickey

A 19 FIRING LINE

A 19.1

First edition, only printing (1971)

Cover title for A 19.1: 5^{11}/$_{16}$″ × 8^{7}/$_{16}$″

[i–ii] 1–11 [12–14]

[1]⁸

Contents: p. i: title; p. ii: blank; pp. 1–11: text; pp. 12–14: blank. Transcription of discussion between Dickey and William F. Buckley, Jr. Collected as *"Firing Line"* in *Night Hurdling*.

Typography and paper: Double columns. 7½″ (7¹¹⁄₁₆″) × 4¹¹⁄₁₆″. No running heads. Wove paper.

Binding: Light yellowish brown wrappers. Front: '[drawing of Buckley by Ronald G. Chapiesky] | [outlined against background] [circle] WILLIAM F. BUCKLEY JR. | [dark grayish brown] FIRING LINE | SOUTHERN EDUCATIONAL COMMUNICATIONS ASSOCIATION'. Back: postage permit. Inside front: copyright and note on series. Inside back: subscription coupon. All edges trimmed. Saddle-stapled.

Publication: Unknown number of copies. Published 25 August (?) 1971. 25¢. Copyright #A387492.

Production: SCETV Network, Columbia, S.C.

Locations: JRB; Lilly; MJB; ScU.

A 20 SORTIES

A 20.1.a

First edition, first printing (1971)

SORTIES

JAMES DICKEY

Doubleday & Company, Inc. | Garden City, New York

1971

A 20.1.a: 5⁷⁄₁₆″ × 8⅛″

Grateful acknowledgment is made to the following for permission to reprint their material:

"Contemporary Poetry" reprinted from *The Self as Agent* edited by J. MacMurray, 1953 by permission of Humanities Press.

"The Son, the Cave, and the Burning Bush" reprinted from *The Young American Poets* edited by Paul Carroll copyright © 1968 by Follett Publishing Company. Used by permission.

"Edward Arlington Robinson" reprinted from *The New York Times Book Review* May 18, 1969. Copyright © 1969 by The New York Times Company.

"The Great American Poet" copyright © 1968 by The Atlantic Monthly Company, Boston, Mass. Reprinted with permission.

Excerpts from *The Distinctive Voice:* Twentieth Century American Poetry edited by W. J. Martz copyright © 1966 by Scott, Foresman And Company. Reprinted by permission of the publisher.

Included in "Spinning the Crystal Ball":
"Fever 103°" by Sylvia Plath, copyright © 1963 by Ted Hughes. From *Ariel* by Sylvia Plath. Reprinted by permission of Harper & Row.

"It Was in Vegas" by James Cunningham reprinted from *The Collected Poems and Epigrams of J. V. Cunningham* © 1971, by permission of The Swallow Press, Chicago.

"Rome" by James Cunningham reprinted from *The Collected Poems and Epigrams of J. V. Cunningham* © 1971, by permission of The Swallow Press, Chicago.

"Approaching Winter" by Robert Bly reprinted from *Silence in the Snowy Fields*, Wesleyan University Press, copyright © 1962 by Robert Bly, by permission of the author.

"Next Day" by Randall Jarrell, reprinted with permission of The Macmillan Company from *The Lost World*, copyright © 1963, 1965 by Randall Jarrell. Originally appeared in *The New Yorker*.

"Motherhood, 1880" by Eleanor Ross Taylor reprinted from her *Wilderness of Ladies* (New York, McDowell, Obolensky, copyright © 1960) with permission of Astor-Honor, Inc.

"After the Late Lynching" by Katherine Hoskins. Copyright © 1956, 1966 by Katherine Hoskins from the book *Excursions* by Katherine Hoskins. Reprinted by permission of Atheneum Publishers.

First stanza of "In Medias Res" by William Stafford, copyright © 1960 by William Stafford. From *Traveling Through the Dark* by William Stafford. Reprinted by permission of Harper & Row.

"Sunday" by Vern Rutsala copyright © 1964 by Vern Rutsala. Reprinted from *The Window*, by Vern Rutsala, by permission of Wesleyan University Press.

"The Long Waters" by Theodore Roethke copyright © 1962 by Beatrice Roethke as Administratrix of the Estate of Theodore Roethke. From *The Collected Poems of Theodore Roethke* reprinted by permission of Doubleday & Company, Inc.

"Song of Caribou, Musk Oxen, Women and Men Who Would Be Manly" originally published in Knud Rasmussen's *Intellectual Culture of the Copper Eskimos* (Copenhagen, Gyldendal, 1932) reprinted from *The Unwritten Song*, edited by Willard R. Trask (New York, Macmillan, 1966).

"The Vision of Adam" by Brewster Ghiselin from his book *Against the Circle* copyright 1946 by E. P. Dutton. Reprinted by permission of the publishers.

[i–xii] [1–3] 4–151 [152–155] 156–164 [165–166] 167–170 [171–172] 173–188 [189] 190–208 [209–210] 211–213 [214] 215–224 [225–226] 227 [228]

Notch binding; unsewn.

Contents: p. i: half title; p. ii: card page; p. iii: title; pp. iv–v: copyrights; p. vi: blank; p. vii: '*To Maxine*'; p. viii: blank; p. ix: contents; p. x: blank; p. xi: half title; p. xii: blank; p. 1: 'PART I | [rule] | Journals'; p. 2: blank; pp. 3–151: text; p. 152: blank; p. 153: 'PART II | [rule] | New Essays'; p. 154: blank; pp. 155–227: text; p. 228: blank.

Journals and 7 essays. Essays: "The Self as Agent" (see B 16), "A Statement of Longing" ("The Son, the Cave, and the Burning Bush"—see B 18), "Two Talks in Washington" ("Metaphor as Pure Adventure," "Spinning the Crystal Ball"), "Two Voices" ("Edwin Arlington Robinson," "The Greatest American Poet: Theodore Roethke"), "One Voice." Journals and "One Voice" previously unpublished. "Edwin Arlington Robinson" is different from the essay of the same title in *Babel to Byzantium*.

Typography and paper: 6¼" (6½"); ragged right margin. 37 lines per page. Running heads: section titles on versos. Wove paper.

Binding: Dark red V cloth (smooth). Spine stamped vertically: '[silver] SORTIES [dark gray] JAMES DICKEY *Doubleday*'. Light green endpapers. Top and bottom edges trimmed; fore-edge rough-trimmed. Dark red and white headbands and footbands.

Dust jacket: Front and spine printed in black against multicolored background. Front: 'SORTIES | Journals | and | New Essays | JAMES | DICKEY'. Spine: '[vertically] SORTIES JAMES DICKEY [horizontally] Doubleday'. Back: photo of Dickey by Christopher Dickey. Front and back flaps have description of *Sorties* and biographical note on Dickey.

Publication: 5,000 copies. Published 10 December 1971. $6.95. Copyright #A291884.

Production: Doubleday, Berryville, Va.; Doubleday, Smithsburg, Md. P. 227: 'M43'.

Locations: Caroliniana (dj); JRB (dj); LC (17 DEC 1971—dj); Lilly (dj); MJB (dj); PSt.

A 20.1.b

Second printing: Garden City, N.Y.: Doubleday, [1972].

Cloth. 2,000 copies. Not seen.

$6.95

SORTIES
Journals
and
New Essays
JAMES
DICKEY

For the past few years, James Dickey has kept a journal in which he recorded his thoughts on a number of literary and non-literary matters. The first part of Sorties is the substance of that journal and as such represents the innermost feelings of one of the most important writers in English today.

Here, the reader finds Mr. Dickey musing on such topics as poets, books, poetry (his trouble with most poetry is that it is too much like poetry; too damn much), music (he's a guitar player), archery (he's just below the championship level), love, age, death, and work (his comments on his new novel, "Death's Baby Machine," are so vivid that the novel seems to take shape right in these pages).

The second part of Sorties consists of essays on poets, such as

(continued on back flap)

SORTIES
Journals
and
New Essays
JAMES
DICKEY

SORTIES   JAMES DICKEY

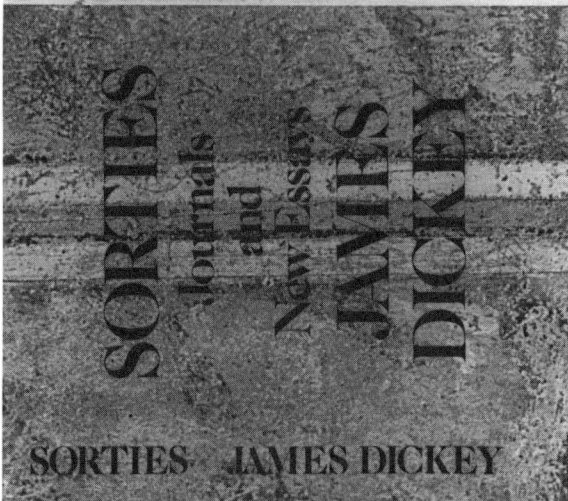

JAMES DICKEY

PHOTO BY CHRISTOPHER DICKEY

JAMES DICKEY

Printed in the U.S.A.

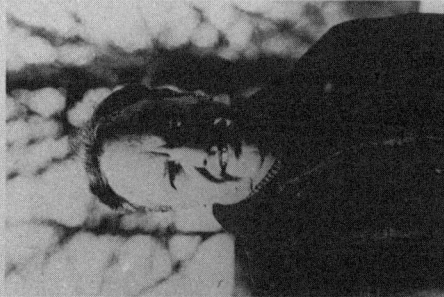

(continued from front flap) Theodore Roethke and Edward Arlington Robinson, the relationship between the poet and the university, the nature and the writing of poetry, poetry written in the first person, and contemporary American poets (Ginsberg, Jarrell, Plath, Sexton, and others).

This is a very frank book (the debunkment of all folk styles that have ever existed in the world comes to a culmination in Bobby Gentry), a very outspoken book (the bellwether of all intellectual cuteness and over-intellectualization is Norman Mailer), a very revealing book (a man cannot pay so much attention to himself as I do without living in hell all the time).

James Dickey won the National Book Award for Poetry for Buckdancer's Choice and received widespread popularity for his bestselling novel, Deliverance. He is the author of four other volumes of poetry and numerous essays and articles.

Dust jacket for A 20.1.a

A 20.1.c

Third printing: Garden City, N.Y.: Doubleday, [1972].

Cloth. 2,000 copies. Not seen.

A 20.1.d

Fourth printing: Baton Rouge: Louisiana State University Press, [1984].

Wrappers. L-206. Also noted in paper-covered boards; presumably a library binding.

A 21 JERICHO

A 21.1

First edition, only printing (1974)

A 21.1: 16″ × 12½″

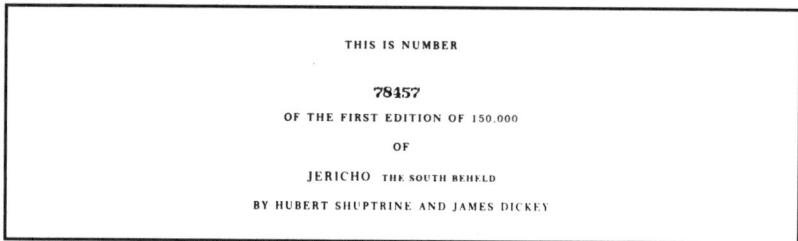

[1–14] 15–17 [18–20] 21–25 [26] 27–29 [30–64] 65–75 [76–110] 111–121 [122–156] 157 [158] 159–165 [166–168]

[1–14]⁶

Contents: pp. 1–2: blank; p. 3: half title; p. 4: blank; p. 5: card page; p. 6: blank; p. 7: title; p. 8: copyright, masthead, and acknowledgments; p. 9: contents; p. 10: blank; p. 11: 14-line epigraph from the Book of Joshua; p. 12: blank; p. 13: 'Introduction'; p. 14: illustration; pp. 15–17: introduction; p. 18: blank; p. 19: 'The | Land | and the | Water'; p. 20: illustration; pp. 21–156: text and illustrations; p. 157: 'Epilogue'; p. 158: blank; pp. 159–165: 'CATA-LOGUE OF THE | PAINTINGS AND DRAWINGS'; p. 166: blank; p. 167: colophon; p. 168: certificate of limitation. Excerpts from *Jericho* were previously published in C 267.

Library of Congress Catalog Card Number: 74-78763

Copyright © 1974 by Oxmoor House, Inc., P. O. Box 2463.
Birmingham, Alabama 35202. All rights reserved.

First Edition published 1974.

Printed in the United States of America.

Conceived, edited and published by Oxmoor House, Inc., Book Division of
The Progressive Farmer Company.

Publication under the direction of:

Leslie B. Adams, Jr., *Vice President and Director*

John Logue, *Editorial Director*

The Publisher wishes especially to acknowledge the contribution made to
this project by the following individuals:

Richard V. Benson, *Marketing Consultant*

Harry H. Lerner, *Graphic Arts Consultant*

James A. Shuptrine, *Artist's Representative*

Grateful acknowledgment is made for permission to reprint the following material:
   Lines from "Big Midnight Special" arranged by Wilma Lee Cooper. Copyright © 1959 by
Acuff-Rose Publications, Inc., Nashville. Used by permission of the publisher. All rights reserved.
   Recipes from *Southern Country Cookbook* by the Editors of *Progressive Farmer* under the
direction of Lena Sturges, Foods Editor. Copyright © 1972 by Oxmoor House, Inc., Birmingham.
   Lines from "The Antique Harvesters" by John Crowe Ransom. Reprinted by permission of
Alfred A. Knopf, Inc., New York, from *Selected Poems*, Third Revised Edition. Copyright © 1955 by
John Crowe Ransom.
   Line from "Lines Written for Allen Tate on His Sixtieth Birthday" by Donald Davidson.
Reprinted by permission of Mrs. Donald Davidson from *The Long Street*, Vanderbilt University
Press, Nashville, 1961. Copyright © 1959 by Donald Davidson.
   Lines from "On a Replica of the Parthenon" by Donald Davidson. Reprinted by permission of
Mrs. Donald Davidson from *Lee in the Mountains and Other Poems*, Houghton Mifflin Company,
Boston, 1938. Copyright © 1935, 1963 by Mrs. Donald Davidson.
   Lines from "Say Good-bye to Big Daddy" by Randall Jarrell. Reprinted by permission of
Farrar, Straus & Giroux, New York, from *The Complete Poems* by Randall Jarrell.
Copyright © 1945, 1969 by Mrs. Randall Jarrell.
   A spoken comment made by Dr. William Y. Elliott to James Dickey.
   Line from "Gold Glade" by Robert Penn Warren. Reprinted by permission of Random House,
Inc., New York, from *Selected Poems: New and Old 1923-1966* by Robert Penn Warren.
Copyright © 1957 by Robert Penn Warren.

Typography and paper: 8½″ (87⁄8″) × 6¹⁵⁄₁₆″. Captions: section titles in left margins of rectos and right margins of versos. Coated wove paper. See colophon.

Binding: White sailcloth covers with very deep red buckram shelfback. Front blindstamped with illustration of fisherman. Spine vertically silverstamped:

'SHUPTRINE • DICKEY Jericho THE SOUTH BEHELD [horizontally] OXMOOR | HOUSE'. Medium gray end papers. All edges trimmed. Red and white headbands and footbands. See colophon. A color print of Shuptrine's "Late Autumn" was laid into the book.

Dust jacket: Front: '[on white panel] HUBERT SHUPTRINE • JAMES DICKEY Jericho | THE SOUTH BEHELD | [color illustration of fisherman]'. Back has statement by Willie Morris and photos of Shuptrine and Dickey with biographical notes. Front flap has statements by Robert Penn Warren, William Styron, and Willie Morris; description of book continued on back flap.

Note 1: Sold in printed mailing box.

Publication: 150,000 copies machine-numbered. Published 10 October (?) 1974. $39.95 before 31 December 1974; $60.00 thereafter. Copyright #A603294.

Production: See colophon.

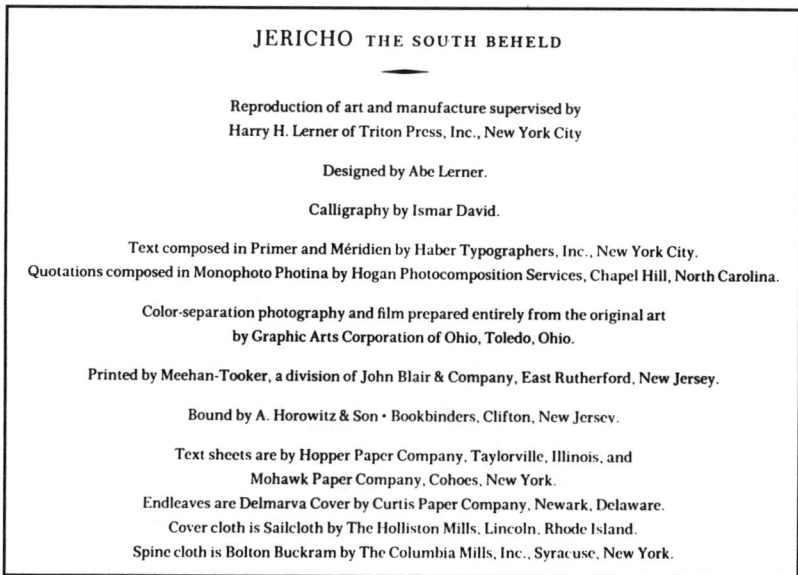

JERICHO THE SOUTH BEHELD
———

Reproduction of art and manufacture supervised by
Harry H. Lerner of Triton Press, Inc., New York City

Designed by Abe Lerner.

Calligraphy by Ismar David.

Text composed in Primer and Méridien by Haber Typographers, Inc., New York City.
Quotations composed in Monophoto Photina by Hogan Photocomposition Services, Chapel Hill, North Carolina.

Color-separation photography and film prepared entirely from the original art
by Graphic Arts Corporation of Ohio, Toledo, Ohio.

Printed by Meehan-Tooker, a division of John Blair & Company, East Rutherford, New Jersey.

Bound by A. Horowitz & Son • Bookbinders, Clifton, New Jersey.

Text sheets are by Hopper Paper Company, Taylorville, Illinois, and
Mohawk Paper Company, Cohoes, New York.
Endleaves are Delmarva Cover by Curtis Paper Company, Newark, Delaware.
Cover cloth is Sailcloth by The Holliston Mills, Lincoln, Rhode Island.
Spine cloth is Bolton Buckram by The Columbia Mills, Inc., Syracuse, New York.

Locations: Caroliniana (dj); JRB (dj—box); LC (CIP 5 FEB 1975); Lilly (dj); PSt (dj). One mis-gathered copy has been located (MJB): 113–114 111–112 117–118 115–116.

Note 2: See Betty Ann Jones, "*Jericho:* The Marketing Story," *Pages: The World of Books, Writers, and Writing* (Detroit: Gale Research, 1976), pp. 248–253.

Dust jacket for A 21.1

A 22 BILL MOYERS' JOURNAL

A 22.1

First edition, only printing (1976)

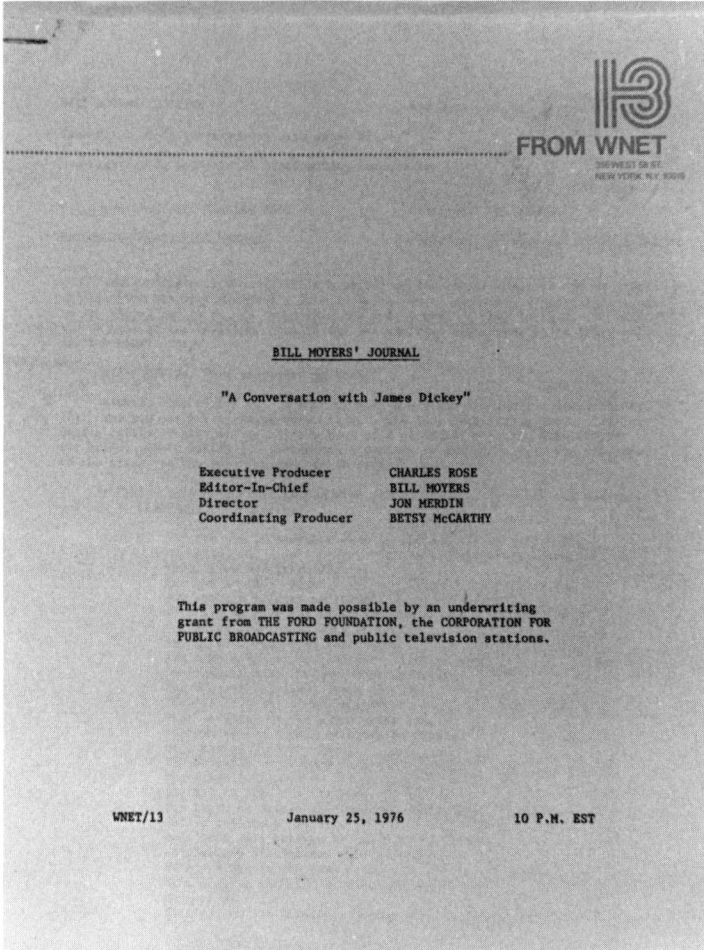

Cover title for A 22.1: 8½″ × 11″; dotted rule and upper right corner in orange [i–ii] [1] 2–16

9 leaves mimeographed on rectos and versos; stapled at upper left. Also 17 leaves mimeographed on rectos only.

Contents: p. i: cover title; p. ii: blank; pp. 1–16: text. Collected as "Conversation on a Dock" in *Night Hurdling*.

Typography and paper: Typescript mimeographed on white paper.

Publication: Distributed by WNET (Channel 13, New York) in conjunction with broadcast on 25 January 1976.

Locations: JRB (9 leaves); Lilly (17 leaves); ScU (17 leaves).

A 23 THE ZODIAC

A 23.1

First edition, only printing (1976)

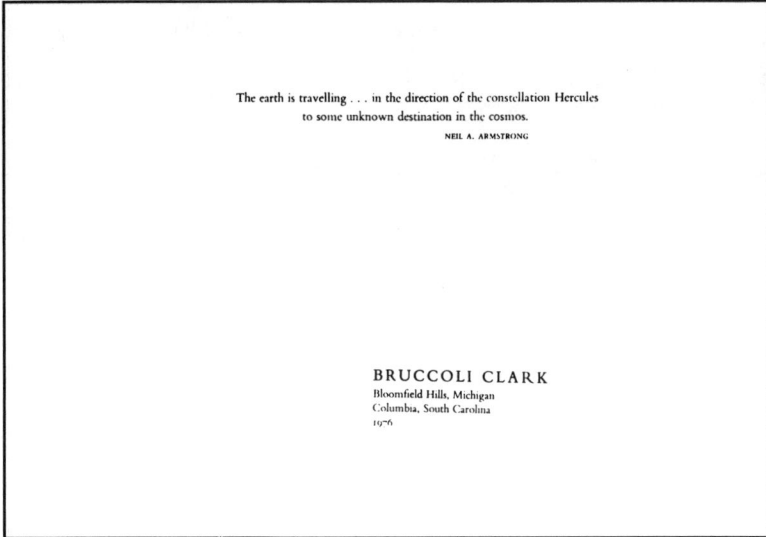

The earth is travelling . . . in the direction of the constellation Hercules
to some unknown destination in the cosmos.

NEIL A. ARMSTRONG

BRUCCOLI CLARK
Bloomfield Hills, Michigan
Columbia, South Carolina
1976

A 23.1: 2-page title; 17⅞″ × 11½″; left

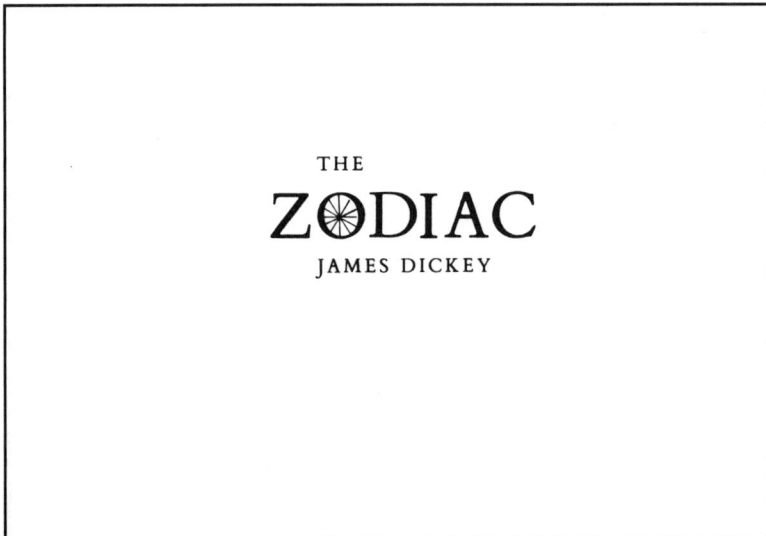

THE

Z☉DIAC

JAMES DICKEY

A 23.1: right; second line in brownish orange, the rest in dark brown

Copyright page: 'THE | ZODIAC | Copyright © 1976 by | *James Dickey*'.

[i–xiv] 1–46 [47–50]

[1–4]⁸; leaf of revised typescript tipped in after first leaf.

Contents: p. i: blank; p. ii: certificate of limitation; pp. iii–iv: blank; p. v: half title; pp. vi–vii: title; p. viii: copyright; p. ix: 'to Walter Schirra'; p. x: blank; p. xi: half title; p. xii: blank; p. xiii: prefatory note by Dickey; p. xiv: blank; pp. 1–46: text; pp. 47–48: blank; p. 49: colophon; p. 50: blank. Poem.

The Zodiac was republished in *The Central Motion* (see E 5).

Typography and paper: 6½″ (6¹⁵⁄₁₆″). No running heads. Maidstone laid paper watermarked 'Hand Made' and 'F J Head', chainlines 1¼″ apart; text printed in dark brown with signs of the zodiac and roman section numbers in brownish orange. See colophon.

Binding: Front covered with medium yellowish brown Elephant Hide paper printed with the signs of the zodiac in pale yellow; shelfback and back bound in light yellowish brown buckram. Spine goldstamped vertically: 'THE ZODIAC DICKEY [horizontal BC device]'. Endpapers same as front. All edges trimmed. Dark yellowish brown and pale yellow headbands and footbands.

Slipcase covered with medium yellowish brown Elephant Hide paper printed with signs of the zodiac in pale yellow on front. Printed yellowish white paper label on front: '[within single-rules frame] THE | ZODIAC | James Dickey'. Shipped in yellowish white unprinted box.

Publication: See certificate of limitation. 61 numbered copies signed by Dickey, each with a leaf of the revised working typescript bound in; 2 unnumbered deposit copies. Published 21 September 1976. $300 prepublication; subsequently raised to $400. Copyright #A773743.

Copy 58 of sixty-one copies of *The Zodiac* signed
by the author, each with a page of the revised working
draft bound in. Two unnumbered copies without a
draft page have been prepared for copyright deposit.

from

James Dickey

Production: See colophon.

Locations: Caroliniana; LC (slipcase without draft leaf—AUG 30 1976); Lilly
(slipcase); MJB (slipcase); ScU (slipcase).

The Zodiac

The type was composed by Heritage Printers in Monotype Bembo. an original Aldine designed in 1929 for the
Monotype Corporation. After letterpress printing by
Heritage on a handmade paper called Maidstone. the
book was bound by Kingsport Press in natural finish
buckram and imported Elephant Hide paper.

The book was designed by Robert. L. Nance.

A 23.2.a₁

Second edition, first printing, first issue (1976)

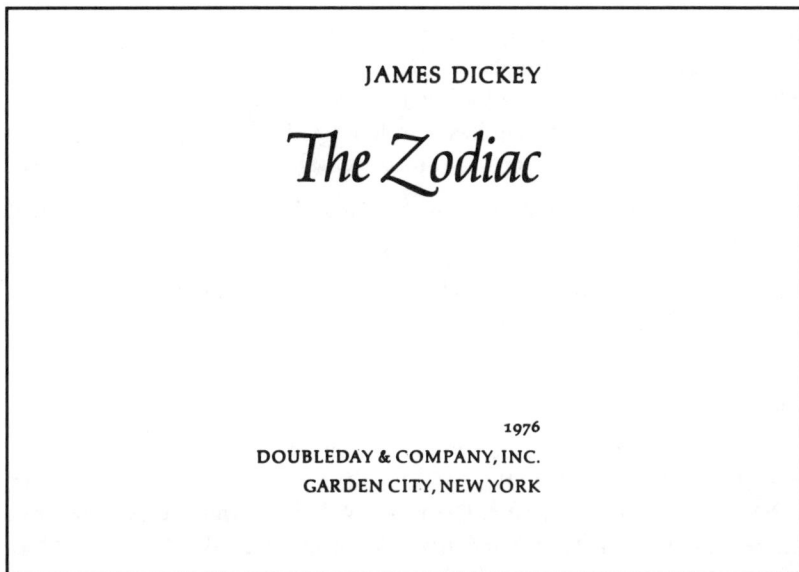

JAMES DICKEY

The Zodiac

1976
DOUBLEDAY & COMPANY, INC.
GARDEN CITY, NEW YORK

A 23.2.a₁: 8¼" × 5⅝"

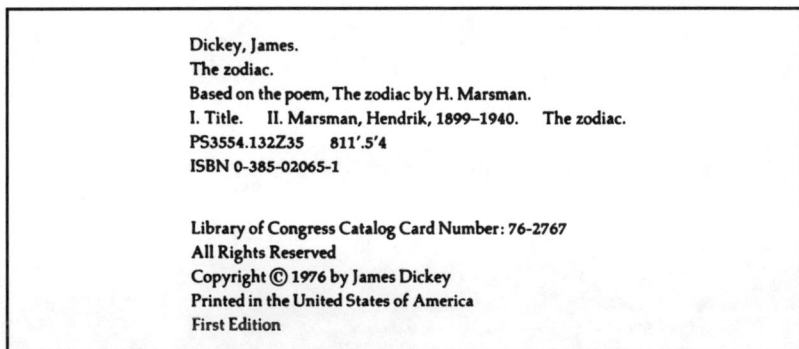

Dickey, James.
The zodiac.
Based on the poem, The zodiac by H. Marsman.
I. Title.   II. Marsman, Hendrik, 1899–1940.   The zodiac.
PS3554.I32Z35   811'.5'4
ISBN 0-385-02065-1

Library of Congress Catalog Card Number: 76-2767
All Rights Reserved
Copyright © 1976 by James Dickey
Printed in the United States of America
First Edition

[1–8] 9–62 [63–64]

[1–4]⁸

Contents: p. 1: half title; p. 2: blank; p. 3: card page; p. 4: blank; p. 5: title; p. 6: copyright; p. 7: author's note and dedication to Hendrik Marsman; p. 8: blank; pp. 9–62: text; pp. 63–64: blank.

Typography and paper: 4³⁄₁₆". No running heads. Wove paper.

Binding: Very red V cloth (smooth). Front goldstamped: '[within circle of zodiac signs] *The Zodiac*'. Spine vertically goldstamped: 'JAMES DICKEY THE ZODIAC DOUBLEDAY'. White endpapers. All edges trimmed.

Dust jacket: Printed on white. Front: '[brown] THE | [brown, orange, purple, and pink] Zodiac | [black] [rule] | BY JAMES DICKEY'. Spine lettered vertically: '[black] THE [brown] Zodiac [black] JAMES DICKEY [purple] Doubleday'. Back same as front. Front flap has description of book. Back flap has note on Dickey. Also noted with title on front and back in shades of orange and lavender.

Publication: 3,000 copies. Published 5 November 1976. $6.00 Copyright #A797112.

Production: Publication Press, Baltimore; Finn Typographical Service, Stamford, Conn.; Doubleday, Berryville, Va.

Locations: Caroliniana (dj); JRB (dj); LC (NOV 11 1976—dj); Lilly (dj— orange and lavender); MJB (dj); PSt.

Proof copy: Light bluish green wrappers; stapled. 7⅜″ × 9⁹⁄₁₆″. Front: 'UN-CORRECTED PROOF | JAMES DICKEY | The Zodiac | 1976 | DOUBLEDAY & COMPANY, INC. | GARDEN CITY, NEW YORK'. Printed paper label over printed wrapper. Label annotated in ink to cancel '2.95 PAPER' and substitute '$30.00 Limited Ed.' Locations: JRB; MJB; ScU (without label).

A 23.2.a₂

Second edition, first printing, English issue (1978)

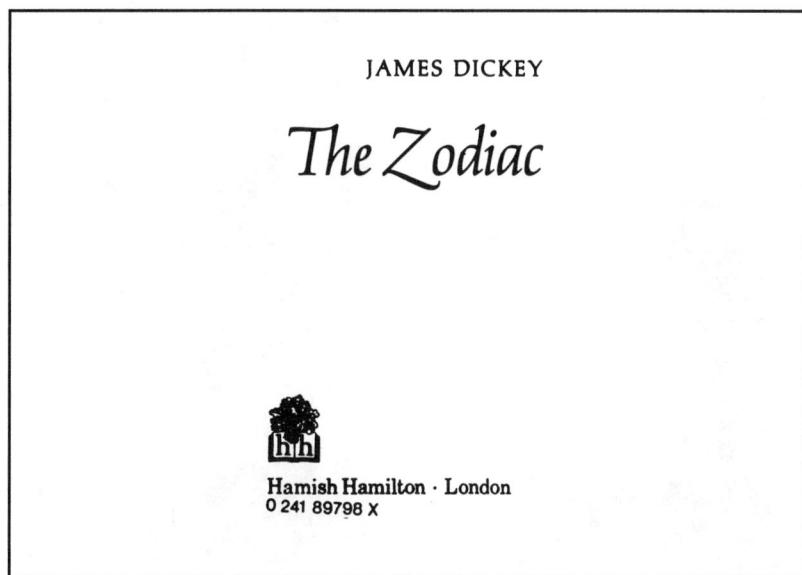

JAMES DICKEY

The Zodiac

[hh logo]

Hamish Hamilton · London
0 241 89798 X

A 23.2.a₂: 8¼″ × 5⅝″

Doubleday printing with 3″ × 1½″ label pasted over title page imprint. Also hh label pasted over imprint on dust jacket spine. Labels pasted on front and back flaps. Slight variation in shades of brown on American and English dust jackets. Unknown number of copies published 15 June 1978.

Locations: JRB (dj); Lilly (dj); MJB (dj); ScU (dj—review slip).

A 23.2.a₃

Second edition, first printing, third issue (1981)

Trade printing with signed leaf on heavy off-white paper tipped in before title leaf.

Slipcase: Very deep red paper-covered boards. Yellowish white label on front: '[within 2 sets of single-rule frames] [very deep red decoration] [black] THE [very deep red decoration] | [black] ZODIAC | [very deep red] JAMES DICKEY'. The books were erroneously shipped in dust jacket; and on 1 June 1981 Doubleday sent a form letter requesting that booksellers remove the jackets before selling the books.

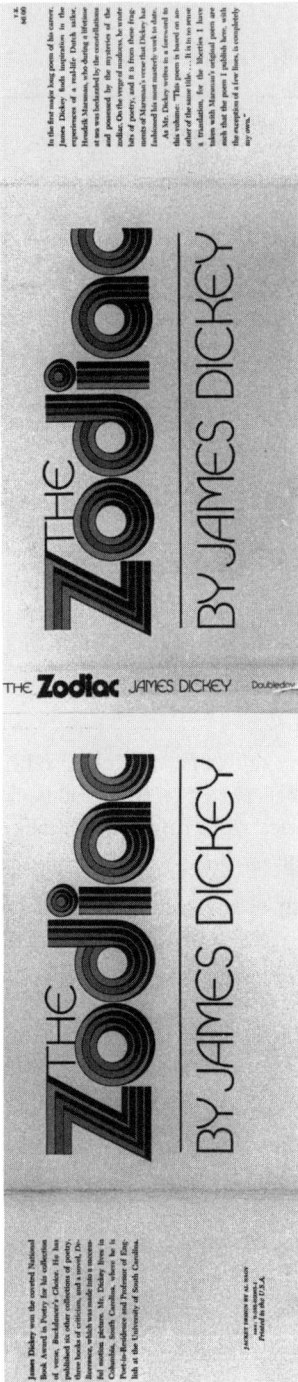

Dust jacket for A 23.2.a_1

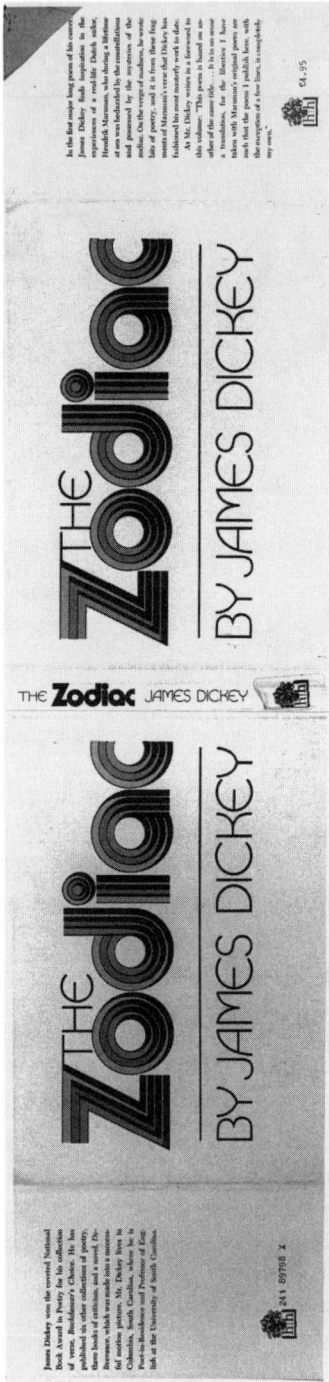

Dust jacket for A 23.2.a_2

Publication: 250 copies. Distributed June 1981. $30.00 The Doubleday limited issue was planned for simultaneous publication with the trade issue, but publication was delayed.

Locations: JRB (dj—boxed); Lilly (boxed); MJB (dj—boxed).

A 23.2.b

Second edition, second printing: Garden City, N.Y.: Doubleday, [1976].

Cloth. 3,400 copies according to Doubleday records. Not seen.

A 23.2.c

Second edition, third printing: Garden City, N.Y.: Doubleday, [1977].

Cloth. 4,800 copies according to Doubleday records. Not seen.

A 24 THE STRENGTH OF FIELDS (POEM)

A 24.1

First edition, only printing (1977)

The Strength of Fields · James Dickey

Bruccoli Clark
Bloomfield Hills, Michigan and
Columbia, South Carolina
1977

A 24.1: 9″ × 6″

Copyright page: 'Copyright © 1977 by James Dickey'.

[1–12]

[1]⁶

Contents: p. 1: title; p. 2: copyright; p. 3: 3-line epigraph from Arnold Van Gennep; pp. 4–11: text; p. 12: certificate of limitation and colophon. Previously published in B 41 and C 276; subsequently collected in *Strength of Fields*.

Typography and paper: See colophon.

Binding: Light yellowish brown wrappers. Front: '[dark red] The Strength of Fields | [medium blue] A poem by James Dickey | written for the inauguration of Jimmy Carter | thirty-ninth President of | The United States of America'. Sewn with light yellowish brown thread. All edges trimmed. Distributed in white envelope printed in gray-blue on front: 'The Strength of Fields • James Dickey | [leaves]'.

This edition consists of 350 numbered copies signed by James Dickey
of which copies I-L are for private distribution

Copy XXIII

Designed and printed at Adagio: The Private Press of Leonard F. Bahr
Harper Woods, Michigan
The type was set by hand in Palatino and printed on a C&P Craftsman press
The paper is Strathmore Americana

The Strength of Fields

A poem by James Dickey
written for the inauguration of Jimmy Carter
thirty-ninth President of
The United States of America

Front cover for A 24.1

Publication: 350 numbered copies signed by Dickey. Published 1 February 1977. $30.00. Copyright #A828339.

Production: See colophon.

Locations: Caroliniana; Lilly; MJB.

A 25 THE OWL KING

A 25.1

First edition, only printing (1977)

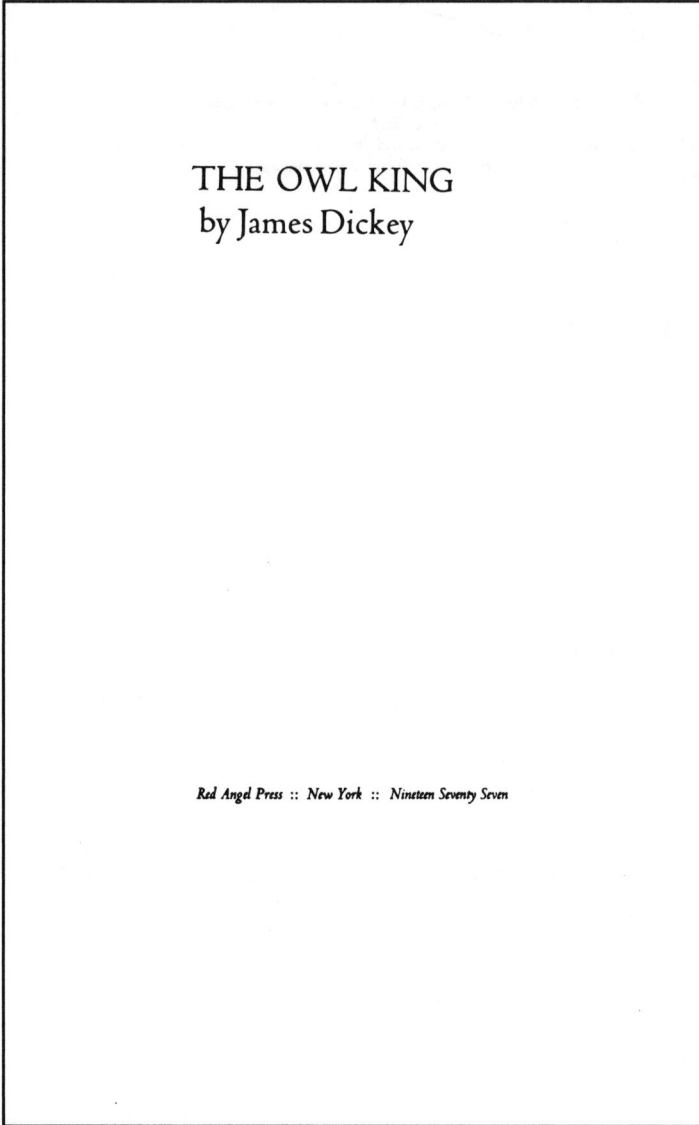

THE OWL KING
by James Dickey

Red Angel Press :: *New York* :: *Nineteen Seventy Seven*

A 25.1: 7¾″ × 12″; title and 'by James Dickey' in blue

Copyright page: 'Copyright © 1962 by James Dickey. Reprinted from "Drowning With | Others" by James Dickey, by permission of Wesleyan University Press.'

[1–24]; frontispiece inserted facing title page. The text of the poem is divided into numbered horizontal sections: I (pp. [a–b] 1 [2] 3 [4] 5–6); II (pp. [a–b] 7–9 [10] 11–12 [13] 14); III (pp. [a–b] 15–23).

[1–2]⁶

Contents: pp. 1–4: blank; p. 5: title; p. 6: copyright; p. 7: section numbers; p. 8: blank; pp. 9–17: text; p. 18: blank; p. 19: certificate of limitation; pp. 20–24: blank. Poem.

Typography and paper: Printed in blue and black. No running heads. Wove paper watermarked 'RIVES'.

Binding: Deep purplish blue V cloth (smooth) front and back with 2 horizontal divisions; yellowish gray B cloth (linen) shelfback. Spine stamped horizontally: '[deep purplish blue] THE OWL KING'. Endpapers same as text. Deckle fore-edge and bottom edge.

Dust jacket: None.

Publication: 100 numbered copies signed by Ronald Keller. Published June 1977. $90.00.

Production: See certificate of limitation.

Locations: Lilly; MJB; ScU.

Note: A sewn folio promotional piece with inserted tissue illustrations was distributed by the publisher. Location: Lilly.

One hundred copies
of this book
were set & printed
by hand at
the Red Angel Press
in New York &
Bremen, Maine.
The typefaces
are Centaur & Arrighi,
the paper is Rives.
The design &
illustrations are by
Ronald Keller.

Number 17
Ronald Keller

I
THE
CALL

Through the trees, with the moon underfoot,
More soft than I can, I call.
I hear the king of the owls sing
Where he moves with my son in the gloom.
My tongue floats off in the darkness.
I feel the deep dead turn
My blind child round toward my calling,
Through the trees, with the moon underfoot,

1

II
THE
OWL
KING

I swore to myself I would see
When all but my seeing had failed.
Every light was too feeble to show
My world as I knew it must be.
At the top of the staring night
I sat on the oak in my shape
With my claws growing deep into wood
And my sight going slowly out
Inch by inch, as into a stone,
Disclosing the rabbits running
Beneath my bent, growing throne,
And the foxes lighting their hair,

7

III
THE
BLIND
CHILD'S
STORY

I am playing going down
In my weight lightly,
Down, down the hill.
No one calls me
Out of the air.
The heat is falling
On the backs of my hands
And holding coldness.
They say it shines two ways.
The darkness is great
And luminous in my eyes.
Down I am quickly going;
A leaf falls on me,
It must be a leaf I hear it
Be thin against me, and now
The ground is level,
It moves it is not ground,
My feet flow cold
And wet, and water rushes
Past as I climb out.
I am there, on the other side.
I own the entire world.

15

Specimen page for A 25.1; top and bottom panels of text in black
with poem titles in blue, middle panel of text in blue with poem title
in black

A 26 GOD'S IMAGES

A 26.1.a

First edition, first printing (1977)

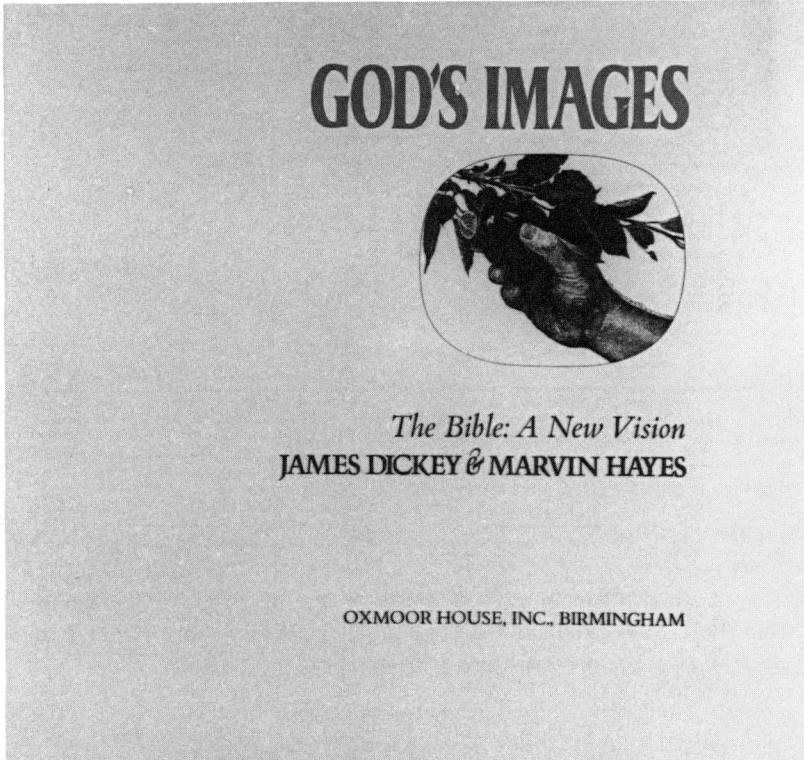

A 26.1.a: 11¾″ × 11″; first line in red

God's Images

ISBN: 0-8487-0479-7
Library of Congress Catalog Card Number: 76-40862
Printed in the United States of America
Copyright © 1977 by Oxmoor House, Inc.
P. O. Box 2463, Birmingham, Alabama 35202
All rights reserved
First Edition

Text copyright © 1977 by James Dickey

Oxmoor House, Inc., is the Book Division of The
Progressive Farmer Company:

Eugene Butler *Chairman of the Board and Editor-in-Chief*
Emory Cunningham *President and Publisher*
Vernon Owens, Jr. *Senior Executive Vice President*
Roger McGuire *Executive Vice President*
Leslie B. Adams, Jr. *Vice President and Director of Book Division*

Conceived, edited, and published by Oxmoor House, Inc.,
under the direction of:

John Logue *Editor-in-Chief*
Ann H. Harvey *Managing Editor*
Robert L. Nance *Production Manager and Designer*

Advisory Board:
Keith Crim, Ph.D., General Editor, *Supplementary Volume, The
    Interpreter's Dictionary of the Bible;* Professor of Philosophy and
    Religious Studies, Virginia Commonwealth University,
    Richmond, Virginia
Hubert H. Harper, Jr., Ph.D., Associate Dean of the Graduate
    School, University of Alabama in Birmingham, Alabama
Father Roland E. Murphy, O. Carm., Professor of Religion,
    The Divinity School, Duke University, Durham, North
    Carolina
Harry M. Orlinsky, Ph.D., Effie Wise Ochs Professor of Bible,
    Hebrew Union College—Jewish Institute of Religion, New
    York, New York
Malcolm L. Peel, Ph.D., Chairman and Professor of Religion,
    Coe College, Cedar Rapids, Iowa

[1–120]

$[1-10]^6$

Contents: p. 1: scroll; p. 2: blank; p. 3: title; p. 4: copyright, masthead, and advisory board; pp. 5–7: 'Foreword'; p. 8: blank; p. 9: 'Old Testament | [lamp]'; pp. 10–116: text and etchings; p. 117: 'Afterword'; pp. 118–119: 'Catalogue of Etchings'; p. 120: colophon and copy number. Excerpts and etchings from *God's Images* were previously published in C 279.

Typography and paper: Text printed in black with initial letter of each chapter and marginal glosses in red. Wove paper. See colophon.

Binding: White B cloth (linen). Front blindstamped: 'GOD'S IMAGES'. Spine stamped vertically in black: 'GOD'S IMAGES [decoration] DICKEY & HAYES Oxmoor'. Black endpapers. All edges trimmed. Black and white headbands and footbands.

Dust jacket: Front: '[two black-and-white etchings of hands] | [black on white panel] GOD'S IMAGES | THE BIBLE: A NEW VISION JAMES DICKEY & MARVIN HAYES'. Spine: '[black] GOD'S IMAGES DICKEY & HAYES [horizontally] Oxmoor | House®'. Back: circular etching and 6 comments on the book; with '0479-7' at lower right. Front flap has comment on book and statement by John Knowles. Back flap has photos of Dickey and Hayes with biographical notes.

```
Design and manufacturing supervision by Robert L. Nance
Production consultant Harry H. Lerner
Text composed in Bembo by Graphic Composition, Inc., Athens, Georgia
Film prepared from the artist's original plates by
Capitol Engraving Company, Nashville, Tennessee
Printed by Rae Publishing Company, Cedar Grove, New Jersey.
Bound by A. Horowitz & Sons · Bookbinders, Fairfield, New Jersey
Text sheets are Special Opaque Vellum Cream by
Beckett Paper Company, Hamilton, Ohio
Endleaves are Multicolor by
Lindenmeyr Paper Corporation, Long Island City, New York
Cover cloth is Natural Finish Payco by
The Holliston Mills, Inc., Kingsport, Tennessee


This is number
18441
of the first edition of GOD'S IMAGES
```

Publication: 25,000 machine-numbered copies. Published 15 October 1977. $19.95 until 31 May 1978; $24.95 thereafter. Copyright #TX364-603.

Production: See colophon.

Locations: Caroliniana (dj); JRB (dj); MJB (dj).

Note: Selections from *God's Images* appeared in *Book Digest*, 4 (November 1977), 146–157.

A 26.1.b

Second printing: New York: Seabury Press, [1978].

Wrappers. $7.95.

Dust jacket for A 26.1.a

A 27 THE ENEMY FROM EDEN

A 27.1

First edition, only printing (1978)

THE ENEMY FROM EDEN

JAMES DICKEY

Illustrated by

RON SAUTER

1978

LORD JOHN PRESS: NORTHRIDGE, CALIFORNIA

A 27.1: 5½″ × 8½″; illustration in brown

THIS first edition of *The Enemy from Eden* is limited to two hundred and seventy-five numbered copies and twenty-six lettered copies, all of which have been signed by the author. The paper is Vicksburgh Vellum and the type Hermann Zapf's Aldus.
Designed and printed by Grant Dahlstrom for the Lord John Press.
This is number **39**

James Dickey [signature]

[i–viii] 1–12 [13–20]

[1]^6 [2–3]^4

Contents: pp. i–iv: blank; p. v: half title; p. vi: blank; p. vii: title; p. viii: 'Copyright © 1978 | *James Dickey*'; pp. 1–13: text; p. 14: blank; p. 15: certificate of limitation; pp. 16–20: blank. Essay. Previously published as "Blowjob on a Rattlesnake" (see C 266); subsequently collected as "The Enemy from Eden" in *Night Hurdling*.

Typography and paper: 5½" (5⅞") × 3½". 28 lines per page. Printed in black with brown illustrations. No running heads. Wove paper.

Binding: Numbered copies: Black, white, and medium blue marbled paper-covered boards. Very dark red buckram shelfback. Front goldstamped on cloth, vertically up: 'THE ENEMY FROM EDEN • JAMES DICKEY'. Medium brown endpapers. All edges trimmed. Lettered copies bound in white buckram with white buckram slipcase.

Publication: See certificate of limitation. 275 numbered copies ($35.00) and 26 lettered copies ($75.00—all signed by Dickey). Published 27 May (?) 1978.

Production: See certificate of limitation.

Locations: Caroliniana (numbered); JRB (numbered); Lilly (numbered and lettered); MJB (numbered); ScU (numbered and lettered).

Note 1:   The author's copy replaces the last line of the certificate of limitation with 'This is the Author's copy' and has a white buckram shelfback. Technically this copy constitutes a separate issue. Location: MJB.

Note 2:   There were 20 presentation copies so identified in the certificate of limitation. Not seen.

THE ENEMY FROM EDEN · JAMES DICKEY

Front cover for A 27.1

A 28 TUCKY THE HUNTER

A 28.1.a₁

First edition, first printing, first issue (1978)

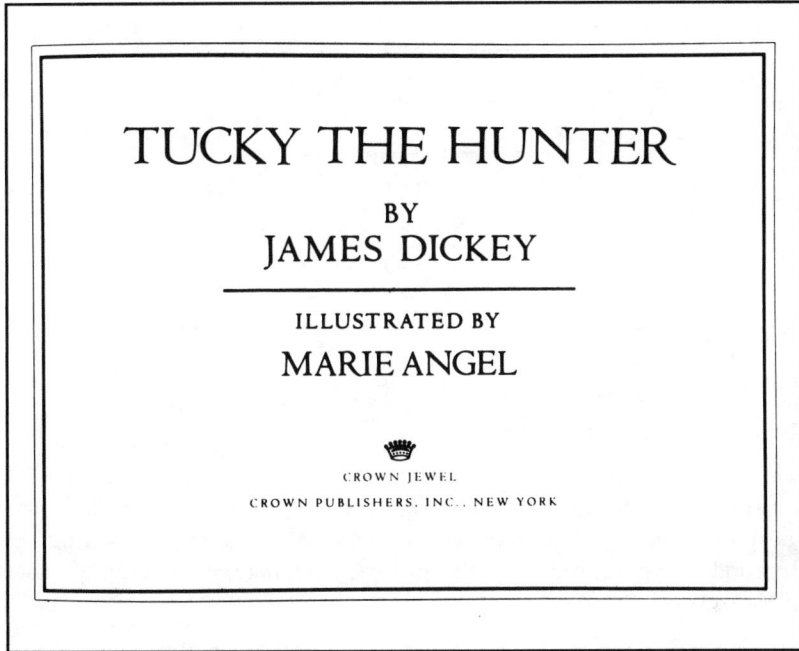

TUCKY THE HUNTER

BY
JAMES DICKEY

ILLUSTRATED BY
MARIE ANGEL

CROWN JEWEL
CROWN PUBLISHERS, INC., NEW YORK

A 28.1.a₁: 8¹¹⁄₁₆″ × 6⁹⁄₁₆″; printed in bluish green, brown, rust, and black

[1–48]

[1–3]⁸

Contents: p. 1: half title in black and rust; p. 2: blank; p. 3: card page in black and rust; p. 4: blank; p. 5: title; p. 6: copyright; p. 7: 'TO | James Bayard Tuckerman Dickey | herein known as Tucky'; p. 8: blank; p. 9: half title in black and rust; p. 10: blank; pp. 11–46: text; p. 47: note on Dickey; p. 48: note on Marie Angel. Poem.

Typography and paper: All text pages illustrated in color. No running heads. Wove paper; watermarked 'Beckett'.

Binding: Strong bluish green V cloth (smooth). Spine goldstamped vertically: 'TUCKY THE HUNTER James Dickey [horizontal crown] CROWN JEWEL'. Back cover goldstamped: '532581'. Medium red endpapers. All edges trimmed.

Dust jacket: Printed on white. Front: '[within bluish green single-rule frame] [bluish green] TUCKY THE HUNTER | [black] by James Dickey | illustrated by Marie Angel | [illustration of bird and flower in color from p. 16]'. Spine: '[bluish green] [vertically] TUCKY THE HUNTER [black] James Dickey [horizontal bluish green crown] [black] CROWN JEWEL'. Back reproduces part of p. 17. Front flap has description of book. Back flap has notes on Dickey and Angel.

Publication: 25,000 copies. Published 11 October 1978. $6.95. Copyright #TX147–259.

Production: Lithochrome, Co., Garden City, N.Y.; Horowitz, Fairfield, N.J.; Haber Typographers, New York.

Locations: Caroliniana (dj); JRB (dj); LC (NOV 15 1978—dj); Lilly (dj); MJB (dj).

Review copy A: Unknown number of bound copies in dust jacket were distributed in advance of publication. P. 1: 'TUCKY THE HUNTER | [rust rule] | [black] This signed, bound proof is one of _____ prepared | especially for prepublication review.' No numbered or signed copies have been located. These copies are on unwatermarked paper and constitute a separate printing. Dust jacket and spine read 'CROWN'—not 'CROWN JEWEL'. Location: MJB.

Review copy B: Unbound book gatherings inserted in dust jacket with review slip laid in. Location: ScU.

TUCKY THE HUNTER
by James Dickey
illustrated by Marie Angel

TUCKY
THE HUNTER
by James Dickey
illustrated by Marie Angel

ISBN: 0-517-55298
$6.95

James Dickey, National Book Award winner for his book of poems *Buckdancer's Choice*, has written a poem about the mind of a child as he hunts the animals of the world with a pop-gun and the mare of his imagination. What emerges is beautiful on the one face and powerful beneath. It is an imagistic celebration of a child's ability to become one with the exuberance of the animal kingdom; it is an evocation of the links that embrace both the mind of the child and the experience of all who love.

(continued on back flap)

TUCKY THE HUNTER · James Dickey · CROWN JEWEL

TUCKY THE HUNTER
BY JAMES DICKEY

E SHOT the bearded barbury goat,

as it sat looking wise,

And, creeping into Eden,

shot the Bird of Paradise.

Illustrated by Marie Angel

(continued from the flap)

Marie Angel's illustrations are a coequal artistic contribution to a joyous and valuable illuminated poem.

James Dickey, in addition to his National Book Award for *Buckdancer's Choice*, is the author of the novel *Deliverance*.

Marie Angel is an award-winning English graphic artist and a highly acclaimed calligrapher.

Crown Publishers, Inc.
One Park Avenue
New York, N.Y. 10016

Dust jacket for A 28.1.a₁

A 28.1.a₂

First edition, first printing, English issue (1979)

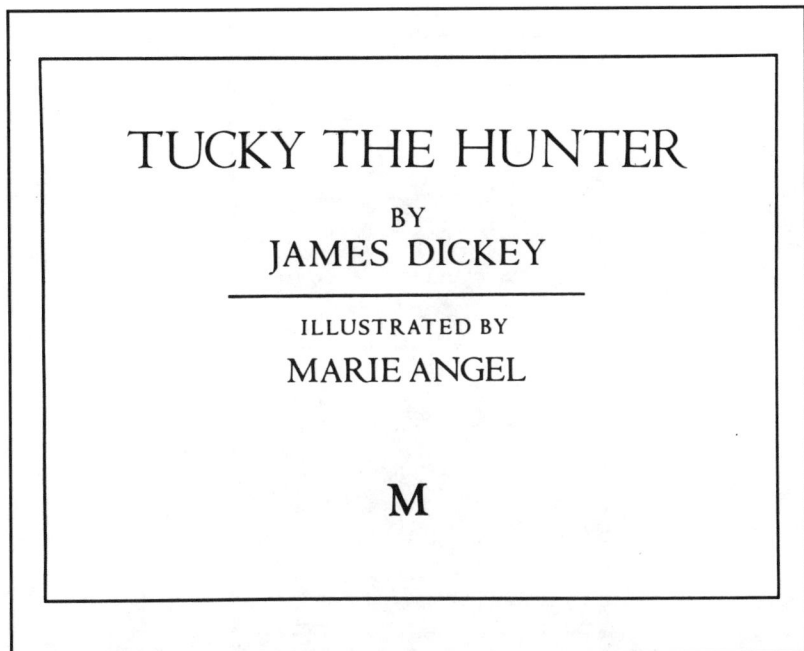

TUCKY THE HUNTER

BY
JAMES DICKEY

ILLUSTRATED BY
MARIE ANGEL

M

A 28.1.a₂: 85%8″ × 65%8″; printed in bluish green, brown, rust, and black

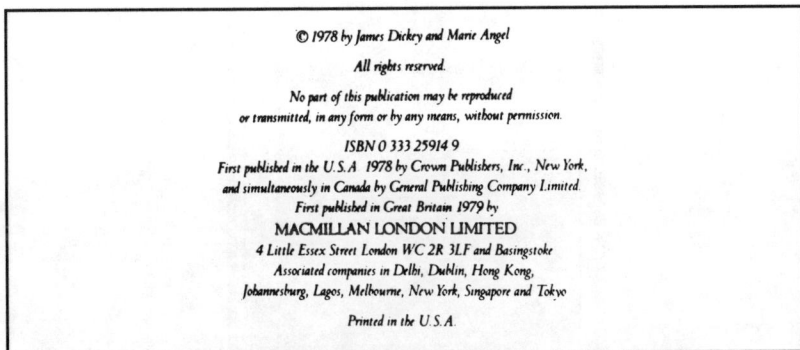

Same pagination and collation as first printing with substitution of English title page and copyright page.

Binding: Strong green paper-covered boards. Spine vertically goldstamped: 'TUCKY THE HUNTER James Dickey [horizontally] M'. White endpapers. All edges trimmed.

Dust jacket for A 28.1.a₂

Front cover:

TUCKY THE HUNTER
by James Dickey
illustrated by Marie Angel

Spine:

TUCKY THE HUNTER   James Dickey   **M**

Half-title / title panel:

TUCKY THE HUNTER
BY JAMES DICKEY

...E SHOT the bearded barbary goat,

     as it sat looking wise,

And, creeping into Eden,

     shot the Bird of Paradise.

Illustrated by Marie Angel

Front flap:

TUCKY
THE HUNTER

He shot the two-horned rhino
with his double-barreled gun,
He shot the dusty python
for sleeping in the sun.

In his dreams, five-year-old Tucky was a hunter. Armed with his pop-gun, he boldly roamed each distant corner of the earth – and beyond – in pursuit of birds and beasts of every kind. But Tucky's prey, like all the creatures of the night, were real only in the dreams when Tucky's mother understood when she spoke his name for him, and sang to him in his bedtime night's alarm.

Written with perception and sensitivity, James Dickey's poem explores the mind of an imaginative small boy and the unique relationship of mother and child, while Marie Angel's glowing pictures perfectly capture and illuminate the vivid world of Tucky's dreams.

Macmillan
£3.95 net

ISBN 0 333 35914 9

TUCKY
THE HUNTER

Back flap:

James Dickey is one of America's leading contemporary poets and a winner of the coveted National Book Award for his volume of poems, Buck-dancer's Choice. He is also the author of the novel, Deliverance, a U.S. best-seller and later a successful film, for which he wrote the screenplay. He is married to his second wife, Deborah, and has two sons and a grandson, Tucky.

Marie Angel studied art at the Croydon School of Art and the Design School of the Royal College of Art. Her work has been widely exhibited and her drawings are in the permanent collections of several libraries and museums, including the Victoria and Albert Museum. She has illustrated a number of books for children, including her Beauty Factory, The Tale of the Faithful Dove and The Tale of Tuppenny. She lives in Wokingham.

Dust jacket: Front and spine same as American dust jacket with substitution of 'M' for Crown imprint on spine. Front and back flaps have new copy. Front flap has description of book. Back flap has notes on Dickey and Marie Angel.

Publication: 6,000 copies. Published 22 February 1979. £3.95.

Production: American sheets with Macmillan title leaf; presumably bound in England.

Locations: Lilly (dj); MJB (dj); ScU.

A 29 VETERAN BIRTH

A 29.1

First edition, only printing (1978)

VETERAN BIRTH

The Gadfly Poems
1947-1949

James Dickey

**Illustrated by
Robert Dance**

Palaemon Press Limited

A 29.1: 5½″ × 7″; first and fourth lines in brownish orange

Copyright page: 'Copyright © 1978 James Dickey | These poems, James Dickey's first-published, ap- | peared in *The Gadfly*, a student literary magazine | at Vanderbilt University, II (Winter 1947), III | (Spring 1948), and IV (Summer 1949).'

[1–16]

[1]^8

Contents: pp. 1–2: blank; p. 3: half title; p. 4: illustration; p. 5: title; p. 6: copyright and acknowledgments; p. 7: note by Dickey; p. 8: illustration; pp. 9–13: text; p. 14: blank; p. 15: certificate of limitation; p. 16: printer's imprint.

4 poems: "Christmas Shopping, 1947," "Sea Island," "King Crab and Rattler," "Whittern and the Kite." All previously published.

Typography and paper: Printed in black and brownish orange. No running heads. Laid paper watermarked 'L AMATRUDA | AMALFI'; chainlines $^{15}/_{16}''$ apart.

Binding: Unprinted black wrappers. Deckle fore-edge and bottom edge. Brown, yellow, beige, and gray marbled wrappers sewn on, with printed white label on front.

VETERAN BIRTH
is printed in an edition of
two hundred and thirty copies.
The type is Caslon,
and the hand-sewn wrappers are
a Swedish marble paper.
Two hundred copies
numbered 1–200 are for sale,
and 30 copies, numbered
i–xxx are for the
use of the author and publisher.
This is number

60

James Dickey

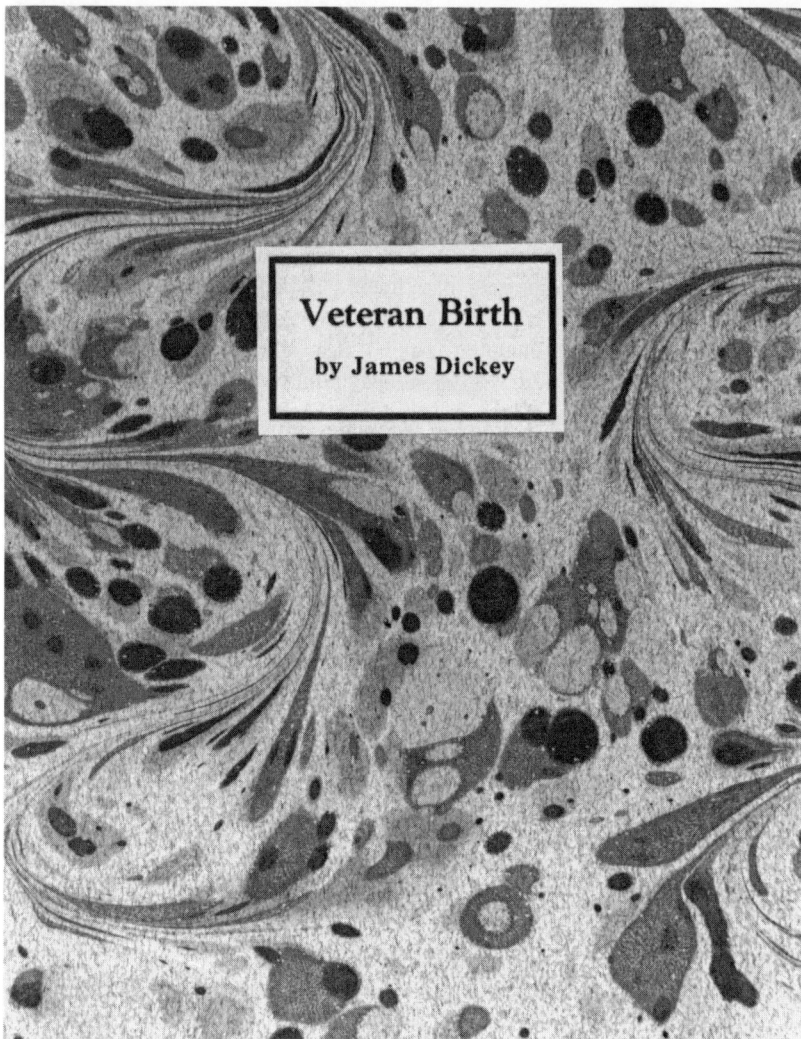

Front cover for A 29.1

Publication: 230 numbered and signed copies. See certificate of limitation. Published 16 October 1978. $20.00

Production: Printed by Heritage Printers, Charlotte, N.C.

Locations: Caroliniana; JRB (unnumbered); Lilly; MJB; ScU.

A 30 MEXICAN VALLEY

A 30.1

First edition, only printing (1978)

Mexican Valley

homage and invention, Octavio Paz

The day works on
                works out its transparent body. With fire, the bodiless hammer,
Light knocks me flat.
                Then lifts me. Hooked on—
to the central flame-stone, I am nothing but a pause between
Two vibrations
                of pressureless glow: Heaven
And trees. Tlaloc help me
                I am pure space:
One of the principle future-lost battlefields
Of light. Through my body, I see my other bodies

Flocking and dancing   fighting each other
With solar joy. Every stone leaps inward, while the sun tears out my eyes
And my Heaven-knifed, stone-drunken heart.
                Yes,
But behind my gone sight is a spiral of wings.
                Now   *now*
My winged eyes are fetched-back and singing: yes singing like buzzards
                From the black-feathered crown-shifts of air
        Have always wished to be singing
                                over this valley.

And I lean over my song
        Within trees, God knows where,
                                in Mexico.
No matter what they say, it is not bad here. No, it is good:
It is better than anything the astronomers can dream up
With their sweaty computers. I've shaved my chest off to be
        Slowly-nearer and now without junk-hair
That is not really me   instantaneously nearer
        Soft universal power! It is warm, it is maybe even a little
Too hot, but glorious here at the center   all the center there is
Before history . . . I send you a searing Yes
From the thousand cross-glittering black-holes of obsidian:
        I am like the *theory* of a blade
        That closes rather than opens   *closes*:
        That sends something back
Other than blood. Among leaves, I have torn out the heart of the sun

        The long-lost Mexican sun.

James Dickey

A 30.1: 8¹⁵⁄₁₆″ × 13″; title and 'James Dickey' in red

Single leaf.

Winston-Salem, N.C.: Palæmon Press, 1978.

On verso: '*This is copy* | *Mexican Valley* © 1978 by James Dickey'.

Previously unpublished poem; subsequently collected in *Head-Deep in Strange Sounds* and *Strength of Fields*.

Paper: Wove; watermarked 'HMP'.

Binding: Published as part of portfolio (marbled paper-covered boards and cloth shelfback with cloth laces).

Publication: Certificate of limitation on separate broadside: 'For Aaron Copland | *on the occasion of his seventy-eighth birthday* | *14 November 1978* | This broadside folio is issued by Palæmon Press Limited | as the personal tribute of the publisher. | Seventy-eight sets, each containing an original poem by | James Dickey, Reynolds Price, and Robert Penn Warren, | and a specially commissioned woodcut by | Ann Carter Pollard, have been prepared and laid into hand- | made folios. Fifty sets, numbered 1–50, | are for public sale, and twenty-eight sets, | numbered *i–xxviii,* are for the use of Mr. Copland, the | poets, the artist, and the publisher. Fourteen | lettered proof copies of the woodcut, out of series, have | been struck by the artist for her personal use. | This is number | [publisher's signature]'. Price of portfolio: $125.00. Each poem is signed by the author.

Locations: JRB (unnumbered copy of "Mexican Valley"); MJB (portfolio and unnumbered copy of "Mexican Valley"); ScU ('COLOR PROOF' of "Mexican Valley").

A 31 IN PURSUIT OF THE GREY SOUL

A 31.1

First edition, only printing (1978)

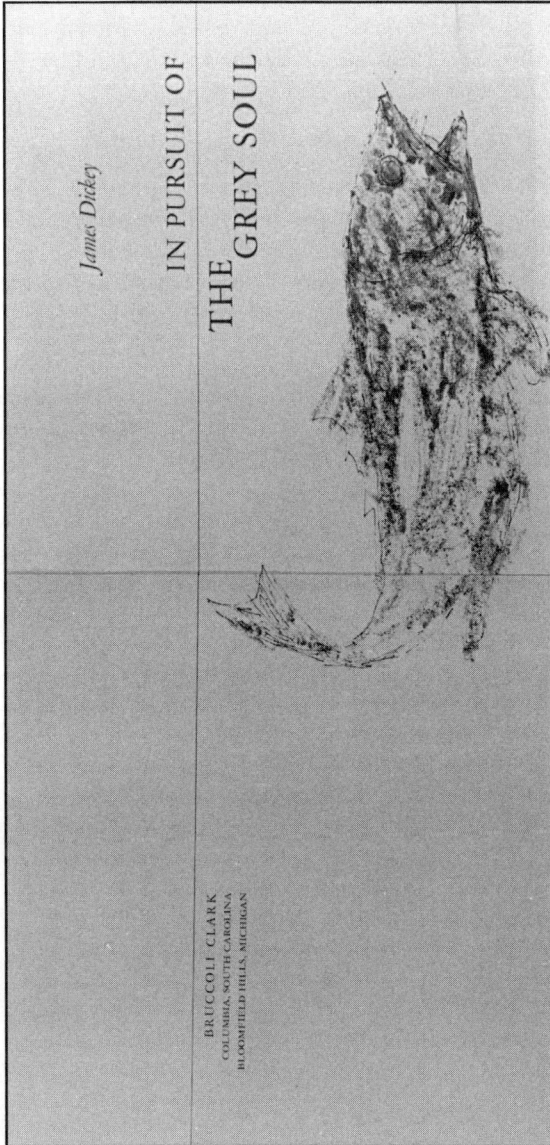

A 31.1: 16" × 8"

Copyright page: 'In Pursuit of the Grey Soul | ISBN: 0-89723-004-3 | [rule] | Copyright © 1978 by | James Dickey'.

[1–32]

[1–4]⁴

Contents: p. 1: certificate of limitation and colophon; pp. 2–3: title; p. 4: copyright; p. 5: half title; pp. 6–31: text; p. 32: blank. Essay. Previously published as "Pursuing the Grey Soul" in C 284; collected as "A Hand-Line: In Pursuit of the Grey Soul" in *Night Hurdling*.

Typography and paper: Illustrations by Robert Nance. No running heads. Wove paper. See colophon.

Binding: Dark bluish gray unprinted wrappers. Very light blue paper portfolio cover. Front: underwater seascape. Spine: '[vertically] IN PURSUIT OF THE GREY SOUL'. All edges trimmed. Unprinted dark bluish gray slipcase with dark blue paper protective fold. Some copies distributed with 2½" × 2½" white printed label on front wrapper or on slipcase: 'IN PURSUIT OF | THE | GREY SOUL | James Dickey | [rule] | BRUCCOLI CLARK'.

Publication: 500 numbered copies. Published 4 December 1978. $35.00 until 1 January 1979; $50.00 thereafter. Copyright #TX263-900.

Production: See colophon.

Locations: Caroliniana (slipcase); JRB (slipcase); Lilly (slipcase); MJB (slipcase).

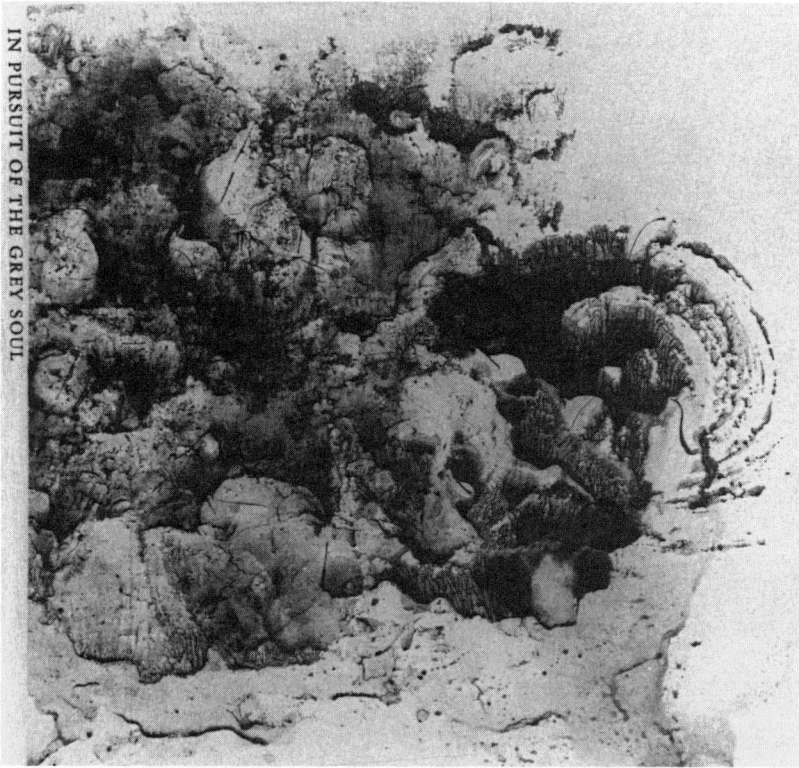

Front cover and spine for A 31.1

IN PURSUIT OF

THE GREY SOUL

Copy **110** of five hundred numbered copies signed by the Author

James Dickey

The type was composed by Heritage Printers in Garamond. After offset printing by Meriden Gravure on SN Text paper, the book was bound by A. Horowitz and Sons in Multicolor.

This book was designed by Robert L. Nance.

A 32 HEAD-DEEP IN STRANGE SOUNDS

A 32.1

First edition, only printing (1979)

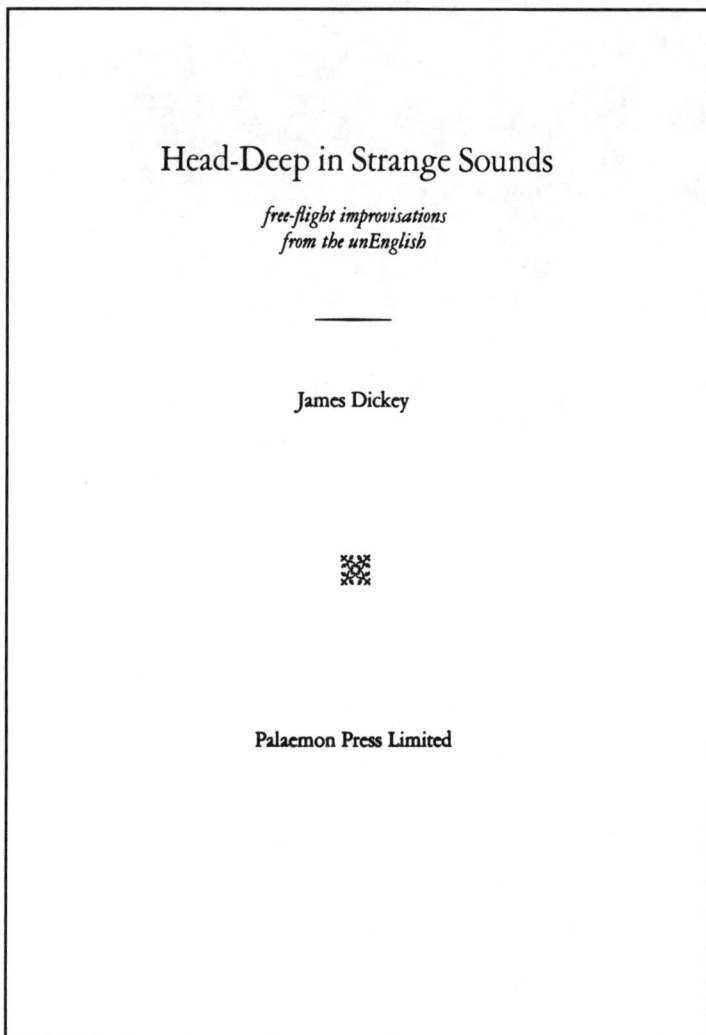

Head-Deep in Strange Sounds

*free-flight improvisations
from the unEnglish*

———

James Dickey

Palaemon Press Limited

A 32.1: 8″ × 10¹⁵⁄₁₆″; first line and decoration in red

Copyright page: 'COPYRIGHT © 1978, 1979 BY JAMES DICKEY'.

[1–10] 11–26 [27–32]

[1–4]⁴

Contents: pp. 1–2: blank; p. 3: half title; p. 4: blank; p. 5: title; p. 6: copyright; p. 7: 'TO MY WIFE DEBORAH | My great love in all languages | all poems, and all times'; p. 8: blank; p. 9: foreword by Dickey; p. 10: blank; pp. 11–26: text; pp. 27–28: blank; p. 29: certificate of limitation; pp. 30–31: blank; p. 32: printer's imprint.

12 poems: "Purgation" (see C 295), "The Ax-God: Sea-Pursuit," "Nameless," "Math," "Judas," "Small Song," "Undersea Fragment in Colons," "Mexican Valley," "Low Voice, Out Loud," "When," "Poem," "A Saying of Farewell." All previously unpublished except "Mexican Valley" (see A 30). "A Saying of Farewell" was reprinted in *New Republic,* 181 (20 October 1979), 36. All of these poems were subsequently included in *Strength of Fields.*

Typography and paper: Poem titles and initial capital of foreword in red. No running heads. Wove paper.

Binding: Medium gray B cloth (linen). Paper label on front: '[within Greek key frame] Head-Deep in Strange Sounds | [very red rule] | [black] *by* James Dickey'. White endpapers. All edges trimmed.

Publication: 575 copies. See certificate of limitation. Published 5 May 1979. $20.00.

Production: Printed by Heritage Printers, Charlotte, N.C.

Locations: Caroliniana; JRB; Lilly; MJB; ScU.

Review copy A: Cover title: 'FOUR POEMS | [ornamental rule] | James Dickey | Privately Printed'. Back cover: 'Twenty-five copies have been prepared for distribution by the poet. | *March 1979*'. Sewn wrappers 7″ × 9¾″. Printed only in black. According to the publisher, "Distributed to selected reviewers prior to publication of *Head-Deep in Strange Sounds.* . . ."

Contents: "Mexican Valley," "Undersea Fragment in Colons," "When," "Low Voice, Out Loud."

Locations: JRB; MJB.

Review copy B: 3 unbound gatherings of page proofs. 7″ × 9¹⁵⁄₁₆″. Printed only in black. Rubberstamped below Dickey foreword: 'REVIEW COPY'. Distributed in yellow envelope with white label: '[printed] PALÆMON PRESS, LTD. | BOX 7527 REYNOLDA STATION | WINSTON-SALEM, NORTH CAROLINA 27109 | [double rules] | [typed] ADVANCE READING PROOF | James Dickey | Head-Deep in Strange Sounds | Publication Date [holograph: March 1979] | Price _____'. Locations: MJB; ScU (label provides '30 March' as publication date and $20 as price).

HEAD-DEEP IN STRANGE SOUNDS
is limited to 475 unnumbered copies
signed by the poet. Fifty additional copies,
hors commerce, are for private distribution: fifteen, lettered A-O, by the poet,
and thirty-five, numbered *i-xxxv*, by the
publisher. *Mexican Valley* first appeared
as part of a broadside tribute to Aaron
Copland from Palaemon Press Limited.

A 33 THE WATER BUG'S MITTENS

A 33.1

First edition, only printing (1979)

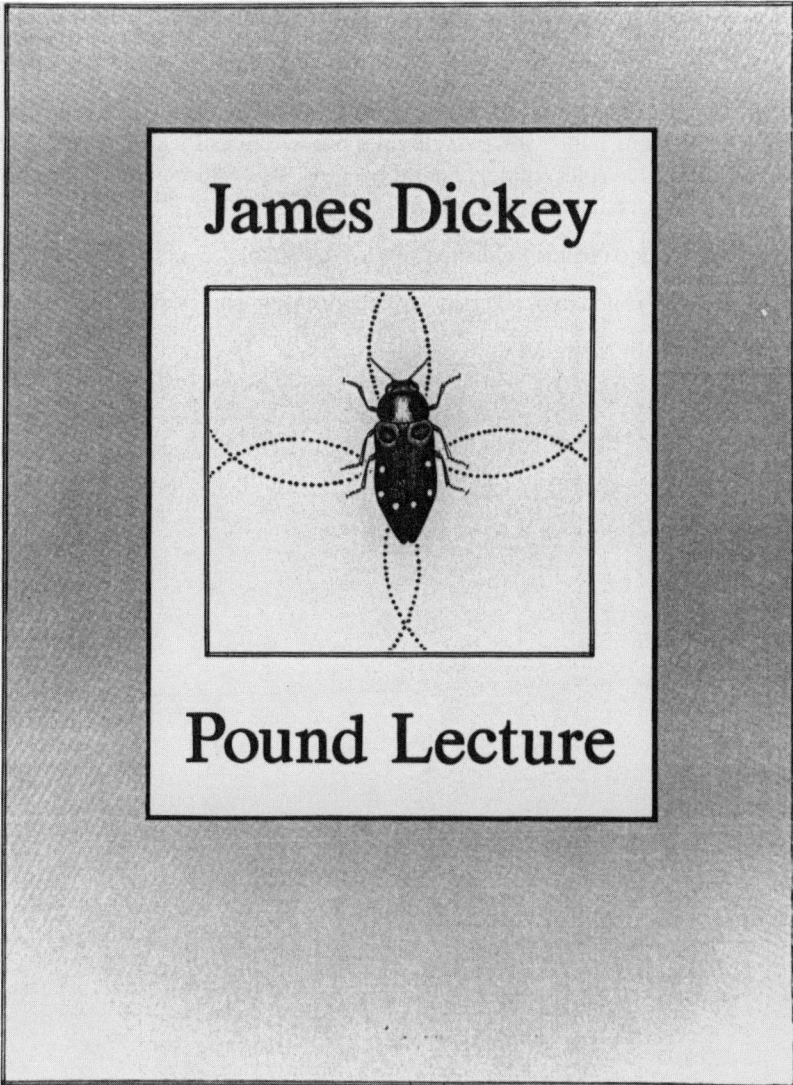

Cover title for A 33.1: 8½″ × 11″; printed in black with gray borders

[1–2] 3–12 [13–16]

[1]⁸

Contents: p. 1: drawing of Ezra Pound above note signed by Margaret New-some, Daniel Pearlman, and Galen Rowe; 'Copyright 1979 James Dickey'; p. 2: blank; pp. 3–12: text headed 'The Water Bug's Mittens | Ezra Pound: What We Can Use | *James Dickey*'; p. 13: 'Notes'; pp. 14–16: blank.

Typography and paper: $9\frac{3}{16}''$ ($9\frac{5}{16}''$) × $5\frac{7}{16}''$. No running heads. Wove paper.

Binding: Wrappers. Front: '[double rules frame] [light gray border] [all the following on white pane within single rules frame] James Dickey | [drawing of bug within double rules frame] | Pound Lecture'. Back: '[decoration] | University of Idaho'. All edges trimmed. Saddle-stapled.

Publication: 250 copies. Published July 1979. $3.00.

Production: Printed by University of Idaho Printing and Duplicating.

Locations: JRB; MJB; ScU.

A 33.2

Limited edition, only printing (1980)

James Dickey

❋

THE
WATER-BUG'S
MITTENS

❋

Ezra Pound: What We Can Use

Bruccoli Clark
Bloomfield Hills, Michigan
Columbia, South Carolina
1980

A 33.2: 7″ × 9⅞″

James Dickey

THE WATER-BUG'S MITTENS

Ezra Pound: What We Can Use

This First Edition Of
THE WATER-BUG'S MITTENS
Is Limited To 350 Copies
Signed by James Dickey.
Copies Numbered 1-300 Are For Sale;
Copies Numbered I-L Are Reserved
For The Author and Publisher.
Copy _139_ .

Designed by Leonard Bahr at the Adagio Press.

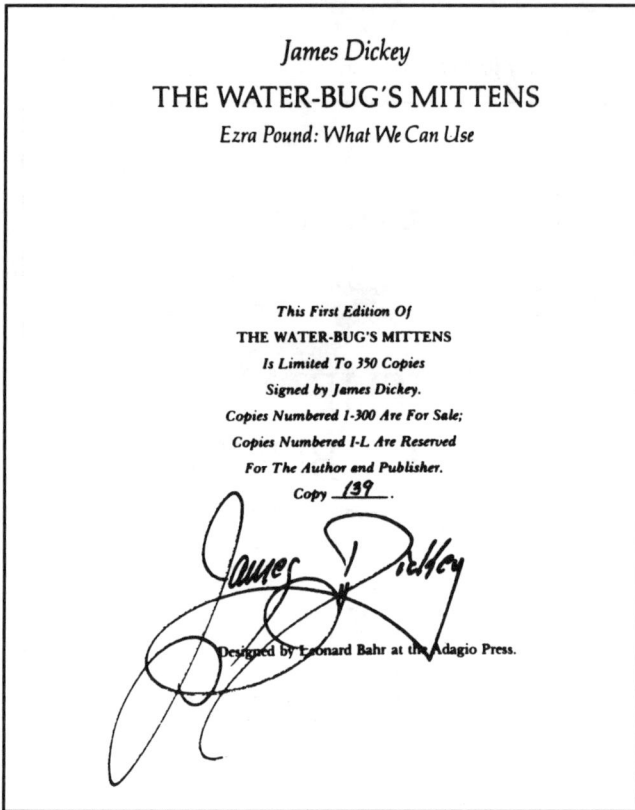

[i–vi] 1–15 [16] 17–18

[1–3]⁴

Copyright page: 'Copyright © 1979 by James Dickey | Originally delivered as the University of Idaho Pound Lecture | in the Humanities, 26 April 1979.'

Contents: p. i: certificate of limitation; p. ii: photo of Pound; p. iii: title; p. iv: copyright; p. v: previously unpublished note by Dickey; p. vi: blank; pp. 1–15: text; p. 16: blank; pp. 17–18: 'Notes'.

Typography and paper: 7¼" (79⁄16") × 45⁄8". 41 lines per page. No running heads. Laid paper; chainlines 1 1⁄16" apart.

Binding: Slightly yellowish brown wrappers printed on front: '*James Dickey* | [gold decoration] | THE | WATER-BUG'S | MITTENS | [gold decoration] | *Ezra Pound: What We Can Use*'. Greenish white endpapers. All edges trimmed.

Publication: 350 numbered copies signed by Dickey; see certificate of limitation. Published 1 March 1980. $20.00. Copyright # TX1-2-325-741.

Production: Printed and bound by Washburn Press, Charlotte, N.C.

Locations: Caroliniana; JRB; Lilly; MJB; PSt; ScU (stamped 'REVIEW COPY').

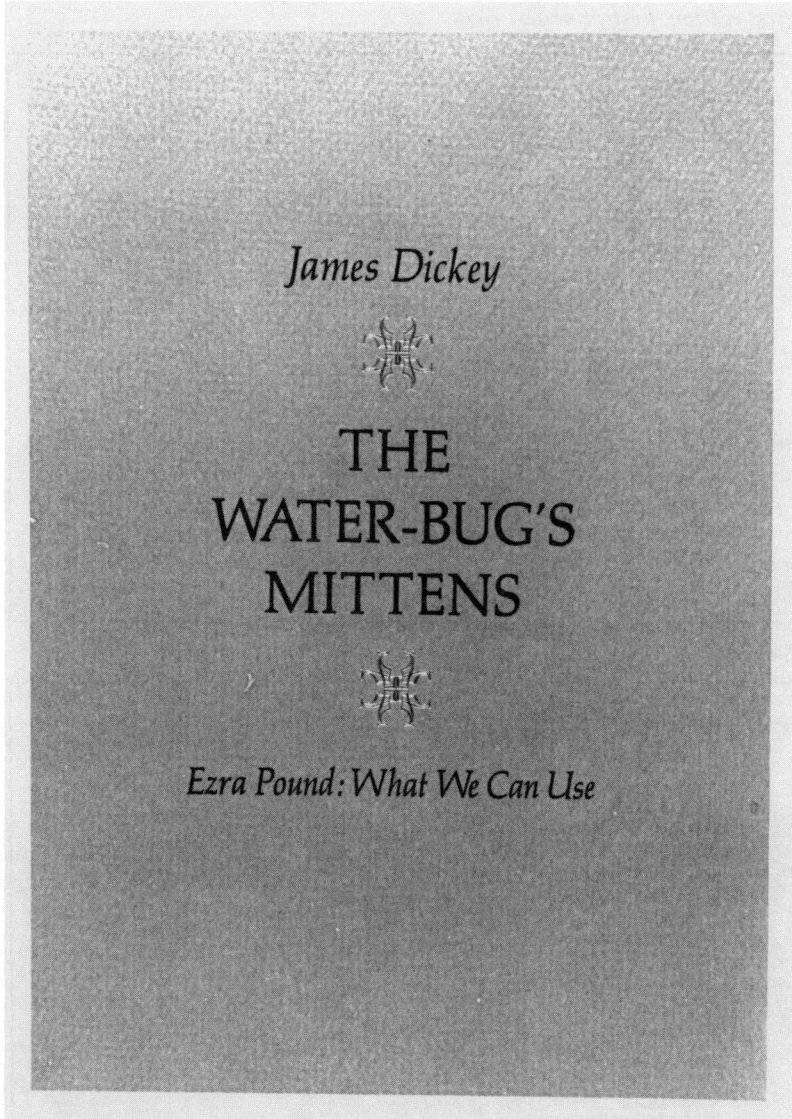

Front wrapper for A 33.2

A 34 THE STRENGTH OF FIELDS (COLLECTION)

A 34.1.a

First edition, first printing (1979)

JAMES DICKEY

The Strength of Fields

1979
DOUBLEDAY & COMPANY, INC.
GARDEN CITY, NEW YORK

A 34.1.a: 8¼″ × 5⁵⁄₁₆″

The title poem, "The Strength of Fields," originally appeared in 1977 in a book called *A New Spirit, a New Commitment, a New America*, by the 1977 Inaugural Committee, published by Bantam Books. Copyright © 1977 by James Dickey.

"I Dreamed I Already Loved You," "Assignation," and "Doing the Twist on Nails," translated by James Dickey, are all from *Stolen Apples*, by Yevgeny Yevtushenko. Translation copyright © 1971 by Doubleday & Company, Inc. Reprinted by permission of the publisher.

Some of the other poems in this volume appeared originally in the following publications: "False Youth: Autumn: Clothes of the Age" (issue of November 1971), "Reunioning Dialogue" (issue of January 1973), and "Exchanges" (issue of September 1970) in *The Atlantic*; "For the Death of Lombardi" in *Esquire*, © 1971 by Esquire, Inc.; "Haunting the Maneuvers," copyright © 1969 by Harper's Magazine, reprinted from the January 1970 issue by permission of *Harper's*; "The Voyage of the Needle" (1978 winter issue) in *Gentlemen's Quarterly*; "The Rain Guitar" (January 8, 1972), "Drums Where I Live" (November 26, 1969), "Root-light, or the Lawyer's Daughter" (November 8, 1969), and "Remnant Water" (March 10, 1973) in *The New Yorker*; "Camden Town" in the 1970 spring issue (Vol. 46, No. 2) of *The Virginia Quarterly*.

"Purgation," "The Ax-God: Sea-Pursuit," "Nameless," "Math," "Judas," "Small Song," "Undersea Fragment in Colons," "Mexican Valley," "Low Voice, Out Loud," "Poem," "When," and "A Saying of Farewell" originally appeared in *Head-Deep in Strange Sounds: Free-Flight Improvisations from the unEnglish*, by James Dickey, published by Palaemon Press, Ltd. Copyright © 1979 by James Dickey. Reprinted by permission of the publisher.

ISBN: 0-385-15809-2
Library of Congress Catalog Card Number 79-3034
Copyright © 1979 by James Dickey
All Rights Reserved
Printed in the United States of America
First Edition

[1–12] 13–56 [57–58] 59–86 [87–88]

[1–4]⁸ [5]⁴ [6]⁸

Contents: p. 1: half title; pp. 2–3: card pages; p. 4: blank; p. 5: title; p. 6: copyright and acknowledgments; p. 7: 'To Deborah | in the new life'; pp. 8–9: contents; p. 10: blank; p. 11: section title; p. 12: blank; pp. 13–86: text; pp. 87–88: blank.

28 poems: The Strength of Fields: "Root-light, or the Lawyer's Daughter," "The Strength of Fields" (see B 41), "Two Poems of the Military" ("Haunting the Maneuvers"—see B 25, "Drums Where I Live"), "The Voyage of the Needle," "The Rain Guitar," "Remnant Water," "Two Poems of Flight-Sleep" ("Camden Town," "Reunioning Dialogue"), "For the Death of Lombardi" (see B 26), "False Youth: Autumn: Clothes of the Age" (see B 33), "For the Running of the New York City Marathon,"* "Exchanges"; Head-Deep in Strange Sounds: Free-Flight Improvisations from the UnEnglish: "Purgation" (see C 295), "The Ax-God: Sea-Pursuit," "Nameless," "Math," "Judas," "Small Song," "Undersea Fragment in Colons," "Mexican Valley," "Low Voice, Out Loud," "Poem," "When," "A Saying of Farewell," "Three Poems with Yevtushenko" ("I Dreamed I Already Loved You"—see B 27, "Assignation"—see B 27, "Doing the Twist on Nails"—see B 27). Asterisks indicate previously unpublished poems.

The Strength of Fields was republished in *The Central Motion* (see E 5).

Typography and paper: 4³⁄₁₆″. 22 lines per page. No running heads. Wove paper.

Binding: Deep blue V cloth (smooth). Spine vertically silverstamped: 'JAMES DICKEY *The Strength of Fields* Doubleday'. White endpapers. All edges trimmed.

Dust jacket: Lettered on white. Front: '[green, light blue, medium blue, and black] The | Strength | of Fields | [black] [rule] | BY JAMES DICKEY'. Back same as front. Spine lettered vertically: '[medium blue] The Strength of Fields [black] JAMES DICKEY [medium blue] Doubleday'. Front flap has comment on book, continued on back flap. Back flap has photo of Dickey by Terry Parke and biographical note.

Publication: 5,000 copies. Published 14 December 1979. $6.00. Price subsequently cut off front flap and replaced with label: '$8.95 | D & CO. INC.' Copyright #TX-431-126.

Production: Doubleday, Smithsburg, Md.; Doubleday, Berryville, Va.

Locations: Caroliniana (dj); JRB (dj—review slip laid in); LC (MAR 17 1980); Lilly (dj); MJB (dj); MJB (dj—price-change label); PSt.

7101
$8.95

The Strength
of Fields
JAMES DICKEY

Here, accompanied by over thirty other poems, is James Dickey's stunning poem "The Strength of Fields," composed expressly for President Carter's 1976 inauguration ceremony. Not since Robert Frost read his *Inaugural Poem* at the induction of President Kennedy in 1960 has an American poet been called upon to serve at a national event of such magnitude.

Mr. Dickey, renowned as one of America's most highly acclaimed and popular poets, has over eight volumes of verse to his credit. His most recent volume, *The Zodiac*, published in 1976, has had an unprecedented impact on a wide variety of readers. His collection *Buckdancer's Choice* was awarded the 1966 National Book Award for poetry. He has also served

(continued on back flap)

The Strength of Fields

BY JAMES DICKEY

The Strength of Fields JAMES DICKEY Doubleday

The Strength of Fields

BY JAMES DICKEY

(continued from front flap)

as Consultant in Poetry to the Library of Congress and is the author of several books of criticism.

James Dickey is Poet-in-Residence and Professor of English at the University of South Carolina. He is presently at work on a new novel, a portion of which has been published in *Esquire* to enthusiastic reader response.

JACKET DESIGN BY AL NAGY
0281
Printed in the U.S.A.

Dust jacket for A 34.1.a

Proof copy: Orangish yellow wrappers; perfect bound. 8″ × 10¾″. Front: 'UNCORRECTED PROOF | JAMES DICKEY | *The Strength of Fields* | 1979 | DOUBLEDAY & COMPANY, INC. | GARDEN CITY, NEW YORK'. Produced by Crane Duplicating, Inc., Barnstable, Mass. Locations: MJB; ScU.

A 34.1.b

Second printing: Garden City, N.Y.: Doubleday, [1980].

Copyright page: '9 . . . 2'. 20,000 copies.

A 34.1.c

Third printing: Garden City, N.Y.: Doubleday, [1980].

Copyright page: '9 . . . 3'.

A 34.1.d

Fourth printing: Garden City, N.Y.: Doubleday, [1980].

2,000 copies according to Doubleday records. Not seen.

A 35 SCION

A 35.1

First edition, only printing (1980)

James Dickey

SCION

Illustrations by Timothy Engelland

THE DEERFIELD PRESS
THE GALLERY PRESS

A 35.1: 5¾″ × 8¾″

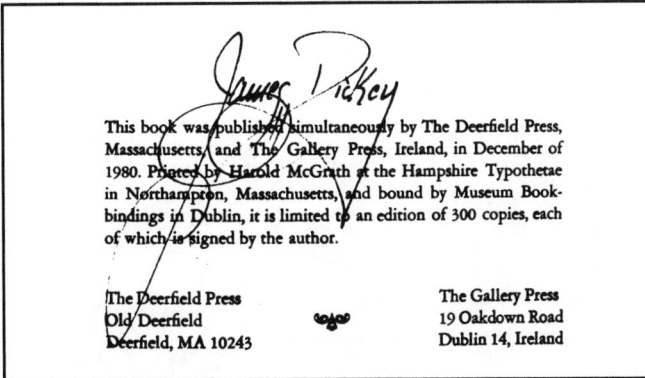

> *[signature: James Dickey]*
>
> This book was published simultaneously by The Deerfield Press, Massachusetts, and The Gallery Press, Ireland, in December of 1980. Printed by Harold McGrath at the Hampshire Typothetae in Northampton, Massachusetts, and bound by Museum Bookbindings in Dublin, it is limited to an edition of 300 copies, each of which is signed by the author.
>
> The Deerfield Press
> Old Deerfield
> Deerfield, MA 10243
>
> The Gallery Press
> 19 Oakdown Road
> Dublin 14, Ireland

[1–16]

[1]^8

Contents: pp. 1–2: blank; p. 3: title; p. 4: 'Copyright, James Dickey, 1980'; p. 5: 'To Deborah'; p. 6: color illustration; pp. 7–11: text, concluding with color illustration; p. 12: blank; p. 13: colophon and certificate of limitation; pp. 14–16: blank.

2 poems: "With Rose, at Cemetery" and "In Lace and Whalebone." Both previously unpublished; subsequently collected under general title "Deborah as Scion" in *Puella*.

Typography and paper: No running heads. Wove paper.

Binding: Black V cloth. Spine vertically goldstamped: 'SCION James Dickey Deerfield [slash] Gallery'. Medium brown endpapers. All edges trimmed.

Dust jacket: Same color as endpapers. Front: 'James Dickey | SCION | [bull within circle]'. Spine: '[vertically] SCION James Dickey Deerfield [slash] Gallery'. Front flap has biographical note on Dickey. Back flap has note on publishers and lists 11 titles in the series.

Publication: See certificate of limitation. 300 unnumbered copies signed by Dickey. Published December 1980. $9.50.

Production: See colophon.

Locations: MJB (dj); ScU.

James Dickey

SCION

SCION   James Dickey   Deerfield/Gallery

James Dickey was born in Atlanta, Georgia, in 1923. His books of poems include *Buckdancer's Choice* which won the National Book Award in 1966, *Poems 1957–67*, *The Zodiac* (1976) and *The Strength of Fields* (1979) which included the 1976 Presidential inauguration poem. *Deliverance* (1970) was a bestselling novel and later an acclaimed film. James Dickey now lives in Columbia, S.C. and is Professor of English and writer in residence at the University of South Carolina.

Illustrations by Timothy Engelland

This book was published simultaneously by The Deerfield Press, Massachusetts, and The Gallery Press, Dublin, in December, of 1980. Printed by Harold McGrath at the Hampshire Typothetae in Northampton, Massachusetts and bound by Gray Parrot by Williams Bookbinding in Dublin, it is limited to an edition of 300 copies, each of which is signed by the author.

In this same series:

The Gift of Gravity by Wendell Berry
Thanks by Robert Creeley
Prisoners by Michael Hamburger
After Lorca by Seamus Heaney
The Snow Winter by Derek Mahon
The Lamp by John Montague
Nether by Richard Murphy
Where Our Voices Broke Off by James Simmons
Out of Season by Louis Simpson
Tiares of Lace by Virgil
  by William Stafford
Four Poems by Máirtín Ó Direáin

Dust jacket for A 35.1

A 36 THE STARRY PLACE BETWEEN THE ANTLERS

A 36.1

Limited edition (1981)

BRUCCOLI CLARK
Bloomfield Hills, Michigan
Columbia, South Carolina
1981

A 36.1: 2-page title, 13½″ × 10″; left

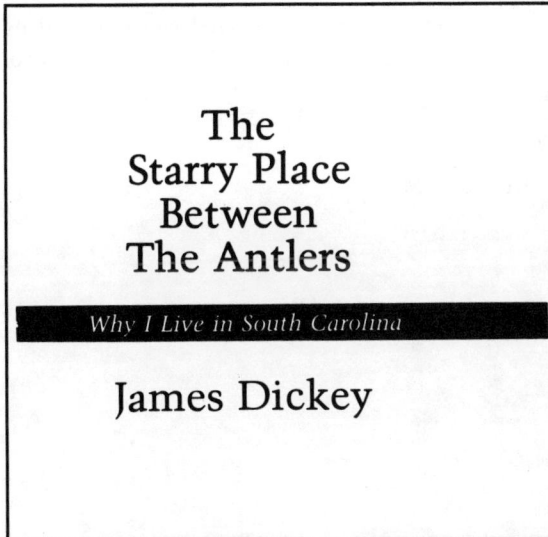

The
Starry Place
Between
The Antlers

Why I Live in South Carolina

James Dickey

A 36.1: right; bar in brown

[i–ii] [1–2] 3–4 [5] 6–12 [13] 14–16 [17–18]

[1]^{10}

Contents: p. i: colophon and certificate of limitation; p. ii–p. 1: title; p. 2:
copyright; pp. 3–4: text; p. 5: photo of Dickey by Terry Parke; pp. 6–12: text;
p. 13: photo of Dickey by Terry Parke; pp. 14–16: text; pp. 17–18: blank. Essay.
Previously published as "Why I Live Where I Live" in C 303; subsequently
collected as "The Starry Place Between the Antlers" in *Night Hurdling.*

Typography and paper: 7″ (7½″); ragged right margin. 31 lines per page.
Printed in black with brown decorations. No running heads. Antique finish
paper.

Binding: Yellowish white unprinted paper covers. Strong yellowish brown
portfolio wrappers. Front: '[dark grayish brown] The | Starry Place | Between |
The Antlers | [outlined on dark grayish brown bar] *Why I Live in South Caro-
lina* | [dark grayish brown] James Dickey'. Bar continued on front flap. All
edges trimmed.

Publication: See certificate of limitation. 500 numbered copies signed by
Dickey. Published simultaneously with trade edition; 15 March 1981. $20.00.
Copyright #TX2-424-793.

Production: See colophon.

Locations: Caroliniana; JRB; Lilly; MJB.

This edition of James Dickey's
The Starry Place Between the Antlers:
Why I Live in South Carolina
was designed by Leonard F. Bahr.
Typography by BC Research in Trump
Mediaeval Roman, designed by
Georg Trump. It was printed
by the R. L. Bryan Company
in Columbia, South Carolina.

This Collector's Edition is limited
to 500 numbered copies signed by
James Dickey.

James Dickey

Copy number 152

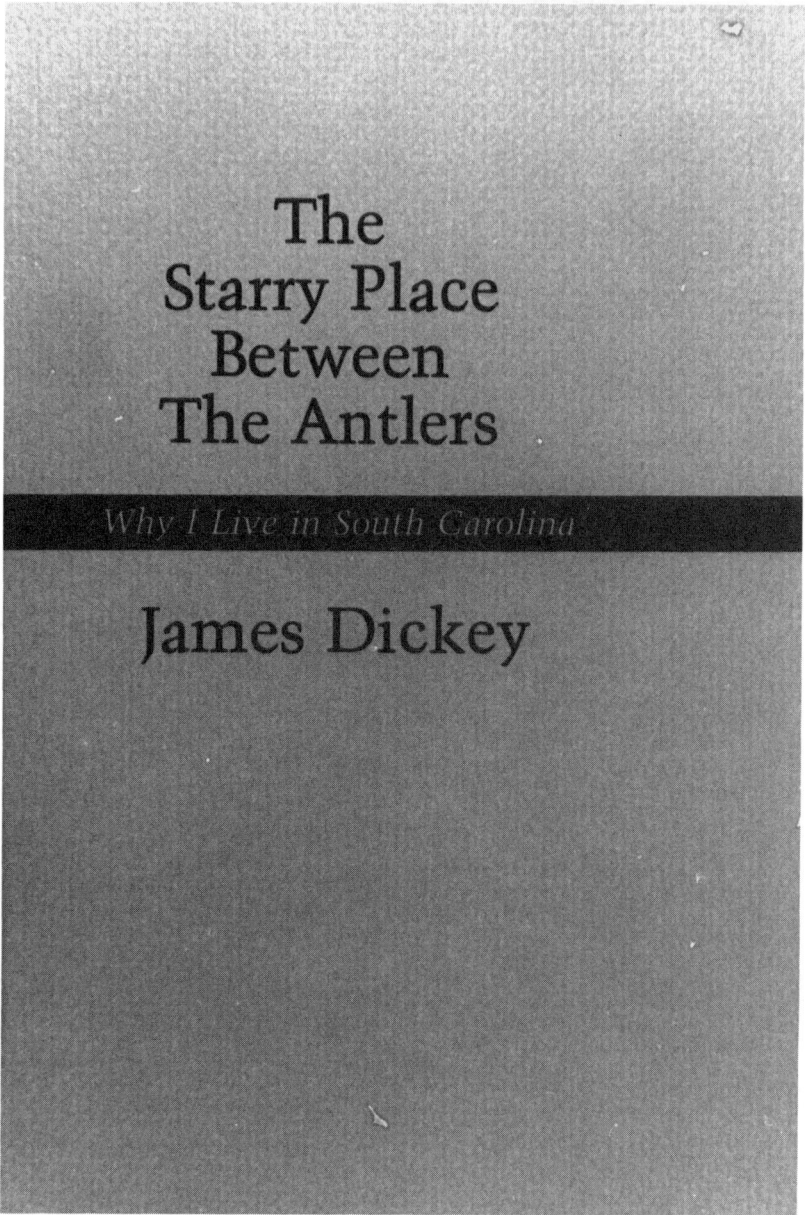

The
Starry Place
Between
The Antlers

Why I Live in South Carolina

James Dickey

Front wrapper for A 36.1

A 36.2

Trade edition, only printing (1981)

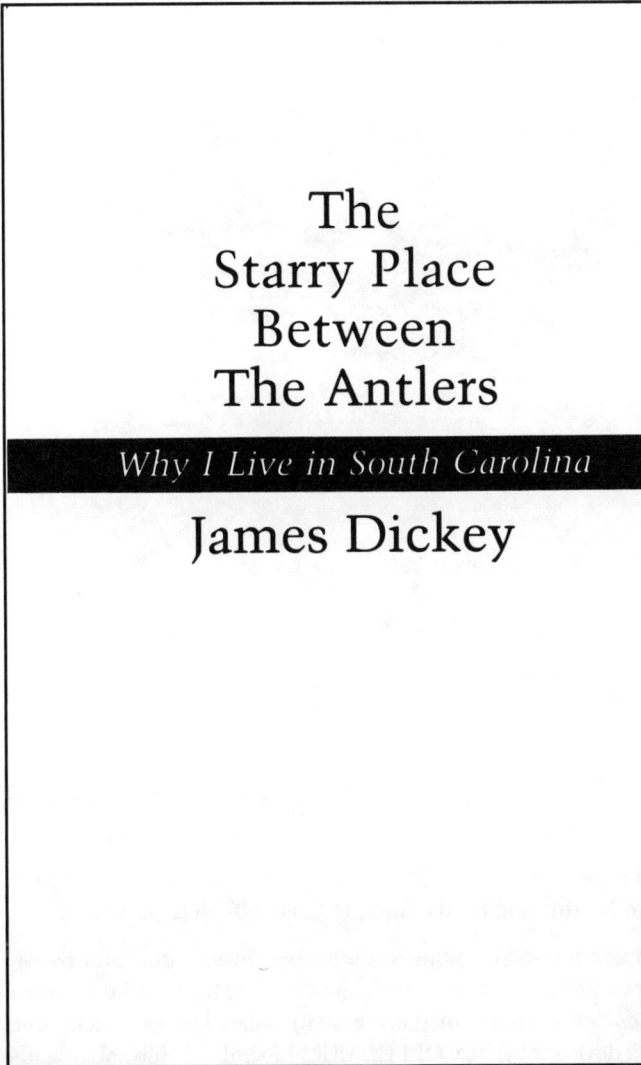

The
Starry Place
Between
The Antlers

Why I Live in South Carolina

James Dickey

Cover title for A 36.2: 5½″ × 8½″; printed in brown on off-white paper

James Dickey on the Horseshoe
at the University of South Carolina

Copyright © James Dickey 1981.
Originally published in *Esquire* magazine,
April 1981.

Photo by Terry Parke.

[1–2] 3–14 [15–16]

[1]⁸

Contents: p. 1: cover title; p. 2: photo of Dickey by Terry Parke and copyright; pp. 3–14: text; p. 15: blank; p. 16: device and publisher's imprint.

Typography and paper: 5¹⁵⁄₁₆″ (6⅜″); ragged right margin. 31 lines per page. Printed in brown. No running heads. Antique finish off-white paper.

Binding: Wrappers printed on same stock as text. Front: '[medium brown] The | Starry Place | Between | The Antlers | [outlined against medium brown] *Why I Live in South Carolina* | [medium brown] James Dickey'. Back: '[medium brown] [BC device] | BRUCCOLI CLARK | Bloomfield Hills, Michigan | Columbia, South Carolina | 1981'. All edges trimmed. Saddle-stapled.

Publication: 5,000 copies. Published simultaneously with limited edition. $2.00.

Production: Printed by the R. L. Bryan Co., Columbia, S.C.

Locations: Caroliniana; MJB; PSt.

A 37 DELIVERANCE (SCREENPLAY)

A 37.1

First edition, only printing (1982)

Deliverance

**By
James Dickey**

Southern Illinois University Press
Carbondale and Edwardsville

A 37.1: 5⅞″ × 8⅞″

Copyright © 1972, 1982 Warner Bros. Inc.
All rights reserved
Printed in the United States of America
Edited by Joyce Atwood
Designed by Kathleen Giencke
Production supervised by Richard Neal

Library of Congress Cataloging in Publication Data

Dickey, James
  Deliverance.

  (Screenplay library)
    I. Title.   II. Series.
  PN1997.D423   812'.54
  ISBN 0-8093-1029-5
  ISBN 0-8093-1030-9 (pbk.)

81-13551
AACR2

[i–x] [1] 2–151 [152–153] 154–157 [158]

Cloth: [1–2]¹⁶ 3⁴ [4–6]¹⁶; wrappers: perfect bound.

Contents: p. i: device; p. ii: list of series titles; p. iii: title; p. iv: copyright; p. v: contents; p. vi: blank; p. vii: 'Foreword'; p. viii: 'Acknowledgments'; p. ix: half title; p. x: 'Credits'; pp. 1–151: text; p. 152: blank; pp. 153–157: 'Afterword' by Dickey; p. 158: blank. Afterword collected as "Bare Bones: Afterword to a Film" in *Night Hurdling*.

Typography and paper: 7″ (7⁷⁄₁₆″); ragged right margin. Printed from camera-ready typescript. Running heads: rectos: 'A Screenplay [folio]'; versos: '[folio] Deliverance'. Wove paper.

Binding: Brownish orange V cloth (smooth). Spine stamped vertically in black: 'Dickey Deliverance [above] Southern Illinois [below] University Press'. White endpapers. All edges trimmed.

Dust jacket: Front: reproduction of movie poster with black-and-white and color stills; printed in brilliant blue, black, medium brown, and brownish orange. Spine lettered vertically: '[black] Dickey [medium brown] Deliverance [black] [above] Southern Illinois [below] University Press'. Back lettered on black background: '[medium brown] Deliverance | By | James Dickey | A Screenplay | [white] Afterword by James Dickey | ISBN 0-8093-1029-5'. Front and back flaps have comment on book.

Wrappers: Front, spine, and back same as dust jacket, except 'ISBN 0-8093-1030' on back.

Publication: 774 cloth and 1,544 wrappers. Simultaneously published 4 January 1982. Cloth: $17.50; wrappers: $6.95. Copyright #TX1-023-535.

Production: Composition by G & S Typesetters; printed and bound by Edwards Brothers, Ann Arbor, Mich.

Locations: Caroliniana (cloth—dj); LC (cloth—CIP 5 DEC 1981); Lilly (cloth—dj); MJB (cloth—dj); MJB (wrappers).

Deliverance

By
James Dickey

A Screenplay

Afterword by James Dickey

Dickey   Deliverance

Southern Illinois
University Press

ISBN 0-8093-1029-5

This is the weekend they didn't play golf.

Deliverance

JON VOIGHT · BURT REYNOLDS "DELIVERANCE"

Dust jacket for A 37.1

A 38 HOW TO ENJOY POETRY

A 38.1–2

First and second editions (1982)

A 38.1–2: 8¼" × 10¹⁵⁄₁₆"

[1–2]

Single sheet printed on both sides. Also published as double-page spread (16½″ × 10¹⁵⁄₁₆″) with blank verso. Priority undetermined.

Essay. Distributed gratis as part of Power of the Printed Word Series by the International Paper Company in 1982. Unknown number of copies. Also published as an advertisement (see C 309). Subsequently collected in *How to Use the Power of the Printed Word,* ed. Billings S. Fuess, Jr. (Garden City, N.Y.: Doubleday/Anchor Press, 1985), pp. 78–83.

Locations: JRB (single-sheet format); MJB (both formats).

A 39 PUELLA

A 39.1

First edition, only printing (1982)

PUELLA

James Dickey

1982
DOUBLEDAY & COMPANY, INC.
GARDEN CITY, NEW YORK

A 39.1: 5⁷⁄₁₆″ × 8⅛″

[1–12] 13–48

[1–3]^8

Contents: p. 1: half title; p. 2: card page; p. 3: title; p. 4: copyright; p. 5: 'To Deborah— | *her girlhood, male-imagined*'; p. 6: blank; p. 7: contents; p. 8: blank; p. 9: 2-line epigraph from T. Sturge Moore; p. 10: blank; p. 11: half title; p. 12: blank; pp. 13–48: text.

19 poems: "Deborah Burning a Doll Made of House-Wood," "Deborah, Moon, Mirror, Right Hand Rising," "Deborah and Deirdre as Drunk Bridesmaids Foot-Racing at Daybreak," "Veer-Voices: Two Sisters Under Crows," "Deborah in Ancient Lingerie, in Thin Oak Over Creek," "Heraldic: Deborah and Horse in Morning Forest," "Springhouse, Menses, Held Apple, House and Beyond," "Ray-Flowers I," "Ray-Flowers II," "Deborah as Scion" ("With Rose, at Cemetery," "In Lace and Whalebone"), "The Lyric Beasts," "Deborah in Mountain Sound: Bell, Glacier, Rose," "Doorstep, Lightning, Waif-Dreaming," "From Time" (see B 59), "The Lode," "Tapestry and Sail," "The Surround," "Summons" (see A 46). All previously published.

Typography and paper: 6¼" (6⁹⁄₁₆"). No running heads. Wove paper.

Binding: Medium purplish red paper-covered boards with dark red V cloth (smooth) shelfback. Spine vertically goldstamped: 'PUELLA JAMES DICKEY DOUBLEDAY'. White endpapers. All edges trimmed.

Dust jacket: Front lettered against white background: 'JAMES | DICKEY | [in orangish yellow within pinkish red circle surrounded by orangish yellow, light brown, and reddish brown circles] Puella'. Spine lettered vertically against orangish yellow: '[pinkish red] JAMES DICKEY PUELLA [white] DOUBLEDAY'. Back has photo of Dickey by Mark Morrow. Front flap has comment on book. Back flap has note on Dickey.

Publication: Unknown number of copies. Published 29 April 1982. $10.95. Copyright #TX936-904.

Production: Doubleday, Berryville, Va.; Halliday Lithograph, West Hanover, Mass.

Locations: Caroliniana (dj); JRB (dj); LC (MAY 6 1982); LC (MAY 11 1982—dj); Lilly (dj); MJB (dj); PSt.

Proof copy: Yellow paper wrappers printed in black. Front: 'Advance uncorrected proofs | JAMES | DICKEY | [in white script] against black circle within three circular frames] Puella | 1982 | DOUBLEDAY & COMPANY, INC. | GARDEN CITY, NEW YORK'. Location: ScU.

530105

JAMES DICKEY

Puella

In these poems a poet encounters his young wife by creating his own version of her childhood, her coming of age, and her passage into womanhood.

In loving his wife, James Dickey became obsessed with imagining her life before they met. Her personality became a means by which he embarked on his own male voyage into the realm of womanhood. PUELLA creates a partly real, partly mythical country in which a young girl/woman discovers her unique relationship with nature, her changing body, her self-image and her enrichening and disturbing fantasies.

In these sensuous, intuitive encounters, the reader discovers—perhaps again or perhaps for the first time—the risks, doubts and energies of a crucial and exhilirating passage.

JAMES DICKEY

JAMES DICKEY   PUELLA   DOUBLEDAY

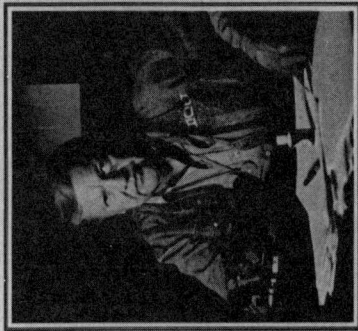

Born in Atlanta, Georgia, in 1923, James Dickey is regarded as one of the major American poets of our time. His works include *Buckdancer's Choice*, winner of the National Book Award for Poetry in 1966; *Poems 1957–1967*; *The Zodiac*; *The Strength of Fields*, which includes the 1976 Presidential Inaugural poem; and the novel *Deliverance*. Mr. Dickey is Poet-in-Residence at the University of South Carolina in Columbia, where he lives.

JAMES DICKEY

A group of poems from PUELLA won the distinguished Levinson Prize from *Poetry* magazine.

AUTHOR PHOTOGRAPH © DOLORES MARK MORRIS
JACKET BY JANET HALVERSON.
Printed in the U.S.A.

ISBN: 0-385-17763-3

Dust jacket for A 39.1

A 39.2

Limited edition (1985)

PUELLA

by James Dickey

Pyracantha Press
School of Art, Arizona State University
Tempe, Arizona
1985

A 39.2: 7¼" × 12¹⁵⁄₁₆"; printed in green with floral decorations in red

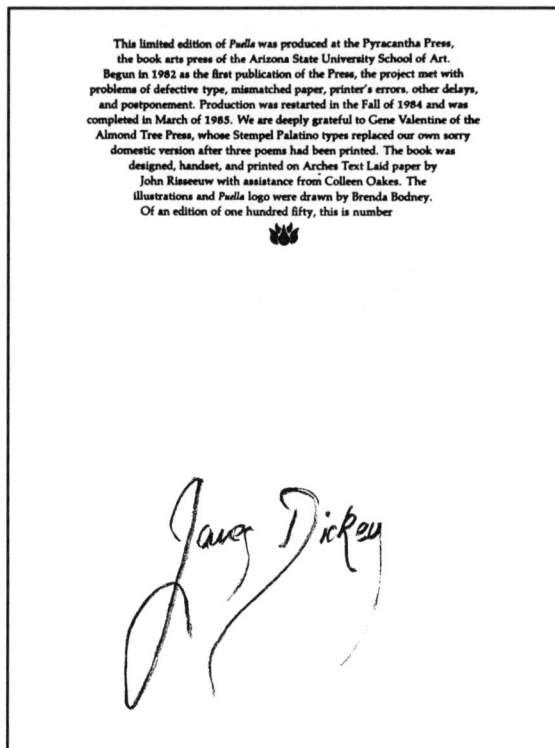

This limited edition of *Puella* was produced at the Pyracantha Press,
the book arts press of the Arizona State University School of Art.
Begun in 1982 as the first publication of the Press, the project met with
problems of defective type, mismatched paper, printer's errors. other delays,
and postponement. Production was restarted in the Fall of 1984 and was
completed in March of 1985. We are deeply grateful to Gene Valentine of the
Almond Tree Press, whose Stempel Palatino types replaced our own sorry
domestic version after three poems had been printed. The book was
designed, handset, and printed on Arches Text Laid paper by
John Risseeuw with assistance from Colleen Oakes. The
illustrations and *Puella* logo were drawn by Brenda Bodney.
Of an edition of one hundred fifty, this is number

[i–xiv] 1–27 [28–32]

[1–3]⁸

Contents: pp. i–iv: blank; p. v: half title; p. vi: frontispiece drawing; p. vii: title; p. viii: 'Copyright © 1982 by James Dickey | Published by special permission of Doubleday & Co., Garden City, New York'; p. ix: 'To Deborah— | *her girlhood, male-imagined*'; p. x: blank; p. xi: contents; p. xii: blank; p. xiii: 2-line epigraph from T. Sturge Moore; p. xiv: blank; pp. 1–27: text; p. 28: blank; p. 29: drawing of flower; pp. 30–31: blank; p. 32: certificate of limitation and colophon.

Typography and paper: 10¼″ (11″). Illustrations, 'Contents', and poem titles in green; red floral decorations on title page and on certificate of limitation/colophon. No running heads. Laid paper, chainlines ¹⁵⁄₁₆″ apart; watermarked 'ARCHES | FRANCE'. See colophon.

Binding: White buckram with black leather shelfback. Front: '[dark green] PUELLA [very red floral decorations] [dark green rule]'. Endpapers same as text. All edges trimmed. Medium green and white headbands and footbands.

Publication: 150 numbered copies signed by Dickey. Published October 1985. $120.00 See certificate of limitation.

Production: See colophon.

Locations: MJB; ScU.

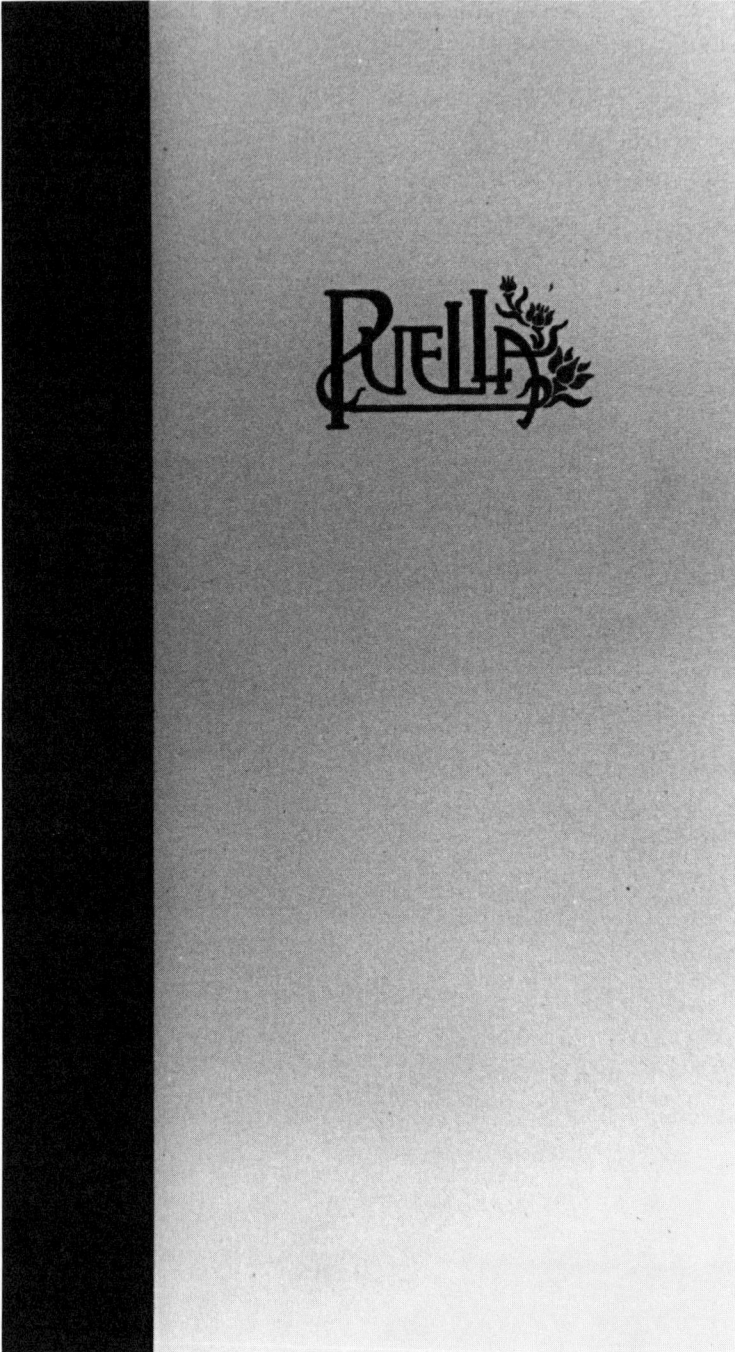

Front cover for A 39.2

A 40 VÄRMLAND

A 40.1

First edition, only printing (1982)

VÄRMLAND

Poems Based On Poems

———◆———

James Dickey

PALAEMON PRESS LIMITED

A 40.1: 6″ × 10″; title and rule in red

[i–ii] [1–4] 5–12 [13–18]

[1]¹⁰

Contents: pp. i–ii: blank; p. 1: title; p. 2: acknowledgments and 'Copyright, 1982, by James Dickey'; p. 3: *'for Robert Penn Warren'*; p. 4: note by Dickey; pp. 5–12: text; pp. 13–14: blank; p. 15: certificate of limitation; pp. 16–18: blank.

   5 poems: "Lakes of Värmland" (with André Frénaud), "Form" (with André Frénaud), "Heads" (with Lucien Becker), "For Having Left the Birds" (with Roland Bouhéret), "Attempted Departure" (with André du Bouchet). All previously unpublished. "Lakes of Värmland," "Heads," and "Attempted Departure" were reprinted in C 321; "Form" was reprinted in *Ploughshares*, 9 (Spring 1983), 16–17.

Typography and paper: No running heads. Wove paper watermarked '[script] Arches'.

Binding: Unprinted black wrappers.

Dust jacket: Red, pink, gold, and green marbled paper. Printed white label on front: '[within red decorative frame] [green] VÄRMLAND | [red French rule] | [green] James Dickey'. Fore-edge and bottom edge rough-trimmed.

Publication: p. 15: 'THIS EDITION IS LIMITED TO ONE HUNDRED AND FIFTY COPIES'. Signed by Dickey. Also 26 lettered copies. Published December 1982. Numbered copies: $45.00. According to *Lovett & Lovett Catalogue No. 5*, "Of this edition, only approximately 50 were issued, and the remainder destroyed."

Production: Undetermined.

Locations: JRB (dj); MJB (dj); ScU (dj).

VÄRMLAND

James Dickey

Front dust jacket for A 40.1

A 41 FOR A TIME AND PLACE

A 41.1

First edition, only printing (1983)

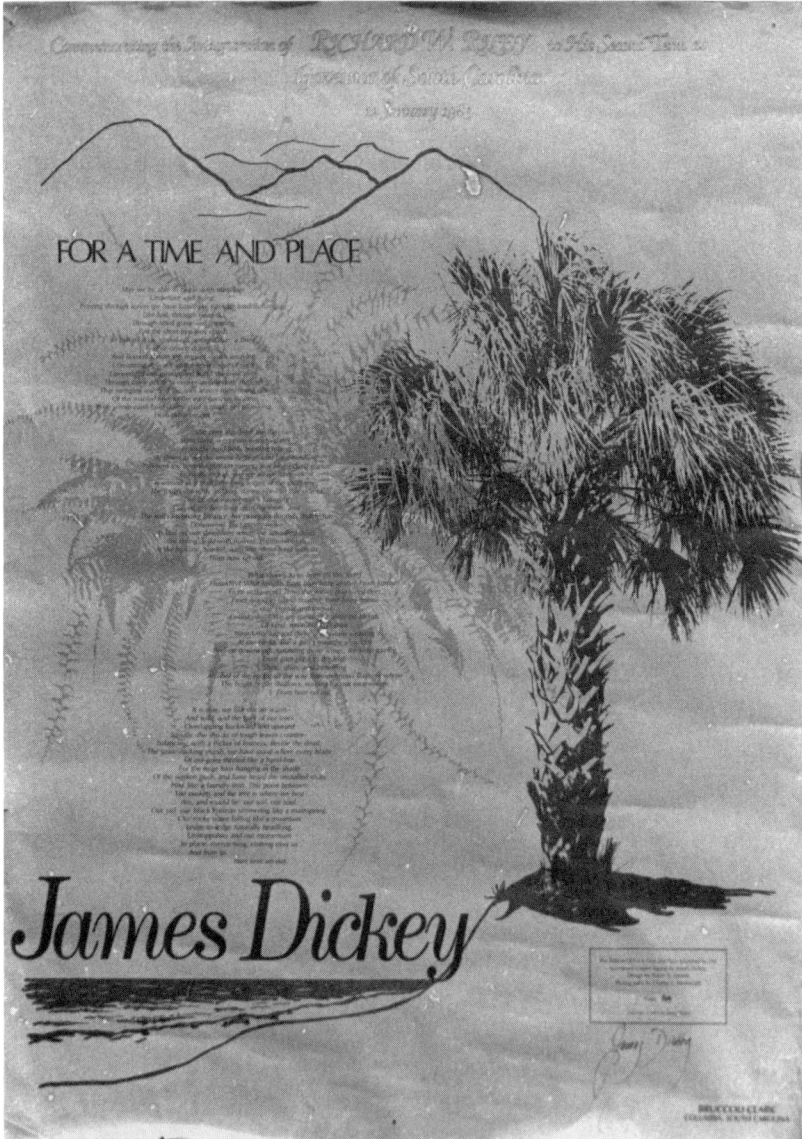

A 41.1: 22″ × 29¾″; printed in silver, navy, and gray

Broadside

Columbia, S.C.: Bruccoli Clark, 1983.

Previously unpublished poem.

Paper: Lavender laid paper; watermarked 'Linenweave Text [logo]'. Right edge deckle.

Publication: 250 numbered copies signed by Dickey. Published 12 January 1983. $25.00. Copyright #TX2-447-994.

Production: Printed by Washburn Press, Charlotte, N.C.

Locations: Caroliniana; JRB; MJB.

A 42 FALSE YOUTH: FOUR SEASONS

A 42.1

First edition, only printing (1983)

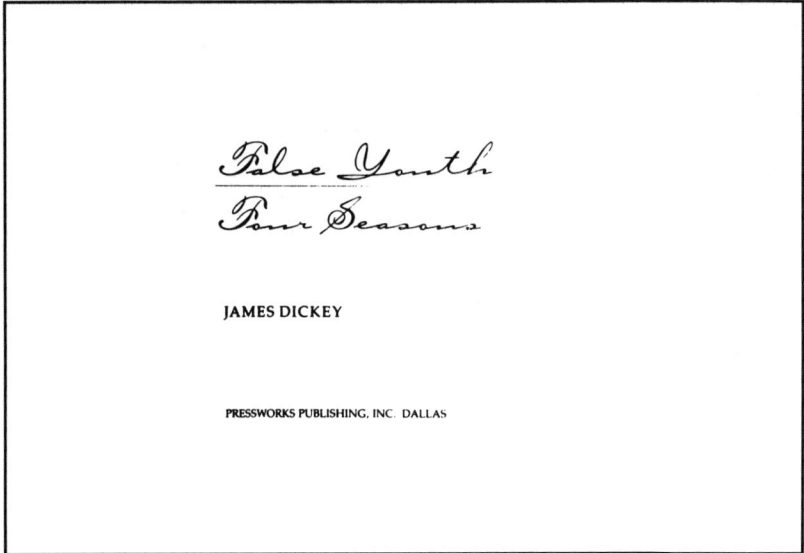

False Youth
Four Seasons

JAMES DICKEY

PRESSWORKS PUBLISHING, INC. DALLAS

A 42.1: 8½″ × 5¹⁵⁄₁₆″; red rule

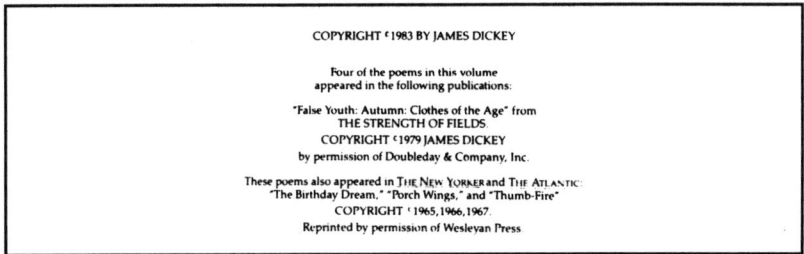

COPYRIGHT © 1983 BY JAMES DICKEY

Four of the poems in this volume
appeared in the following publications:

"False Youth: Autumn: Clothes of the Age" from
THE STRENGTH OF FIELDS
COPYRIGHT © 1979 JAMES DICKEY
by permission of Doubleday & Company, Inc.

These poems also appeared in THE NEW YORKER and THE ATLANTIC:
"The Birthday Dream," "Porch Wings," and "Thumb-Fire"
COPYRIGHT © 1965, 1966, 1967.
Reprinted by permission of Wesleyan Press.

[i–viii] [1–2] 3–5 [6–10] 11–18 [19–20] 21–23 [24–26] 27–28 [29–30] 31–33 [34–42]

[A–B]⁸ [C]⁸ (C5+1). Certificate of limitation inserted.

Contents: pp. i–ii: blank; p. iii: half title; p. iv: blank; p. v: title; p. vi: copyright and acknowledgments; p. vii: 'To Deborah and Bronwen | [red rule] | — *that power to those who make me glad* | T. Sturge Moore'; p. viii: blank; p. 1: '[red rule] | [script] The Birthday Dream'; p. 2: illustration; pp. 3–33: text; p. 34: blank; p. 35: colophon and certificate of limitation; pp. 36–42: blank.

Front cover for A 42.1

5 poems: "The Birthday Dream," "Spring: The Olympian," "Summer: Porch-Wings," "Autumn: Clothes of the Age," "Winter: Thumb-Fire." All previously published. "False Youth: Summer: Porch-Wings" was previously collected as "False Youth: Summer" in *Poems 1957–1967;* "False Youth: Winter: Thumb-Fire" was previously collected as "False Youth: Winter" in *Poems 1957–1967.*

Typography and paper: 4⁹⁄₁₆". Captions in margins: rectos: '[folio] | [red rule] | [poem title]'; versos: '[folio] | [red rule] | [section title]'. Laid paper, chainlines 1³⁄₁₆" apart; watermarked 'TWEEDWEAVE'.

Binding: White paper-covered boards with white V cloth (smooth) shelfback. Front goldstamped: '[60 within laurel wreath] | [script] James Dickey'. Spine goldstamped vertically: 'FOUR SEASONS: FALSE YOUTH *James Dickey*'. Brownish gray endpapers. All edges trimmed.

Dust jacket: Unprinted clear plastic.

Publication: 226 numbered or lettered copies signed by Dickey. See certificate of limitation. Published March 1983. $60.00.

Production: Printed by Capital Printing, Austin, Tex.

Locations: Caroliniana; JRB; LC (MAR 07 1983); MJB.

A43 NIGHT HURDLING

A 43.1.a₁

First edition, first printing, trade issue (1983)

A 43.1.a₁: 2-page title, 11¾″ × 8¹⁵⁄₁₆″; left

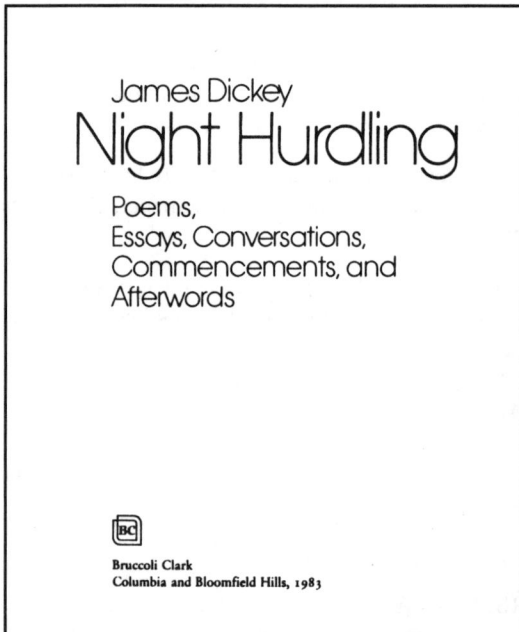

James Dickey
Night Hurdling

Poems,
Essays, Conversations,
Commencements, and
Afterwords

Bruccoli Clark
Columbia and Bloomfield Hills, 1983

A 43.1.a₁: right

Copyright © 1983 by James Dickey

"The Geek of Poetry" © 1979 by the New York Times Company. Reprinted by Permission.

"Conversation on a Dock" Copyright WNET/13, Bill Moyers's Journal, 1976.

"The Enemy from Eden" first appeared in *Esquire*. "Purgation" first appeared in *Head-Deep in Strange Sounds: Free Flight Improvisations from the Unenglish*, Palaemon Press, Ltd. "Craters" and "Farmers" first appeared in the *American Poetry Review*. "The Starry Place Between the Antlers" first appeared in *Esquire* under the title "Why I Live in South Carolina." "Excellently Bright" first appeared in *Harper's Bazaar*. "Imagination and Pain" first appeared in *Mademoiselle*. "The Weathered Hand and Silent Space" aka "Robert Penn Warren's Courage" first appeared in the *Saturday Review*. "The Geek of Poetry" first appeared in the *New York Times Book Review*. "The Unreflecting Shield" is reprinted from *F. Scott Fitzgerald: Poems 1911-1940*, copyright © James Dickey, 1981. Afterword to *Through the Wheat* by James Boyd reprinted by permission of Southern Illinois University Press. "Bare Bones" first appeared in *Deliverance*, a screenplay, Southern Illinois University Press. "Preface to *The Early Motion*" and "Preface to *Falling, May Day Sermon, and Other Poems*" is used by permission of Wesleyan University Press. Acknowledgment is made to the Ecco Press for permission to include the "Afterword" from their edition of *Babel to Byzantium*. The "Afterword" was first published in *Antaeus*.

"Delights of the Edge" was first published in *Mademoiselle*. "Night Hurdling" aka "James Dickey's Glory" first appeared in *Esquire*. "Body, Backstretch, and the Outside Man" aka "Why Men Drive" first appeared in *Playboy*. "Complicity" aka "Female Sexuality" first appeared in *Mademoiselle*. "In Texas" aka "Ritual Magic" was first published in the *Lone Star Review*; interview by Paul Christensen. "In North Carolina" aka "Getting to the Gold" first appeared in the *Arts Journal*; interview by Terry

Roberts. "In Virginia" first appeared in *Shenandoah Review*; interview by C. Kizer and J. Boatwright. "In Mademoiselle" aka "The Poet Tries to Make a Kind of Order" was first published in *Mademoiselle*. "In New York" is reprinted by permission of *New York Quarterly*; craft interview by William Packard.

"At Home" first appeared in *Writers Yearbook 1981*, Writers Digest; interview by Bruce Joel Hillman.

Lines from Robert Penn Warren's "Tell Me a Story" from *Selected Poems 1923-1975* reprinted by permission; copyright Random House, Inc. Lines from Robert Lowell's "Waking Early Sunday Morning" from *Selected Poems* reprinted by permission; copyright Farrar, Straus & Giroux. Lines from Theodore Roethke's "The Far Field" from *Collected Poems* reprinted by permission; copyright Doubleday.

Library of Congress Cataloging in Publication Data

Dickey, James.
  Night hurdling.

  "A Bruccoli Clark book."
  I. Title.
PS3554.I32N5   1983   811'.54   83-7096
ISBN 0-89723-038-8
ISBN 0-89723-040-X (lim. ed.)

[1–vii] viii–xi [xii] [1] 2–7 [8] 9–17 [18] 19–27 [28] 29–111 [112] 113–217 [218] 219–321 [322] 323–356

Perfect binding.

Contents: p. i: half title; pp. ii–iii: title; pp. iv–v: copyright and acknowledgments; p. vi: 'To Bronwen | and to Matt— | *for her coming* | *his continuing*'; pp. vii–viii: contents; pp. ix–xi: 'Introduction'; p. xii: blank; pp. 1–355: text; p. 356: colophon.

4 poems, 9 interviews, 34 essays and addresses: "Introduction,"* "The Enemy from Eden"; *Poems:* Age—"Purgation" (see C 295), Nature—"The Eagle's Mile," Double-Tongue—"Craters" (with Michel Leiris), "Farmers" (with André Frénaud); *Low Country:* "The Starry Place Between the Antlers," "Excellently Bright, or Shell Roads"; *Writers and Beholders:* "The Water-Bug's Mittens: Ezra Pound: What We Can Use," "Imagination and Pain," "The Weathered Hand and Silent Space," "The Unreflecting Shield" (see B 57), "Blood Zero" (see B 56), "Through the Wheat" (see B 46), "The Geek of Poetry," "Devastation in the Arroyo" (see B 67), "Visions in the Invisible Dimension,"* "Bare Bones: Afterword to a Film," "Conversation on a Dock," "An Acceptance"; *Some Statements on Poetry:* "Preface to *The Early Motion*," "Preface to *Falling, May Day Sermon, and Other Poems*," "Afterword to *Babel to Byzantium*" (see A 11.1.e), "The G. I. Can of Beets, the Fox in the Wave, and the Hammers Over Open Ground"; *Lines: "Firing Line,"* "A Hand-Line: In Pursuit of the Grey Soul"; *Courage as an Ideal:* "Delights of the Edge," "Style and Chance,"* "Upthrust and Its Men"*; *Some Personal Things:* "Night Hurdling" (see B 45), "Starting

JAMES DICKEY

night hurdling

POEMS, ESSAYS,
CONVERSATIONS,
COMMENCEMENTS,
AND AFTERWORDS

JAMES DICKEY night hurdling

By
James Dickey

In Pursuit of the Grey Soul
500 signed copies, $35

**The Starry Place Between the Antlers:
Why I Live in South Carolina**
500 signed copies, $20

The Water-Bug's Mittens
300 signed copies, $20

The Eagle's Mile
A poster poem, 75 signed copies, $20

The Zodiac
Manuscript edition, 41 signed copies, $400

For a Time and Place
A poster poem, 250 signed copies, $20

Bruccoli Clark
2006 Sumter Street
Columbia, S.C. 29201

Jacket design by Quentin Fiore
Book cover photo by Leonhard Copeland

Dust jacket for A 43.1.a₁

from Buckhead: A Home Address,"* "Play for Voices: Log of a Stationary Navigator,"* "Body, Backstretch, and the Outside Man," "The Grass Mountain Kid: Family Camping Exposed," "The Wild Heart,"* "Complicity"; *Talking It Out:* "In Texas," "In North Carolina," "In Virginia" (see B 32), "In *Mademoiselle*," "In Louisiana," "In New York," "At Home: The Voices of James Dickey"; *Commencements and Other Tentatives:* "Computerized Rape and the Vale of Soul-Making," "Guilt as Blackmail,"* "Horsemeat and the New Mind" (see B 17), "Three Girls Outgoing." Asterisks indicate previously unpublished material.

Typography and paper: 6⁹⁄₁₆″ (7¹⁄₁₆″) × 3¹⁵⁄₁₆″. 37 lines per page. Running heads: rectos: title of selection; versos: section titles. Wove paper.

Binding: Dark blue V cloth (smooth). Spine vertically silverstamped: 'JAMES DICKEY night hurdling [horizontally] [seal] | BRUCCOLI CLARK'. Later copies have blindstamped hurdler on front. Black endpapers. All edges trimmed. Brilliant purplish blue and white headbands and footbands.

Dust jacket: Front and spine lettered in white against blue background. Front: 'JAMES | DICKEY | night | hurdling | POEMS, ESSAYS, | CONVERSATIONS, | COMMENCEMENTS, | AND AFTERWORDS | [hurdler]'. Spine: '[vertically] JAMES DICKEY night hurdling [horizontally] [seal] | BRUCCOLI CLARK'. Back has photo of Dickey and Bronwen Dickey by Leonhard Copeland. Front flap has previously unpublished statement by Dickey, description of book, and note on Dickey. Back flap lists other Dickey books published by Bruccoli Clark.

Publication: 3,250 copies. Published 15 October 1983. $19.95. Copyright #TX2-370-105.

Production: See colophon.

Locations: JRB (first binding—dj); LC (OCT 13 1983—dj); Lilly (second binding—dj); MJB (both bindings—dj); PSt (second binding).

Proof copy: Blue paper wrappers. Front: 'UNCORRECTED PROOF | JAMES DICKEY | Night Hurdling | Poems, | Essays, Conversations, | Commencements, and | Afterwords | [hurdler] | PUBLICATION _____ JULY 1983 | TENTATIVE PRICE _____ $14.95 | Bruccoli Clark | Columbia and Bloom-

356

This book was designed by Quentin Fiore; production was supervised by Fred M. Kleeberg. It was composed in Sabon type by BC Research in Columbia, S.C.; and printed and bound by R. R. Donnelley & Sons, Harrisonburg, Virginia.

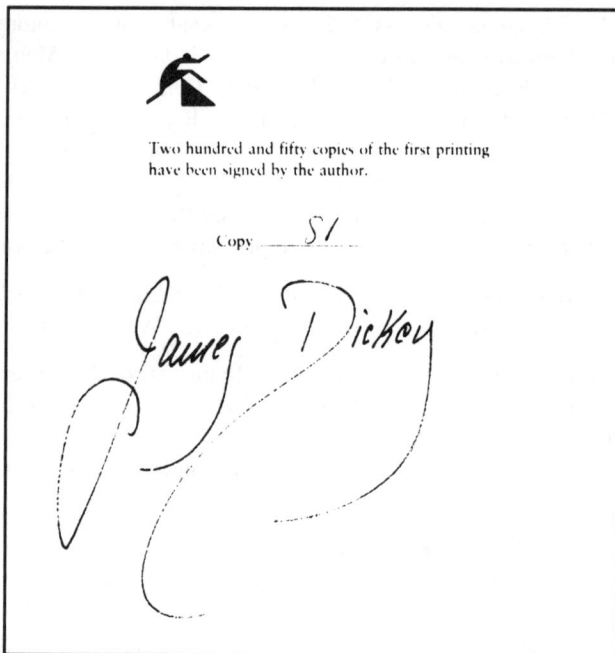

field Hills'. Produced by Crane Duplicating Service, Barnstable, Mass. Locations: JRB; MJB; ScU.

A 43.1.a$_2$

First edition, first printing, limited issue

Same as trade issue but with limitation leaf tipped in before p. i.

Binding: Paper-covered boards with pattern of white hurdlers against very purplish blue background. Dark blue cloth shelfback. Spine stamped in white same as trade issue.

Dust jacket: Unprinted glassine jacket.

Production: Bound by Hoster Bindery, Hatboro, Pa.

Publication: 250 numbered copies signed by Dickey. Published simultaneously with trade issue. $40.00.

Locations: Caroliniana; JRB; MJB.

A 44 BRONWEN, THE TRAW, AND THE SHAPE-SHIFTER

A 44.1

First edition, only printing (1986)

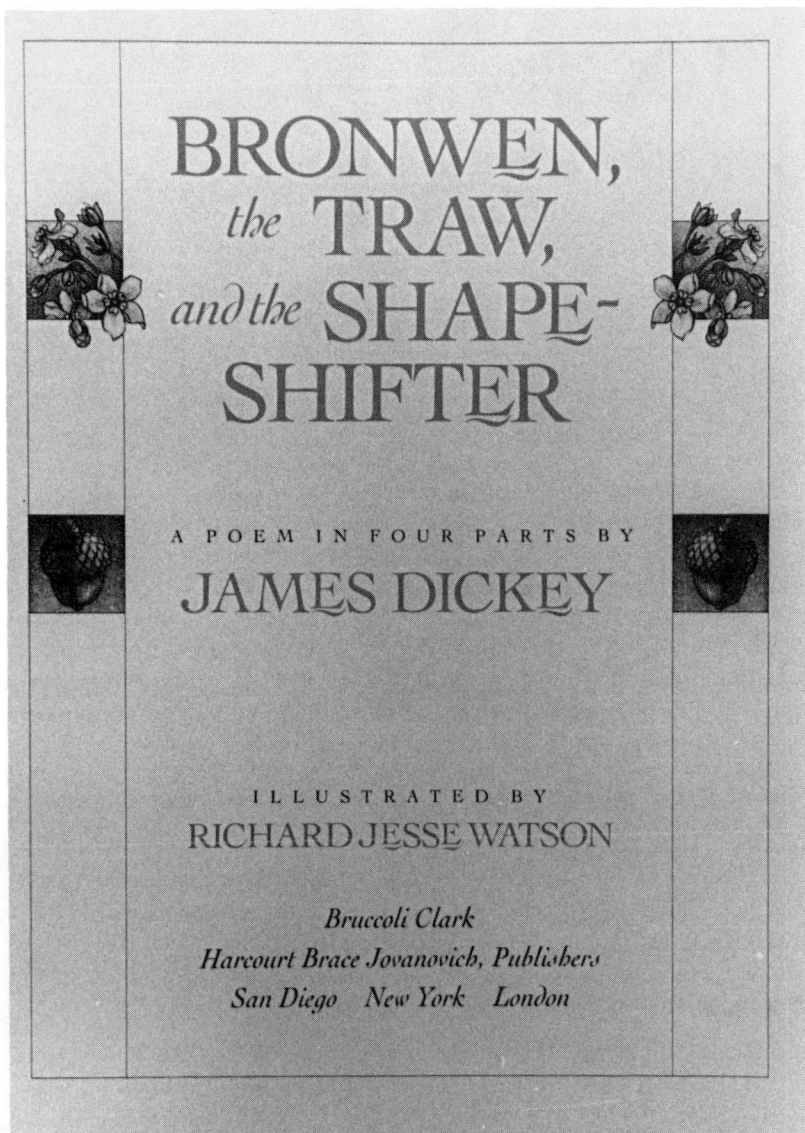

BRONWEN,
the TRAW,
and the SHAPE-
SHIFTER

A POEM IN FOUR PARTS BY
JAMES DICKEY

ILLUSTRATED BY
RICHARD JESSE WATSON

Bruccoli Clark
Harcourt Brace Jovanovich, Publishers
San Diego New York London

A 44.1: 8¹⁵/₁₆″ × 11½″; lines 1–4, 6, 8 in brown

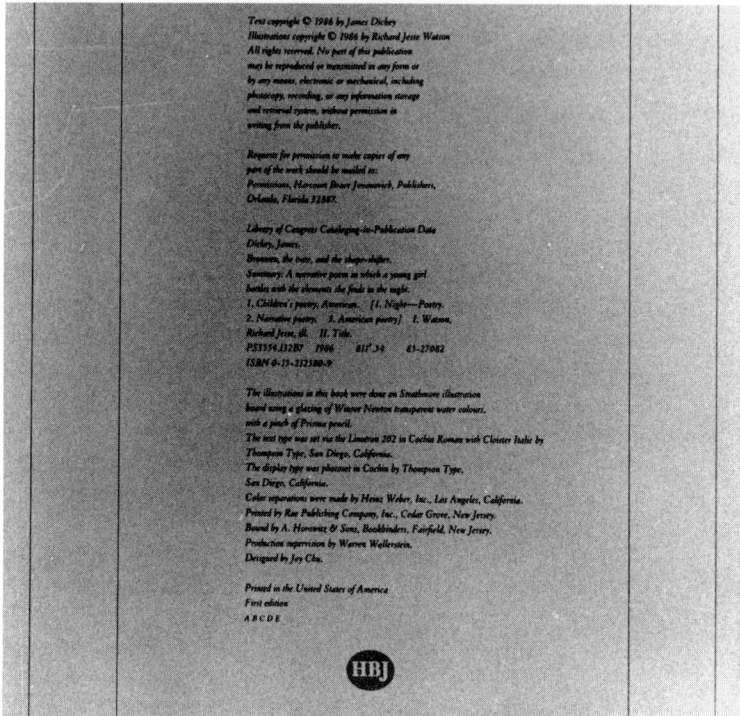

[1–32]

[1–2]^8

Contents: p. 1: title; p. 2: copyright; p. 3: 'TO BRONWEN AND HER MOTHER | IN THE ELEMENTS | —J.D. | FOR JESU, JOY OF MY DESIR-ING | —R.J.W.'; pp. 4–32: text and illustrations. Poem.

Typography and paper: No running heads. Coated wove paper.

Binding: Light blue paper-covered boards. Front blindstamped: 'BRONWEN, | *the* TRAW, | *and the* SHAPE- | SHIFTER'. Light yellowish brown V cloth shelfback. Spine: '[deep yellowish brown] [vertically] Dickey [slash] Watson BRONWEN, *the* TRAW, *and the* SHAPE-SHIFTER [horizontal HBJ device] Harcourt Brace Jovanovich'. Back: '[deep yellowish brown] 0-15-212580-9'. Deep yellowish brown endpapers. All edges trimmed.

Dust jacket: Front: '[in black on white panel] BRONWEN, *the* TRAW, | *and the* SHAPE-SHIFTER | [color illustration of Bronwen] | [in black on white panel] A POEM IN FOUR PARTS BY | JAMES DICKEY | ILLUSTRATED BY | RICHARD JESSE WATSON'. Spine: '[vertically in black] Dickey [slash]

Watson BRONWEN, *the* TRAW, *and the* SHAPE-SHIFTER [horizontal HBJ device] Harcourt Brace Jovanovich'. Back has colored floral illustration and 'ISBN 0-15-212580-9'. Front flap has description of book. Back flap has biographical notes on Dickey and Watson with statement by Dickey. "The Parents' Choice Award" gold foil label printed in black was subsequently pasted on the front dust jacket.

Publication: 20,000 copies. Published 10 September 1986. $13.95. Copyright #TX1-926-084.

Production: Printed by Rae Publishing Co., Cedar Grove, N.J.; bound by A. Horowitz & Sons, Fairfield, N.J.

Locations: JRB (dj); LC (AUG 18 1986); Lilly (dj); MJB (dj).

Review copy: Unbound gatherings inserted in dust jacket. Location: MJB.

BRONWEN, *the* TRAW, *and the* SHAPE-SHIFTER

A POEM IN FOUR PARTS BY
JAMES DICKEY
ILLUSTRATED BY
RICHARD JESSE WATSON

Dickey/Watson BRONWEN, *the* TRAW, *and the* SHAPE-SHIFTER Harcourt Brace Jovanovich

ISBN 0-15-212580-9

Dust jacket for A 44.1

A 45 ALNILAM

A 45.1.a₁

First edition, first printing, trade issue (1987)

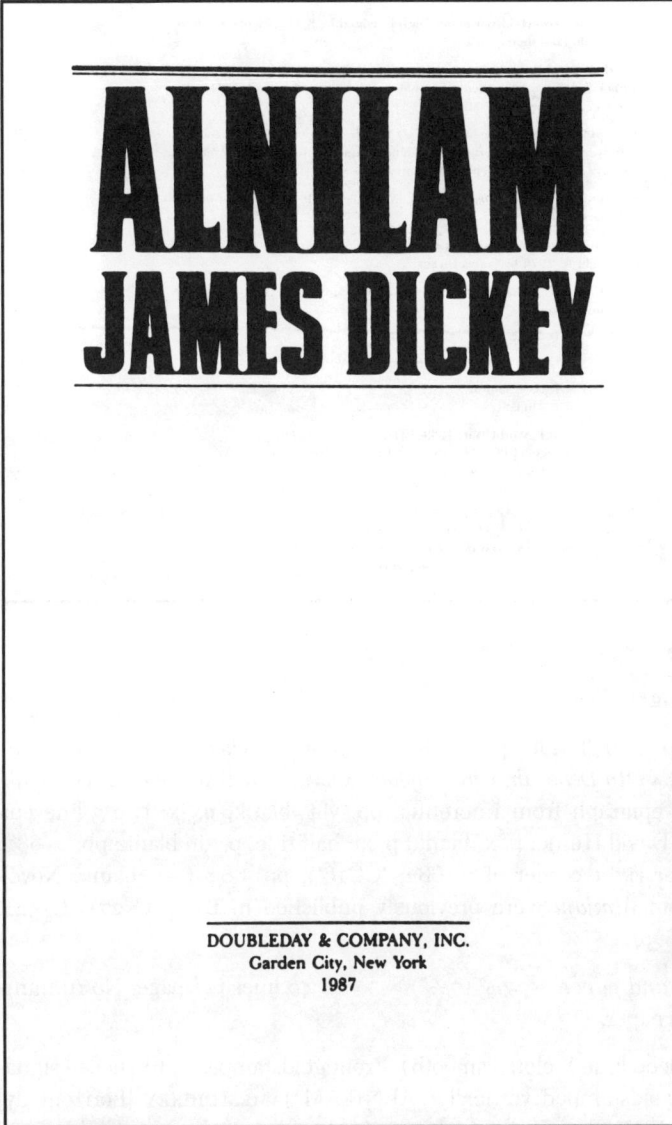

ALNILAM
JAMES DICKEY

DOUBLEDAY & COMPANY, INC.
Garden City, New York
1987

A 45.1.a: 6″ × 9⅛″

Library of Congress Cataloging-in-Publication Data

Dickey, James.
  Alnilam.

  1. World War, 1939–1945—Fiction. I. Title.
PS3554.I32A78   1987   813'.54   86–19699
ISBN 0-385-06549-3

[i–xii] 1–682 [683–684]

Notch binding; unsewn.

Contents: p. i: half title; p. ii: '*Also by James Dickey*'; p. iii: title; p. iv: copyright; p. v: '*to Deborah, Christopher, Kevin, and Bronwen*'; p. vi: blank; p. vii: 6-line epigraph from Lucretius; pp. viii: blank; p. ix: two 3-line epigraphs from David Hume; p. x: blank; p. xi: half title; p. xii: blank; pp. 1–682: text (at lower right corner of p. 682: '$\overline{\text{CC16}}$'); pp. 683–684: blank. Novel. Excerpts from *Alnilam* were previously published in B 84, C 271, C 324, C 341, and C 342.

Typography and paper: 7³⁄₁₆″ (7½″) × 7⁵⁄₁₆″. 40 lines per page. No running heads. Wove paper.

Binding: Deep blue V cloth (smooth). Front goldstamped with Dickey signature. Spine goldstamped vertically: 'ALNILAM JAMES DICKEY [horizontally] DOUBLEDAY'. Endpapers printed on one side only in light greenish blue and white pattern of squares and circles. All edges trimmed.

ALNILAM
JAMES DICKEY

A NOVEL BY THE AUTHOR OF DELIVERANCE

JAMES DICKEY

ALNILAM JAMES DICKEY

DOUBLEDAY

ALNILAM
JAMES DICKEY

In *Deliverance*, his classic work of fiction, James Dickey took us on an unforgettable odyssey into the heart of the American wilderness. Now, America's foremost poet and man of letters takes us on a very different journey. A startling rite of passage through the worlds of darkness and sight, ALNILAM is a stunning portrait of one man's encounter with the truth about his son and, in turn, himself.

Early in World War II, Frank Cahill learns that his son, whom he has never met, has crashed in an Air Corps training accident and is presumed dead. Though recently blind as the result of adult diabetes, Cahill travels to the camp and learns of Joel's mysterious demise and enigmatic life. It is not entirely certain that Joel is really dead; his body has not been recovered and some of his fellow cadets think they have seen him, or sensed his presence. Yet there, Joel is a hero, the center of Alnilam, a secret group named for the middle star in the belt of Orion, the hunter constellation. As the cadets follow Joel's doctrines—or
(continued on back flap)

(continued from front flap)
what they believe them to be—they are in quest of complete knowledge of the air—the ultimate flight as "precision mysticism"—to join the mechanical with the physical and the spiritual.

Through passages as brilliant and unsummarizable as those by Saint Exupéry, Dickey writes about the experience of flying, using air symbolically as Melville used water in *Moby Dick*. In certain key passages Dickey has chosen to tell part of the story in parallel columns, from the point of view of Dark and Light. In the Dark portions we learn what is going on in the heightened perceptions of Cahill, the blind man; in the Light we observe the action's forms from the point of view of those who can see—the world of inner vision as opposed to the apparent world. Together they form ALNILAM, Dickey's most important work to date.

Born in Atlanta, Georgia, in 1923, James Dickey is regarded as one of the major authors of our time. His first novel, *Deliverance*, was a national bestseller and an important motion picture. Mr. Dickey is the recipient of a Guggenheim fellowship and received the National Book Award for his 1967 volume of poetry, *Buckdancer's Choice*. His other books of poetry include *Puella*, *The Zodiac*, and *The Strength of Fields*. Currently, he is poet-in-residence at the University of South Carolina in Columbia, where he lives with his wife and daughter.

Printed in the U.S.A.

Dust jacket for A 45.1.a

Dust jacket: Front: '[below white stars on blue background] [embossed] [dark blue] ALNILAM | [black rule] | [dark gray] A NOVEL BY THE AUTHOR OF [black] DELIVERANCE | [black rule] | [red] JAMES DICKEY'. Spine: '[vertically against white] [dark blue] ALNILAM [red type, black rules] J̲A̲M̲E̲S̲ D̲I̲C̲K̲E̲Y̲ [horizontally in black] DOUBLEDAY'. Back: photo of Dickey by Stathis Orphanos and 'ISBN: 0-385-06549-3'. Front flap has description of *Alnilam* continued on back flap with biographical note on Dickey; '0687' at foot of back flap.

Production: Doubleday, Berryville, Va.

Publication: 125,000 copies. Published 5 June 1987. $19.95. Copyright #TX2-086-335.

Locations: Caroliniana (dj); JRB (dj); Lilly (dj); MJB (dj); PSt.

Proof copy: Uncorrected proof perfect-bound in gray-beige wrappers with all-over pattern of silver circles. Front: 'ALNILAM | [rule] JAMES DICKEY | DOUBLEDAY & COMPANY, INC. | Garden City, New York | 1987'. Spine: '[vertically] A̲L̲N̲I̲L̲A̲M̲ PUB. DATE: June 1987 [above] DOUBLEDAY & COMPANY, INC. [below] GARDEN CITY, NEW YORK'. Back: description of *Alnilam* and three blurbs for *Deliverance*. First page of text has publication information. Locations: JRB; MJB; ScU.

A 45. 1.a₂

First edition, first printing, limited issue (1987)

Same as trade issue but with limitation leaf tipped in before p. i.

Binding: Red buckram goldstamped with Dickey's signature on front. Spine same as trade issue. Blue headband.

Slipcase: Red buckram-covered boards with reproduction of dust jacket front pasted on front of slipcase; rectangular gold label printed in black: '$125.00 | ISBN: 0-385-24258-1'.

Publication: 150 numbered copies signed by Dickey. Published simultaneously with trade issue. $125.00.

Locations: MJB; ScU.

A 45.1.b

First edition, second printing (Book-of-the-Month Club): Garden City, N.Y.: Doubleday, 1987.

Distributed by BOMC as an alternate selection in July 1987. 'FIRST EDITION' slug removed from copyright page. Three-piece binding with medium blue paper-covered boards and darker blue V cloth shelfback; goldstamped. Blindstamped rectangle at bottom of cloth shelfback on back cover.

A 45.2.a

Second edition, first printing: New York: Pinnacle, [1988].

Copyright page: 'First Pinnacle Books printing: August, 1988'. Wrappers. $4.95. #1-55817-086-3.

A 46 SUMMONS

A 46.1

First edition, only printing (1988)

A 46.1: 12″ × 15″; reddish brown decorations, rules, and publication information

Broadside.

Columbia, S.C.: Bruccoli Clark Layman, 1988.

First publication of Dickey's revision of the final poem of *Puella*.

Paper: Off-white laid paper.

Publication: Certificate of limitation: '*One Hundred Numbered Copies For Sale And* | *Twenty Lettered Copies For Private Distribution,* | *All Signed By The Author.*' Published 15 January 1988. $50.00. TX 2-400-510.

Production: Washburn Press, Charlotte, N.C.

Locations: Caroliniana (lettered); JRB (lettered); LC (lettered); MJB (lettered).

A 47 WAYFARER

A 47.1.a

First edition, first printing (1988)

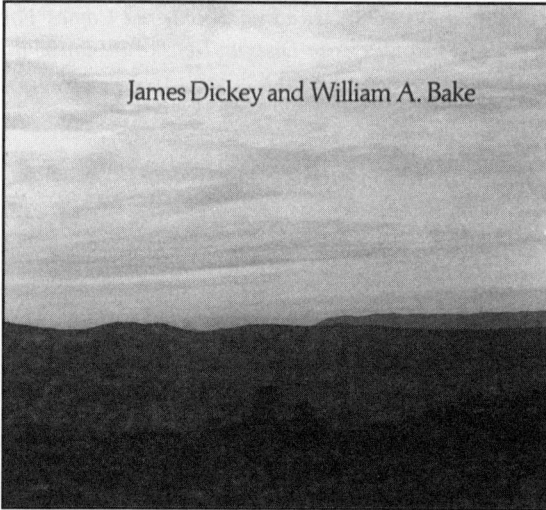

A 47.1.a: 2-page title, 23¾″ × 11¹⁵⁄₁₆″; left; authors' names in deep purplish red on color photo

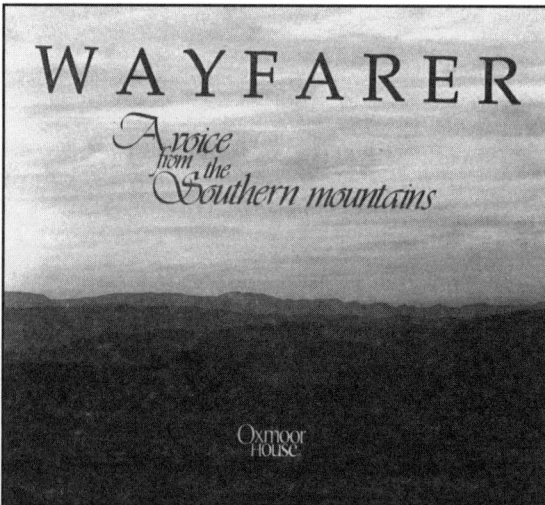

A 47.1.a: right; title in deep purplish red, subtitle in gray-blue, imprint in white—all on color photo

Photographs © 1988 William A. Bake
Text © 1988 James Dickey

Published by Oxmoor House, Inc.
Book Division of Southern Progress Corporation
P.O. Box 2463, Birmingham, Alabama 35201

All rights reserved. No part of this book may be
reproduced in any form or by any means without
the prior written permission of the publisher, ex-
cepting brief quotations in connection with reviews
written specifically for inclusion in magazines or
newspapers.

Library of Congress Catalog Number: 86-62282
ISBN: 0-8487-0691-9
Manufactured in the United States of America
First Edition

Editor-in-Chief: John Logue
Executive Editor: Candace N. Conard
Production Manager: Jerry Higdon
Associate Production Manager: Rick Litton
Art Director: Bob Nance

Wayfarer

Editor: Mary Jean Haddin
Editorial Assistant: Margaret Allen Northen
Production Assistant: Theresa L. Beste

Last five lines on page 97 excerpted from "Antique
Harvesters," *Selected Poems* by John Crowe Ransom.
Reprinted by permission of Alfred A. Knopf, Inc.

PAGE i: *Fantasy on My Window*
      ii: *Wayfarer*
      iv: *Fire in the Sky*

[i–x] [1–2] 3–5 [6] 7–10 [11] 12 [13] 14–15 [16] 17–24 [25] 26–27 [28] 29–33 [34] 35–37 [38] 39–43 [44] 45–51 [52] 53–57 [58–60] 61 [62] 63–71 [72] 73–81 [82] 83–89 [90] 91 [92] 93 [94] 95–97 [98] 99 [100] 101–103 [104] 105 [106–107] 108 [109–116] 117 [118] 119–121 [122–126] 127 [128] 129 [130–135] 136 [137] 138 [139–140] 141–142 [143] 144–148 [149–153] 154–156 [157] 158–159 [160] 161 [162] 163 [164–166] 167–168 [169] 170 [171–172] 173 [174–176] 177 [178–182]

$[1–12]^8$

Contents: p. i: photo of ferns; pp. ii–iii: photo and half title; pp. iv–v: title; p. vi: copyright; pp. vii–viii: photos; p. ix: dedications by William A. Bake and Dickey; pp. x–1: photos and half title; p. 2: photo; pp. 3–97: text and photos; pp. 98–178: photos; pp. 179–181: '*Catalogue* | OF PHOTOGRAPHS'; p. 182: colophon.

Typography and paper: No running heads. Vintage Velvet paper.

Binding: 3-piece binding. Deep purplish red V cloth (Arrestox A) front, spine, and back with 3⅞" light blue-gray paper-covered boards front and back. Front blindstamped vertically up: 'WAYFARER'. Spine silverstamped verti-cally down: 'WAYFARER *Dickey & Bake* [horizontally] Oxmoor | House₉'. Light

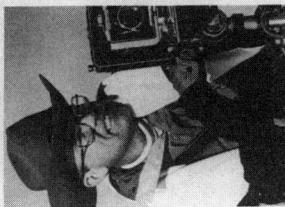

Dust jacket for A 47.1.a

blue-gray Rainbow Felt endpapers. All edges trimmed. White headbands and footbands.

Dust jacket: Front printed over color photograph of mountain road: '[deep purplish red] *James Dickey & William A. Bake* | WAYFARER | [beige script] A voice | from | the | Southern mountains'. Spine: '[vertically down] [deep purplish red] WAYFARER [beige] *Dickey & Bake* [horizontally] Oxmoor | House₍ᵣ₎'. Back: black-and-white photos of Bake and Dickey. Front flap: description of book; '10390088'. Back flap: biographical notes on Dickey and Bake; biographical note quotes Dickey. NB. The jacket folds in on itself at top and bottom. Later copies have price changed to $50.00 by label on front flap.

Publication: 55,000 copies. Published in October 1988. $40.00 before 31 December 1988; $50.00 thereafter.

Production: Composition by Media Services, Birmingham, Ala. Manufactured by Arcata Graphics, Kingsport, Tenn. See colophon.

Locations: JRB (dj); MJB (dj).

Note: The 1989 *Wayfarer* calendar sold by Oxmoor House includes nothing by Dickey.

Designed by Bob Nance

Composition by Media Services
Birmingham, Alabama

Color by Capitol Engraving Company
Nashville, Tennessee

Manufactured by Arcata Graphics
Kingsport, Tennessee

Text paper is Vintage Velvet from Westvaco
New York, New York

Endpaper is Rainbow Felt from Ecological Fibers
Lunenburg, Maine

Binding material is Arrestox A from ICG
Kingsport, Tennessee

A 48: THE VOICED CONNECTIONS OF JAMES DICKEY

A 48.1.a

First edition, first printing (forthcoming 1989)

The Voiced
Connections of

James Dickey

Interviews and Conversations

Edited by
Ronald Baughman

University of South Carolina Press

A 48.1.a: 6″ × 9″

The Voiced Connections of James Dickey: Interviews and Conversations, ed. Ronald Baughman. Columbia: University of South Carolina Press, 1989. FORTHCOMING.

This volume will include a preface by Dickey and the following items: "An Interview with James Dickey" (see D 7); "Things Happen: An Interview with Dickey" (see D 26); Nancy Malone, "Poet with Power: James Dickey" (see D 35); Francis Roberts, "James Dickey: An Interview" (see D 39); John Logue, "James Dickey Describes His Life and Works as He 'Moves Toward Hercules' " (see D 98); David L. Arnett, "An Interview with James Dickey" (see B 66, D 184); "Interview: James Dickey" (see D 177); Glenn Helgeland, "James Dickey: The Archer's Author" (see D 151); Wayne Holmes, Joseph Costello, Mark Greenberg, and Randy McConnell, "James Dickey at Drury College" (see D 433); Geoffrey Norman, "*Playboy* Interview: James Dickey" (see D 159); Donald J. Greiner, " 'That Plain-Speaking Guy': A Conversation with James Dickey on Robert Frost" (see B 36); L. L. Simms, "Interview with James Dickey" (see D 187); Jim Townsend, "Dickey" (see D 223); W. C. Barnwell, "James Dickey on Yeats: An Interview" (see D 225); Phil Patton, "Interview: James Dickey" (see D 231); Earl Turner, "An Interview with . . . James Dickey" (see D 259); Peggy Friedmann and Betty Bedell, "A Conversation with James Dickey" (see D 265); Ron McFarland, "An Interview with James Dickey" (see D 285); L. Elisabeth Beattie, "James Dickey Rides Again" (see D 335); "An Interview with James Dickey" (see B 64); William W. Starr, "An Interview with James Dickey" (see B 70); Leslie Bates, "Recovering the Cosmos: Poet James Dickey at 60" (see D 352); Bettye Givens, "Interview with James Dickey" (see D 361); William Page, "River City Interview with James Dickey" (see D 367); Hank Nuwer, "James Dickey: Limitations and Infinities" (see D 379); Gordon Van Ness, "Living Beyond Recall: An Interview with James Dickey" (see D 414); William W. Starr, "*Alnilam:* James Dickey's Novel Explores Father and Son Relationships" (see D 416); Bob Gingher, "James Dickey Talks About Story Behind *Alnilam*" (see D 425). All first-book appearances except for the four interviews cross-referenced to Section B.

AA. Supplement

AA 1 JAMES DICKEY READS HIS POEMS
  1968

A Presentation of the Cultural Affairs Office of
the American Embassy, London in association
with Rapp and Whiting Limited.

JAMES
DICKEY
reads
his
POEMS

AMERICAN EMBASSY AUDITORIUM - FRIDAY, APRIL 26, 1968

Cover title for AA 1: 5″ × 8½″; lines 4–8 in blue

194

Cover title.

London: American Embassy, 1968.

[1–4]

[1]²

Contents: p. 1: title; p. 2: "The Head-Aim"; p. 3: note on Dickey; p. 4: "The Flash." Poems.

Printed on tannish green laid paper; watermarked '[crown] | [script] Glaston-bury'.

Unknown number of copies distributed gratis at the American Embassy, London, 26 April 1968. Reading sponsored by the Cultural Affairs Office of the American Embassy and Rapp & Whiting.

Locations: MJB; MoSW; ScU.

AA 2 A BIRTH—
1973

— James Dickey —

A Birth

Inventing a story with grass,
I find a young horse deep inside it.
I cannot nail wires around him;
My fence posts fail to be solid,

And he is free, strangely, without me.
With his head still browsing the greenness,
He walks slowly out of the pasture
To enter the sun of his story.

My mind freed of its own creature,
I find myself deep in my life
In a room with my child and my mother,
When I feel the sun climbing my
Shoulder

Change, to include a new horse. —

AA 2: 8½″ × 11″

Broadside.

Pittsburgh: International Poetry Forum, 1973.

Facsimile of Dickey manuscript poem. Off-white paper. Unknown number of copies; distributed gratis at Dickey's reading in Pittsburgh, 3 October 1973.

Locations: JRB; MJB.

Note: Facsimile also published in *The International Poetry Forum Collectors Deskbook 1984* (Pittsburgh, 1983).

AA 3 KNOCK
1977

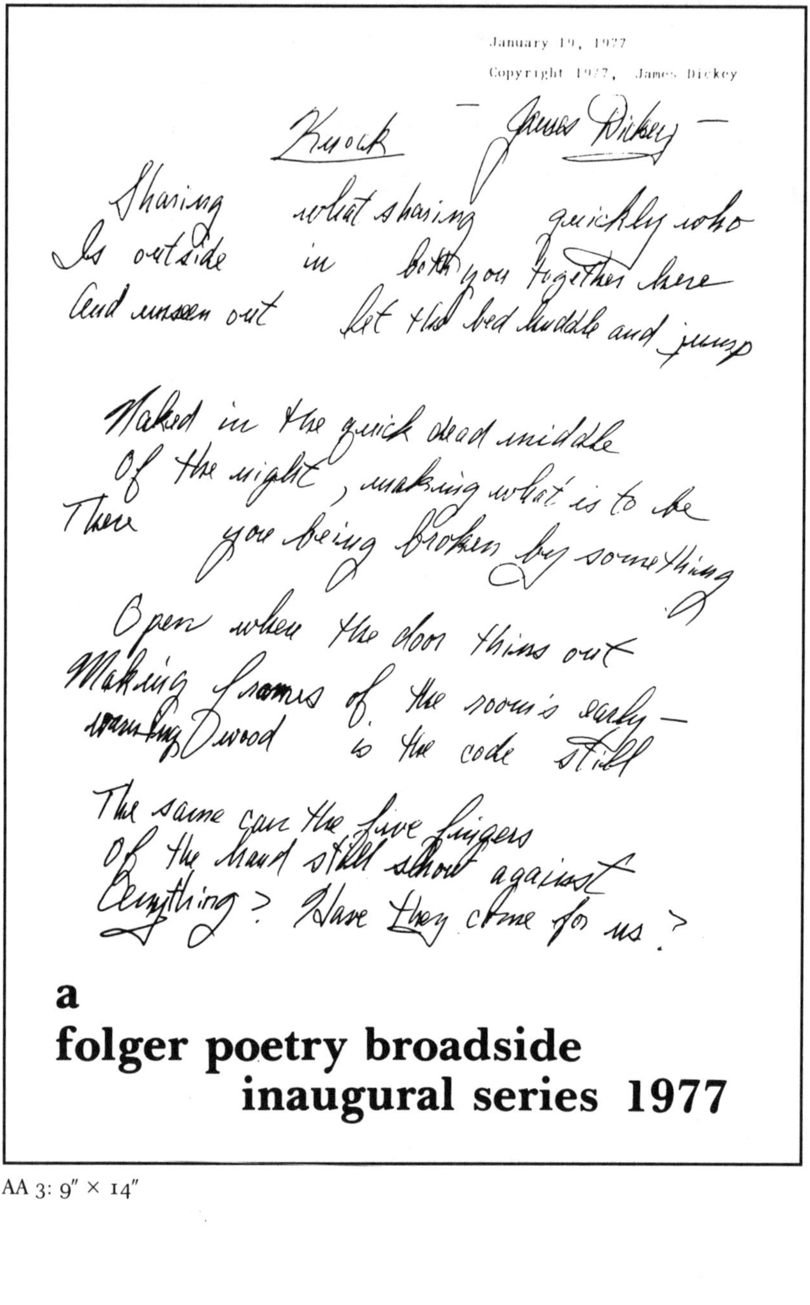

January 19, 1977

Copyright 1977, James Dickey

Knock — James Dickey —

Sharing what sharing quickly who
Is outside in both you together here
And unseen out let the bed huddle and jump

Naked in the quick dead middle
Of the night, making what is to be
There you being broken by something

Open when the door thins out
Making frames of the room's early-
~~warming~~ wood is the code still

The same can the five fingers
Of the hand still shout against
Anything? Have they come for us?

a
folger poetry broadside
inaugural series 1977

AA 3: 9″ × 14″

Broadside.

Washington, D.C.: Folger Shakespeare Library, 1977.

Facsimile of Dickey manuscript poem. Off-white antique finish paper.

1,000 copies; distributed gratis at Dickey's reading at the Folger Shakespeare Library, 19 January 1977.

Locations: JRB; MJB.

AA 4 THE SHARK AT THE WINDOW
1977

THE SHARK AT THE WINDOW— *(for my brother's marriage)*

ii

Brother in the window welcome,
Welcome brother at the seatrap
Glass. Near ghost, your lacquered
Shade drops off and waits—
Aqueous, breathclouded, seeming.
Our centers meet.

iii

Flesh that would have stood in finished grainfields
(The round hard thumb, the eye, the wheaten hair)
In the pollened, trampled fore of Tartar horse,
And to the slung and sighflown spin of blade have
Sung, as it brownly, brightly cropped
Matted and cruel lives
                    stood off from you once
In aquarium glass. We watched it from our uncertain place,
And watched its next-to, brotherly image, and the fraught
Protected waters for a sign.
                    Balanced,
A huge and casual leaf
Fall, through shivered trays of stacked
Autumnal light
Our symbol subsided to us.
We marked behind our shapes of breath
The smeared and old man's mouth, the slatted
Gills, the absolute and unknown terror,
The closest conch that might be trembled into.

Driving home from your wedding in light-
blunting fog, the road I inchmeal held
Dropt instantly, I could not guess it, great
White sail-settled and drew, and I gained there
A sanctum of midnight cloud, a float of trusts.

More than the repartitions of the womb, my brother,
That pilgrim-place has cast our centered bloods:
Renewal, oneness are there; our semblances fail.
We enter to find ourselves the same in love,
In kinship, as the tussled cloth about
A river-reed's needle, a stitching snag, can
Never alter, but renders Platonist and caddis
Fly the selfsame cordonnet, as of point-laced, ancient,
Vital hair, though the water move
More calmly than the waters of a grape, or mull
Sienna-spread and vastly wild
Under ephemerae of mule and leaf.

It was fear first pressed
Us through that pearled and helical threshold where
No adumbrations pass.

Expecting the dark, we found the shapen cupping
Resplendent with the light we made.

Gray and pink volution wore
Our whispers back in rounds.

A single voice became in those one-weltered sounds.

In the shell of the bridal
Chamber, in the still sump of midnight,
Know without fear

This with her.

James Dickey

AA 4: 14½″ × 14½″: illustration in red

Single leaf.

Winston-Salem, N.C.: Palæmon Press, 1977. Palæmon Broadside #6.

Verso: '*THE SHARK AT THE WINDOW by James Dickey* | *is printed in an edition of 126 copies.* | *100 copies numbered 1–100 are for sale.* | *26 lettered copies are for distribution.* | *Original graphic by Robert Dance.* | *This is copy   *'. Also copyright and acknowledgment. All copies signed by Dickey. Poem.

Published 27 February 1977. $10.00.

Locations: Lilly; MJB; ScU.

Note: Out-of-series copies and proof copies of Palæmon Press publications were offered for sale. See *Lovett & Lovett Booksellers Catalogue No. 5* (Winston-Salem, N.C.).

AA 5 BUCKDANCER'S CHOICE
1979

Buckdancer's Choice

So I would hear out those lungs,
The air split into nine levels,
Some gift of tongues of the whistler

In the invalid's bed: my mother,
Warbling all day to herself
The thousand variations of one song;

It is called Buckdancer's Choice.
For years, they have all been dying
Out, the classic buck-and-wing men

Of traveling minstrel shows;
With them also an old woman
Was dying of breathless angina,

Yet still found breath enough
To whistle up in my head
A sight like a one-man band,

Freed black, with cymbals at heel,
An ex-slave who thrivingly danced
To the ring of his own clashing light

Through the thousand variations of one song
All day to my mother's prone music,
The invalid's warbler's note,

While I crept close to the wall
Sock-footed, to hear the sounds alter,
Her tongue like a mockingbird's break

Through stratum after stratum of a tone
Proclaiming what choices there are
For the last dancers of their kind,

For ill women and for all slaves
Of death, and children enchanted at walls
With a brass-beating glow underfoot,

Not dancing but nearly risen
Through barnlike, theatrelike houses
On the wings of the buck and wing.

James Dickey

[signature: James Dickey]

Of an edition of thirty copies, twenty-six, signed A-Z are for private
distribution by H. H. Bradshaw, Jr. to his friends. Christmas 1979. Four
copies, numbered I-IV, are for the use of the publisher. This is copy *?*.
PALAEMON PRESS LIMITED

AA 5: 11 $^{15}/_{16}$″ × 22$^{7}/_{8}$″; title and 'James Dickey' in red

Broadside.

Winston-Salem, N.C.: Palæmon Press, 1979.

Laid paper; chainlines 1″ apart. Certificate of limitation: 'Of an edition of thirty copies, twenty-six, lettered A–Z, are for private | distribution by H. H. Bradshaw, Jr. to his friends, Christmas 1979. Four | copies, numbered I–IV, are for the use of the publisher. This is copy | PALÆMON PRESS LIM-ITED'. Signed by Dickey. Not for sale. Poem.

Locations: MJB (out-of-series); ScU (R and IV).

AA 6 THE AX-GOD: SEA-PURSUIT
1980

The Ax-God: Sea-Pursuit

—after Alfred Jarry

On the horizon, through the steam of exhausted blast-furnaces   fog   Yes
Pure Chance blows, as though it were really itself   blows
Not very well, and moans and shakes bells.

These are the sounds that invented salt. But, listen,
Waves, we are among the arced demons you are hiding

In the visiting green gullies of your mountains.
Where the shoreline clamps a lost quivering over all
Of us, a huge and shadow-cast shape looms over muck.
We crawl round his feet, loose as lizards,

While, like a filthy Caesar on his chariot,
Or on a marble, leg-crossing plinth,
Carving a whale-boat from a tree-trunk, he . . .

Well, in that branching boat, he'll run
Us down, league for league   down   down to
The last of the sea's center-speeding
Center-spreading and ropeless knots.   Green   blue   white
Time space distance: starting from the shore

His arms of unhealable, veined copper   over us
Raise to Heaven a breathing blue ax.

James Dickey

LIMITED TO SEVENTY-FIVE NUMBERED COPIES OF WHICH THIS IS NUMBER   *13*
COPYRIGHT © 1980 BY JAMES DICKEY

AA 6: 9″ × 14″; title and 'James Dickey' in red

Broadside.

Winston-Salem, N.C.: Palæmon Press, 1980.

Off-white wove paper; watermarked 'BFK RIVES'.

Included in double-slipcase set of broadsides celebrating Robert Penn Warren's seventy-fifth birthday. Certificate of limitation on separate broadside: '[red and black] FOR ROBERT PENN WARREN~ 24 • IV • 80~OF SEVENTY- | FIVE SETS PUBLISHED, FIFTY-FIVE ARE FOR PUBLIC SALE. | FIFTEEN AD-DITIONAL COPIES OF THE WOODCUT ARE FOR | THE USE OF THE ARTIST. THIS IS SET NO.   . | [illegible signature] | . . . *wer kann aber auch einem grossen Dichter genug dan-* | *ken, dem kostbarsten Kleinod einer Nation?*— | Ludwig van Beethoven to Bettina von Arnim, April 1811'. "The Ax-God" broadside signed by Dickey. Poem. Price for the set: $250.00.

Locations: MJB; ScU ('1st proof').

Note: Also includes poems by A. R. Ammons, Fred Chappell, Richard Eber-hart, George Garrett, John Hollander, William Meredith, Reynolds Price, Rosanna Warren, and Richard Wilbur.

AA 7 SOME CONTEMPORARIES
1980

Foreword to
DICTIONARY OF LITERARY BIOGRAPHY
American Poets
Since World War II

∽

SOME CONTEMPORARIES
by James Dickey

Within history, each Time of literature, doing what it can with its limits and its depths—straining to push back the limits, to realize and survive the depths—hears like the marathoner's compulsive nursery-rhyme, as on the exaggerated necessity of breath itself, essential questions pertaining to value: How good is our poetry? What do we have to show, *really*? What is great? What is useful? What figure, what style, is dominant?

Since T. S. Eliot there has been no other poet of comparable sway. Yet even during the time of his most complete ascendency there was a determined backlash against his ideas: against the "classical" theory of the Objective Correlative there was a Romantic counterthrust; against "autotelic art," an emphasis on subjectivism, an insistence on the primacy of individual response, the unique perspective, the Life. D. H. Lawrence was the most persuasive—and vociferous—poet of this tendency, Herbert Read its theorist and defense counsel. American poetry has had its counterpart of this gut-and-bedrock struggle; the dichotomy has been apparent in the poetry and the implied attitudes of Robert Lowell and Theodore Roethke.

Lowell began as an extreme formalist, deriving from Eliot via his most astute American followers, the "New Critics" who were Lowell's teachers and champions: John Crowe Ransom, Allen Tate, and Lowell's contemporary, Randall Jarrell. Lowell's assertiveness, his compressed and confident power, his rush, his gift of phrase, are vivid and outstanding virtues, and are strongly his own. His later "confessional" work is looser and far less memorable, yet this is the aspect of Lowell most attractive to his imitators. They have not attempted to emulate the formal tension and authority of his best poems, but have fixed on the fatally seductive and perennially available resource of self-pity manifest in his weakest verse. It is paradoxical that Lowell's profoundly creative historical sense, his mastery of verse form, his *natural* tone of imperious and urgent authority, gave way progressively to the most obvious elements of romanticism, including sentimentality, smugness, and an extraordinarily confusing reversal of values in which personal suffering is equated with authenticity. The most influential poet of this persuasion may, however, turn out to be not Lowell

Head title for AA 7: 7″ × 9¹⁵⁄₁₆″

Head title.

Detroit: Gale Research, 1980.

French fold: pp. 1–3: text—"Foreword" to *Dictionary of Literary Biography 5;* p. 4: 8 *Dictionary of Literary Biography* titles.

Light orangish yellow paper.

p. 3: '*500 Copies* | *For Friends of* | *Gale Research and Bruccoli Clark.* | *Copy* _____ | *Copyright © 1980 Gale Research Co.*' Unknown number of copies signed by Dickey. See B 53.

Locations: Caroliniana (signed); JRB (signed); LC (signed); Lilly (signed); MJB (signed).

AA 8 IN THE CHILD'S NIGHT
1981

IN THE CHILD'S NIGHT

On distant sides of the bed
We lie together in the winter house
Trying to go away.

Something thinks, "You must be made for it,
And tune your quiet body like a fish
To the stars of the Milky Way

To pass into the star-sea, into sleep,
By means of the heart of the current,
The holy secret of flowing."

Yet levels of depth are wrestling
And rising from us; we are still.
The quilt pattern—a child's pink whale—

Has surfaced through ice at midnight
And now is dancing upon
The dead cold and middle of the air

On my son's feet:
His short legs are trampling the bedclothes
Into the darkness above us

Where the chill of consciousness broods
Like a thing of absolute evil.
I rise to do freezing battle

With my bare hands.
I enter the faraway other
Side of the struggling bed

And turn him to face me.
The stitched beast falls, and we
Are sewn warmly into a sea-shroud

It begins to haul through the dark.
Holding my son's
Best kicking foot in my hand,

I begin to move with the moon
As it must have felt when it went
From the sea to dwell in the sky,

As we near the vast beginning,
The unborn stars of the wellhead,
The secret of the game.

James Dickey

TWENTY COPIES HAVE BEEN PRIVATELY PRINTED FOR
JAMES AND DEBORAH DICKEY, MAY 1981. *LAVS DEO!*

AA 8: 7″ × 14¹¹/₁₆″; title and statement of limitation in
red

Broadside.

Winston-Salem, N.C.: Palæmon Press, 1981.

Statement of limitation: 'TWENTY COPIES HAVE BEEN PRIVATELY PRINTED FOR | JAMES AND DEBORAH DICKEY, MAY 1981. LAVS DEO!' Poem.

Locations: JRB; MJB; ScU.

Second edition: Statement of limitation: 'TWENTY COPIES HAVE BEEN PRIVATELY PRINTED FOR | JAMES AND DEBORAH, 19•IX•81. *LAVS DEO!*' Location: ScU.

AA 9 THE EAGLE'S MILE
1981

AA 9: 19″ × 34¾″; title, dedication, and 'James Dickey' in red

Broadside.

Columbia, S.C. & Bloomfield Hills, Mich.: Bruccoli Clark, 1981.

Limited printing:

250 numbered copies signed by Dickey. $20.00. White laid paper; chainlines ¹⁵⁄₁₆″ apart. Right edge deckle. Publisher's brownish red label on verso. Poem.

Trade printing:

500 copies printed in red and black on gold burlap-finish paper. $6.00. Both printings published 15 June 1981.

Locations: Caroliniana (limited and trade); JRB (trade); Lilly (limited); MJB (limited and trade).

AA 10 STATEMENT ON *SOME SORT OF EPIC GRANDEUR*
1981

Some Sort of Epic Grandeur

It would be easy to say that Fitzgerald's life, with its early total triumph and late total defeat, its symbolization of the Twenties spirit—and *this* as symbolic of the promise and defeat of the American dream—is really Fitzgerald's greatest work: inimitable, tragic, and true. But *that* would not be true. The triumph of Fitzgerald's existence is not the story of his life, as fascinating and harrowing as that story is, but is in his work, in the highly personal quality of his linguistic skill, his instinctive mastery of craft, his understanding of fictional people and their situations, and the larger implications of these.

Mr. Bruccoli's biography is principally the account of a rare and always threatened talent, undermined by unavoidable circumstances and personal relationships, particularly that with his wife, but also by his losing struggle in the world of literary reputation, the fickleness of the mass audience, his ambiguous relationship to money, and thus to the meaning of America itself. It is the account of a man who very early became a professional writer, a successful businessman and entrepreneur of letters, but who by the most courageous and tenacious means held to the essence of his gift: held out for the masterpieces he believed he could create, despite anything and everything that happened to him, was done to him, or that he did to himself.

Fitzgerald's biography is and will remain the story of a doomed, tragic talent—or, as I personally would say, genius—which underwent an almost unbelievable number of setbacks, but which survived, no matter what. Mr. Bruccoli is always able to look through the events themselves to the essential fact about Fitzgerald: his existence as an artist, and not only to how it came about, but what it came to. "Some sort of epic grandeur" is exactly what Fitzgerald had. It is a perfect title for this book, for the grandeur is there, in the struggle to create memorable work. I fully expect that this will be the indispensable biography of a very great American writer, for the spirit of the man is in the facts, and these, as gathered and marshalled by Matthew Bruccoli over 25 years, are all we will ever need. But more importantly, they are *what* we need.

–*James Dickey*

AA 10: 8¹⁵/₁₆″ × 5¹⁵/₁₆″

Single leaf.

New York & London: Harcourt Brace Jovanovich, 1981.

Recto: photo of F. Scott Fitzgerald; verso: previously unpublished Dickey statement on *Some Sort of Epic Grandeur* by Matthew J. Bruccoli. Distributed gratis.

Two printings: first printing omits photo credit.

Locations: JRB (both); LC (first); Lilly (second); MJB (both).

AA 11 EXCERPT FROM "THE STRENGTH OF FIELDS"
1984

Hunger, time and the moon:
The moon lying on the brain
                              as on the excited sea   as on
The strength of fields.   Lord, let me shake

With purpose.   Wild hope can always spring
From tended strength.   Everything is in that.
    That and nothing but kindness.   More kindness, dear Lord
Of the renewing green.
                    That is where it all has to start:
With the simplest things.   More kindness will do nothing less
    Than save every sleeping one
        And night-walking one

Of us.
My life belongs to the world. I will do what I can.

AA 11: 12″ × 16¾″

Broadside.

Columbia, S.C.: South Carolina Educational Television, 1984.

Color illustration; poem text printed in green.

1,000 numbered copies signed by Dickey distributed to donors to the South Carolina Educational Television Endowment fund-raising drive in December 1984. Apparently additional unsigned copies were also distributed.

Locations: JRB; MJB (numbered and signed).

AA 12 EXCERPT FROM *BRONWEN, THE TRAW, AND THE SHAPE-SHIFTER*
1986

AA 12: 18¾″ × 17¾″; title in red, HBJ logo in brown

Broadside.

San Diego, New York, & London: Harcourt Brace Jovanovich, 1986.

5,000 copies distributed gratis in May 1986 preceding publication of the book.

16 lines of verse from Book 4 of *Bronwen, the Traw, and the Shape-Shifter*.

Locations: JRB; MJB; ScU.

AA 13 McNEESE STATE UNIVERSITY POSTER
1986

AA 13: 22″ × 34″

Broadside.

White on black.

Lake Charles, La.: McNeese State University, 1986.

Poster for Dickey's reading, 11 November 1986. Reprints entire text of poem "The Heaven of Animals."

Location: MJB.

B. First-Appearance Contributions to Books and Pamphlets

Titles in which material by Dickey appears for the first time in a book or pamphlet written or edited by another author, arranged chronologically. Previously unpublished items are so identified. For publications that also include previously collected Dickey material, that information is stipulated. Only the first printings of these books are described, but the British editions are also noted. Locations are provided for scarce items.

B 1 SOUNDINGS
1953

[two-page title; against background of quadrangles] SOUNDINGS | 1953
SOUNDINGS | SPONSORED BY OWEN WISTER LITERARY SOCIETY |
WRITINGS FROM THE RICE INSTITUTE SOUNDINGS

500 numbered copies.

Poem: "Utterance I," pp. 114–115. Previously unpublished.

Locations: JRB; MJB.

B 2 SOUTH
1961

SOUTH: | MODERN SOUTHERN LITERATURE | IN ITS CULTURAL SET-
TING | EDITED BY | LOUIS D. RUBIN, JR., and ROBERT D. JACOBS |
[device] | Dolphin Books | Doubleday & Company, Inc. | Garden City, New
York

1961. Copyright page: 'First Edition'. Wrappers. #C316.

Essay: "Notes on the Decline of Outrage," pp. 76–94. Previously unpublished.

B 3 NEW WORLD WRITING
1962

21 | NEW | WORLD | WRITING | [seal] | J. B. LIPPINCOTT COMPANY |
Philadelphia & New York

1962. Copyright page: 'FIRST EDITION'. Published in cloth and wrappers.

Poems: "The Crows," "Wall and Cloud," and "A Poem About Bird-Catching by
One Who Has Never Caught a Bird," pp. 50–54. All previously unpublished.

221

B 4 BEST POEMS OF 1962
1963

BEST POEMS | of 1962 | BORESTONE MOUNTAIN | POETRY AWARDS |
1963 | *A Compilation of Original Poetry* | *published in* | *Magazines of the*
English-speaking World | *in 1962* | FIFTEENTH ANNUAL ISSUE | VOL-
UME XV | PACIFIC BOOKS, PUBLISHERS • PALO ALTO, CALIFORNIA |
1963

Poems: "A Letter," "By Canoe Through the Fir Forest," and "The Dusk of
Horses" are first book appearances; "Armor" was previously collected.

B 5 CONTEMPORARY AUTHORS
1965

[script] Contemporary | Authors | A BIO-BIBLIOGRAPHICAL GUIDE TO |
CURRENT AUTHORS AND THEIR WORKS | JAMES M. ETHRIDGE |
BARBARA KOPALA | Editors | [script] volumes 11–12 | *GALE RESEARCH*
COMPANY • THE BOOK TOWER • DETROIT 26, MICHIGAN

1965.

Statement, p. 111. Previously unpublished.

B 6 PITZER COLLEGE YEARBOOK
1965

PITZER COLLEGE | [college seal] | *1964–1965*

Claremont, Calif.: Pitzer College, 1965. Wrappers.

Facsimile of TLS (28 February 1965), p. 71. Previously unpublished.

Location: JD.

B 7 SELECTED POEMS OF EDWIN ARLINGTON ROBINSON
1965

SELECTED | *POEMS* | *of* | *Edwin Arlington* | *Robinson* | [rule] | [rule] | ED-
ITED BY | MORTON DAUWEN ZABEL | With an introduction by James
Dickey | [rule] | THE MACMILLAN COMPANY, NEW YORK | Collier-
Macmillan Limited, London

1965. Copyright page: 'First Printing'.

Essay: "Edwin Arlington Robinson: The Many Truths," pp. xi–xxviii. Previously unpublished. Collected as "Edwin Arlington Robinson" in *Babel to Byzantium*.

B8 BEST POEMS of 1965
1966

BEST POEMS | of 1965 | BORESTONE MOUNTAIN | POETRY AWARDS | 1966 | *A Compilation of Original Poetry* | *published in* | *Magazines of the English-speaking World* | *in 1965* | EIGHTEENTH ANNUAL ISSUE | VOLUME XVIII | PACIFIC BOOKS, PUBLISHERS • PALO ALTO, CALIFORNIA | 1966

Poems: "False Youth: Summer" and "Sustainment" are first book appearances; "The Celebration" was previously collected.

B9 THE DISTINCTIVE VOICE
1966

[script] the distinctive voice | [roman] TWENTIETH-CENTURY AMERICAN POETRY | WILLIAM J. MARTZ • RIPON COLLEGE | [rule] | SCOTT, FORESMAN AND COMPANY

1966.

Statement, pp. 227–228, was previously unpublished. Five poems—"The Lifeguard," "In the Mountain Tent," "Cherrylog Road," "The Shark's Parlor," and "Reincarnation (II)"—were previously collected.

B10 MASTER POEMS OF THE ENGLISH LANGUAGE
1966

MASTER | POEMS | OF THE ENGLISH LANGUAGE | [rule] | *Over one hundred poems* | *together with Introductions* | *by leading poets and critics* | *of the English-speaking world* | EDITED BY | Oscar Williams | [device] | TRIDENT PRESS | *New York 1966*

Essays on Christopher Smart's "A Song to David," pp. 339–340; Matthew Arnold's "Dover Beach," pp. 713–715; Gerard Manley Hopkins's "The Wreck of the Deutschland," pp. 801–803; Francis Thompson's "The Hound of

Heaven," pp. 817–819; and William Carlos Williams's "The Yachts," pp. 901–902. All previously unpublished.

Note: Dickey's essay on Hopkins was reprinted as the introduction to *The Wreck of the Deutschland* (Boston: Godine, 1971).

B 11 POETS ON POETRY
1966

POETS | ON | POETRY | *Edited by HOWARD NEMEROV* | BASIC BOOKS, INC., PUBLISHERS | *New York   London*

1966.

Essay: "The Poet Turns on Himself," pp. 225–238. Previously unpublished.

Note: This essay was subsequently published as a pamphlet (Portree, Isle of Skye: Aquila Publishing, 1982).

B 12 DINNER MENU
1966

Untitled dinner menu for Atlanta Music Club Guild, 4 December 1966.

Folio.

Poem: "Le Salut aux Beaux Arts," p. 2. Previously unpublished.

Entire text reprinted in Kathryn Grayburn, "New Guild Salutes Creative Arts at Formal Dinner," *Atlanta Constitution*, 6 December 1966, p. 21.

Location: JD.

B 13 AMERICAN CHRISTMAS
1967

Edited by | Webster Schott & Robert J. Myers | AMERICAN CHRISTMAS | Second Edition | Hallmark Cards, Incorporated | Kansas City, Missouri, 1967

Copyright page: 'Second Edition'.

Poem: "The Christmas Towns," pp. 79–80. Previously unpublished; not included in first edition.

B 14 TEACHING IN AMERICA
1967

TEACHING IN AMERICA | Proceedings of the 5th Annual Conference | April 2–4, 1967—Washington, D.C. | National Committee for | Support of the Public Schools

1967. Wrappers.

Essay: "Education Via Poetry," pp. 33–43, was previously unpublished. Possible first book appearance for poem "Dark Ones"; two other poems—"Them, Crying" and "The Night Pool"—were previously collected.

B 15 THREE AMERICAN POETS
1967

[all lettering in white] LIFE [within single-rule frame] EDUCATIONAL RE-PRINT 9 | THREE | AMERICAN | POETS | [photos of Moore, Lowell, and Dickey] | [left] Marianne | Moore | [center] Robert | Lowell | [right] James | Dickey

After January 1967. Wrappers; cover title.

Paul O'Neil, "The Unlikeliest Poet," pp. 10–15. Quotes Dickey.

B 16 THE GREAT IDEAS TODAY 1968
1968

THE | GREAT IDEAS | TODAY | 1968 | [rule] | WILLIAM BENTON *Publisher* | ENCYCLOPÆDIA BRITANNICA, INC. | *Chicago • London • Toronto • Geneva • Sydney • Tokyo • Manila*

1968.

Essay: "The Self as Agent," pp. 90–97. Previously unpublished.

Note: Also distributed as offprint: *The Year's Developments in the Arts and Sciences A Symposium on Contemporary Poetry Reprinted from The Great Ideas Today 1968.*

B 17 THE UNIVERSITY AND THE NEW INTELLECTUAL
ENVIRONMENT
1968

The University | *and the New* | *Intellectual Environment* | HENRY DAVID
AIKEN | MICHAEL WALZER | ARTHUR ERICKSON | JAMES DICKEY |
MACMILLAN OF CANADA • TORONTO | ST. MARTIN'S PRESS • NEW
YORK | *in Association with York University* | 1968

Essay: "The New Literature," pp. 67–84, was previously unpublished. Delivered as one of the Frank Gerstein Lectures. Collected as "Horsemeat and the
New Mind" in *Night Hurdling.*

B 18 THE YOUNG AMERICAN POETS
1968

THE YOUNG AMERICAN POETS | A BIG TABLE BOOK | Edited By Paul
Carroll | Introduction By James Dickey | Follett Publishing Company | Chicago
New York

1968. Copyright page: 'First printing'. Published in cloth and wrappers.

Essay: "The Son, the Cave, and the Burning Bush," pp. 7–10. Previously
unpublished.

B 19 THE NEW YORKER BOOK OF POEMS
1969

[rule] | [decorative rule] | The New Yorker | Book of Poems | Selected by the
Editors | of The New Yorker | [decorative rule] | [rule] | [Viking ship device] |
NEW YORK • THE VIKING PRESS

1969.

Poem "Madness," pp. 407–410, is a first book appearance; fourteen other
poems—"Buckdancer's Choice," "Bums, on Waking," "By Canoe Through the
Fir Forest," "Cherrylog Road," "Coming Back to America," "The Dusk of
Horses," "Falling," "Fence Wire," "Goodbye to Serpents," "The Ice Skin,"
"The Lifeguard," "The Movement of Fish," "The Shark's Parlor," and "Slave
Quarters"—were previously collected.

B 20 THE WRITER AND HIS TRADITION
1969

[gray] [four-leaf clover and decorated sun with face] | [black] *April 17–19, 1969 The University of Tennessee* [slash] *Knoxville* | [gray] The | Writer | And His | Tradition | [black] FESTIVAL PROCEEDINGS | Edited by | Robert Drake, Festival President [vertically, up] 1969 Southern Literary Festival

1969. Wrappers.

Panel discussion by Cleanth Brooks, Reynolds Price, Robert Drake, and Dickey, pp. 11–30. Previously unpublished.

B 21 CONTEMPORARY POETS OF THE ENGLISH LANGUAGE
1970

CONTEMPORARY POETS | OF THE | ENGLISH | LANGUAGE | WITH A PREFACE BY | C. DAY LEWIS | EDITOR | ROSALIE MURPHY | DEPUTY EDITOR | JAMES VINSON | ST. MARTIN'S PRESS | NEW YORK

1970.

Published simultaneously by St. James Press: 'CONTEMPORARY POETS | OF THE | ENGLISH | LANGUAGE | WITH A PREFACE BY | C. DAY LEWIS | EDITOR | ROSALIE MURPHY | DEPUTY EDITOR | JAMES VINSON | ST JAMES PRESS | CHICAGO   LONDON'.

Biographical-critical entry on Dickey by Ralph J. Mills, Jr., pp. 295–297; Dickey comments were probably previously unpublished.

B 22 THE NEW YORK TIMES BOOK OF VERSE
1970

The New York Times | BOOK OF VERSE | [decoration] | Edited by Thomas Lask | [decoration] | A NEW YORK TIMES BOOK | The Macmillan Company, New York, N.Y. | Collier-Macmillan Ltd., London

1970. Copyright page: 'FIRST PRINTING'.

Poem: "Under Oaks," p. 122.

B 23 THIS IS MY BEST
1970

America's 85 Greatest Living Authors Present | THIS IS MY BEST | IN THE
THIRD QUARTER OF THE CENTURY | [rule] | Edited by Whit Burnett |
1970 | DOUBLEDAY & COMPANY, INC., GARDEN CITY, NEW YORK

Copyright page: 'FIRST EDITION'.

Letter to Burnett explaining choice of "May Day Sermon . . . ," p. 65. Previously unpublished.

B 24 TRANSLATIONS BY AMERICAN POETS
1970

[script] Translations by | American Poets | [roman] EDITED BY JEAN
GARRIGUE | OHIO UNIVERSITY PRESS • ATHENS

1970.

Poem: "The Angel," pp. 80–89; Dickey's translation of Louis Emié's "L'Ange."
This poem is not the same as C 21. Previously unpublished.

B 25 BEST POEMS OF 1970
1971

Best Poems of 1970 | Borestone Mountain | Poetry Awards 1971 | [rule] | A
Compilation of Original Poetry | Published in Magazines of the | English-
Speaking World in 1970 | Twenty-third Annual Issue | Volume XXIII | Pacific
Books, Publishers, Palo Alto, California | 1971

Poem: "Haunting the Maneuvers," pp. 30–31.

B 26 LOMBARDI
1971

[two-page title; left] LOMBARDI • | [right] Edited by | John Wiebusch | Epi-
logue by | James Dickey | Photography by | Vernon Biever | A National Football
League Book | Follett Publishing Company | Chicago, Illinois

1971. In slipcase.

Poem: "For the Death of Lombardi," pp. 206–210. See C 253.

B 27 STOLEN APPLES
1971

[within frame of pages and books] [script] Stolen Apples | *Poetry by* | YEVGENY YEVTUSHENKO | *With English adaptations by* | JAMES DICKEY | GEOFFREY DUTTON | LAWRENCE FERLINGHETTI | ANTHONY KAHN | STANLEY KUNITZ | GEORGE REAVEY | JOHN UPDIKE | RICHARD WILBUR | *1971* | *Doubleday & Co., Inc.* | *Garden City, New York*

Copyright page: '*First Edition after a Limited Edition of 250 copies*'.

Adaptations by Dickey with Anthony Kahn: "Pitching and Rolling," pp. 17–19; "Assignation," pp. 30–32; untitled—"In aircraft, the newest, inexorable models . . . ," pp. 37–38; "Doing the Twist on Nails," pp. 39–49; untitled—"I dreamed I already loved you . . . ," pp. 48–40; untitled—"Poetry gives off smoke . . . ," pp. 67–69; "In the Wax Museum at Hamburg," pp. 70–73; "Idol," pp. 90–91; "Old Bookkeeper," pp. 92–93; "Kamikaze," pp. 103–105; "At the Military Registration and Enlistment Center," pp. 108–110; and "The Heat in Rome," pp. 119–123. All except "Kamikaze" were previously unpublished.

Limited issue: New York: Doubleday, 1971. 250 numbered copies signed by Yevtushenko. Boxed. Published simultaneously with trade issue.

London: W.H. Allen, 1972.

New York: Doubleday Anchor, 1972. Wrappers. A0–48.

London: Panther, 1973. Wrappers. #586 03725 X.

B 28 CRAFT SO HARD TO LEARN
1972

Craft So Hard | To Learn | Conversations with Poets and Novelists | About the Teaching of Writing | *Conducted by* JOHN GRAHAM | *Edited by* GEORGE GARRETT | MORROW PAPERBACK EDITIONS | *Distributed by* | *William Morrow & Company, Inc.* | New York 1972

Interview, pp. 81–87. Previously unpublished.

B 29 JAMES DICKEY A CHECKLIST
1972

[two-page title] DICKEY JAMES DICKEY JAMES DICKEY JAMES DICKEY JAMES DICKEY JAMES DICKEY [left: photo of Dickey] [right] A CHECK-

LIST | Compiled by Franklin Ashley | Introduction | by | James Dickey | [device] A BRUCCOLI ◇ CLARK BOOK | PUBLISHED BY GALE RESEARCH COMPANY, BOOK TOWER, DETROIT, 1972

Copyright page: *'First Printing'*.

"Introduction," p. xi. Previously unpublished.

B 30 STEPHEN CRANE IN TRANSITION
1972

STEPHEN CRANE | IN TRANSITION | *Centenary Essays* | [decoration] | *Edited, with an Introduction and Afterword, by* | JOSEPH KATZ | [device] | Northern Illinois University Press | DEKALB

1972.

Essay: "Stephen Crane," p. vii. Previously unpublished.

B 31 CREATIVE RESPONSES FOR COMPOSITION
1973

[within triple rules frames with corner decorations] CREATIVE | RESPONSES FOR | COMPOSITION | Mary I. Schuster | *Donnelly College* | CONSULTING EDITORS: | Gregory Cowan and Elisabeth McPherson | *Forest Park Community College* | [logo] | Random House, | New York

1973. Copyright page: 'First Edition | 987654321'. Wrappers.

Essay: "A Poet Witnesses a Bold Mission," pp. 128–129.

B 32 JAMES DICKEY: THE EXPANSIVE IMAGINATION
1973

JAMES DICKEY: | THE EXPANSIVE IMAGINATION | A Collection of Critical Essays | edited by Richard J. Calhoun | [device] | *EVERETT* [slash] *EDWARDS, inc.* | POST OFFICE BOX 1060 | DELAND, FLORIDA 32720

1973.

Carolyn Kizer and James Boatwright, "A Conversation with James Dickey," pp. 1–33. Collected as "In Virginia" in *Night Hurdling*.

B 33 MEANING
1973

[within single-rule frame] MEANING: | A COMMON GROUND | OF LIN-
GUISTICS | AND LITERATURE | [rule] | IN HONOR OF | NORMAN C.
STAGEBERG | [rule] | PROCEEDINGS OF A | UNIVERSITY OF NORTH-
ERN IOWA CONFERENCE | HELD APRIL 27–28, 1973 | Edited by | Don L.
F. Nilsen | University of Northern Iowa | [rule]

1973.

Poem: "False Youth: Autumn: Clothes of the Age," p. 157.

B 34 THE WRITER'S VOICE
1973

THE | WRITER'S | VOICE | CONVERSATIONS WITH | CONTEMPORARY
WRITERS | [rule] | Conducted by John Graham | Edited by George Garrett |
WILLIAM MORROW & COMPANY, INC. | New York 1973

Interview, pp. 228–247. Previously unpublished.

B 35 THE CRAFT OF POETRY
1974

THE CRAFT | OF POETRY | Interviews from | *The New York Quarterly* |
[NYQ monogram] | WILLIAM PACKARD, EDITOR | DOUBLEDAY & COM-
PANY, INC., GARDEN CITY, NEW YORK 1974

Copyright page: 'First Edition'. Published in cloth and wrappers.

"Craft Interview with James Dickey," pp. 131–151. Collected as "In New York"
in *Night Hurdling*.

Note: *The Craft of Poetry* was republished as *The Poet's Craft,* ed. William
Packard (New York: Paragon House, [1987]).

B 36 FROST CENTENNIAL ESSAYS
1974

FROST | CENTENNIAL ESSAYS | COMPILED BY | THE COMMITTEE ON
THE | FROST CENTENNIAL | OF THE UNIVERSITY | OF SOUTHERN
MISSISSIPPI | UNIVERSITY PRESS OF MISSISSIPPI | JACKSON

1974.

Donald J. Greiner, " 'That Plain-Speaking Guy': A Conversation with James Dickey on Robert Frost," pp. 51–59. Previously unpublished. Collected in *The Voiced Connections of James Dickey*.

B 37 PREFERENCES
1974

[thick and thin rules] | PREFERENCES | *51 American poets* | *choose poems from their own work and from the past* | *commentary on the choices* | *and an introduction by* | RICHARD HOWARD | *photographs of the poets by* | THOMAS VICTOR | THE VIKING PRESS • NEW YORK | [thin and thick rules]

1974.

Dickey provided no new material for this book; but he selected "The Sheep Child" and an excerpt from Christopher Smart's *Jubilate Agno,* pp. 52–58.

B 38 JOHN KEATS'S PORRIDGE
1975

[rule] JOHN KEATS'S | PORRIDGE | [rule] Favorite Recipes of | American Poets | [rule] | *Victoria McCabe* | [rule] | UNIVERSITY OF IOWA PRESS | [rule]

1975.

Cream vichyssoise, p. 31. Previously unpublished.

B 39 PAGES
1976

[brown] Pages | [black] THE WORLD OF BOOKS, WRITERS, AND WRIT-ING | [brown rule] | [black] 1 | [brown rule] | [black] MATTHEW J. BRUC-COLI | *Editorial Director* | C. E. FRAZER CLARK, JR. | *Managing Editor* | GALE RESEARCH COMPANY • BOOK TOWER • DETROIT, MICHIGAN 48226 | [brown rule]

1976.

"Notes for Works in Progress," pp. 8–19; material for *Alnilam.* Previously unpublished.

B 40 CONVERSATIONS WITH WRITERS
1977

Conversations • Volume 1 | Conversations | with | Writers | [decoration] | Vance Bourjaily   Robert Hayden | James Dickey   Mary Welsh Hemingway | William Price Fox   Ring Lardner, Jr. | John Gardner   Wallace Markfield | Brendan Gill   Donald Ogden Stewart | Edward Gorey   Thomas Tryon | Robert Penn Warren | A Bruccoli Clark Book | Gale Research Company | Book Tower • Detroit, Michigan 48226

1977.

Interview with Matthew J. Bruccoli, pp. 24–45. Previously unpublished.

Note: Also excerpted in promotional brochure for *Conversations* series; distributed before the volume was published: 'Conversations With • Volume 1 | Conversations | with | Writers | [decoration] | [10 names in double columns] | A Bruccoli Clark Book | Gale Research Company | Book Tower • Detroit, Michigan 48226'.

1977. Wrappers.

Locations: JRB; MJB.

B 41 "A NEW SPIRIT, A NEW COMMITMENT, A NEW
          AMERICA"
          1977

"A NEW SPIRIT, | A NEW COMMITMENT, | A NEW AMERICA" | [black] THE INAUGURATION OF | PRESIDENT JIMMY CARTER | AND | VICE PRESIDENT WALTER F. MONDALE | THE 1977 | INAUGURAL COMMITTEE | [rule] | BANTAM BOOKS | [rooster]

New York, 1977. Copyright page: 'January 1977'. Wrappers.

Poem: "The Strength of Fields," p. 90.

B 42 CLOSE-UPS
          1978

[title page printed on black; all the following within frame of white double rules and dots] [white] CLOSE-UPS | [light gray] INTIMATE PROFILES | OF MOVIE STARS | BY THEIR | CO-STARS, DIRECTORS, | SCREENWRIT-

ERS | AND FRIENDS. | EDITED BY DANNY PEARY | [medium gray]
WORKMAN PUBLISHING, | NEW YORK

1978. Copyright page: 'First printing November 1978 | 10 . . . 1'.

Essay: "Charles Bronson: Silence Under the Fist," pp. 417–419.

Previously unpublished.

B 43 DEAR SCOTT
1978

[red] Dear Scott | [black rule] | [blue] Compiled by Scott Deindorfer | [black]
Workman Publishing, New York

1978. Copyright page: 'First printing May 1978'.

Message from Dickey quoting John Dryden's translation of *The Aeneid,* unpaged. Previously unpublished.

B 44 THE *POETRY* ANTHOLOGY
1978

THE | *POETRY* | ANTHOLOGY | 1912–1977 | [tapered rule] | *Sixty-five Years
of America's Most* | *Distinguished Verse Magazine* | [James Thurber drawing of
winged horse] | EDITED BY | *Daryl Hine & Joseph Parisi* | HOUGHTON
MIFFLIN COMPANY | BOSTON 1978

Poem "After the Night Hunt," pp. 381–382, is a first book appearance. Three
other poems—"The Landfall," "Inside the River," and "Venom"—were previously collected.

B 45 THE READING COMMITMENT
1978

The | Reading | Commitment | MICHAEL E. ADELSTEIN | UNIVERSITY OF
KENTUCKY | JEAN G. PIVAL | UNIVERSITY OF KENTUCKY | [HBJ de-
vice] | HARCOURT BRACE JOVANOVICH, INC. | NEW YORK SAN
DIEGO CHICAGO SAN FRANCISCO ATLANTA

1978. Wrappers.

Essay: "James Dickey's Glory," pp. 80–82. Collected as "Night Hurdling" in
Night Hurdling.

B 46 THROUGH THE WHEAT
1978

Lost American Fiction | *Edited by* Matthew J. Bruccoli | Through | the Wheat | *A Novel by* | THOMAS BOYD | *Afterword by* | James Dickey | SOUTHERN ILLINOIS UNIVERSITY PRESS | *Carbondale and Edwardsville* | Feffer & Simons, Inc. | *London and Amsterdam*

1978.

"Afterword," pp. 267–272, was previously unpublished. Collected as "Through the Wheat" in *Night Hurdling*.

B 47 THE ADVENTURES OF TOM SAWYER . . .
1979

The Adventures of | Tom Sawyer | and | The Adventures of | Huckleberry Finn | [decorations] | by Mark Twain | *With an Introduction by* | *James Dickey* | [device] | A SIGNET CLASSIC | NEW AMERICAN LIBRARY | [rule] | TIMES MIRROR | New York, London, and Scarborough, Ontario

1979. Copyright page: 'First Signet Classic Printing, May, 1979'. Wrappers. #CJ 1198.

"Introduction: Boys of the River-God," pp. v–x. Previously unpublished.

B 48 ALL IS BRILLIG
1979

ALL IS BRILLIG | (or ought to be) | by Allen Tate | [tapered rule] | Preface by | James Dickey | [decoration] | Palæmon Press Limited

1979. Wrappers. 200 numbered copies.

"Preface" dated February 10, 1979, p. [3]. Previously unpublished.

Locations: JRB; MJB.

Note: Tate's poem was also published as a broadside by Palæmon Press—but with no material by Dickey.

B 49 FOUNTAIN OF YOUTH
1979

Fountain | of | Youth | By | Robert S. Lowrance, Jr. | HARVEY DAN ABRAMS | Publisher, Atlanta

1979.

"Introduction," p. [v]. Previously unpublished.

Locations: JRB; MJB.

B 50 JAMES DICKEY: SPLINTERED SUNLIGHT
1979

JAMES DICKEY: | SPLINTERED SUNLIGHT | Interviews, Essays, | and
Bibliography | Edited by Patricia De La Fuente | Associate Editors: Donald E.
Fritz | Jan Seale | Living Author Series No. 2 | School of Humanities | Pan
American University | Edinburg, Texas

1979. Wrappers.

Dickey interview with Will Davis and others, pp. 6–23. Previously unpublished.

B 51 NEW ACQUIST OF TRUE EXPERIENCE
1979

James Gould | Cozzens | New Acquist of True Experience | [rule] | *Edited by* |
Matthew J. Bruccoli | [rule] | Southern Illinois University Press | *Carbondale
and Edwardsville* | Feffer & Simons, Inc. | London and Amsterdam

1979.

Statement, pp. 128–129. Previously unpublished.

B 52 OF POETRY AND POETS
1979

OF POETRY   Richard | AND POETS   Eberhart | University of Illinois
Press   *Urbana Chicago London*

1979.

"Foreword," pp. ix–xii. Previously unpublished.

B 53 DICTIONARY OF LITERARY BIOGRAPHY 5
1980

Dictionary of Literary Biography • Volume Five | American Poets | Since World
War II | Part 1: A–K | Edited by Donald J. Greiner | *Unversity of South*

Carolina | Foreword by James Dickey | A Bruccoli Clark Book | Gale Research Company • Book Tower • Detroit, Michigan 48226 | 1980

"Foreword," pp. ix–x, was also published as "Some Contemporaries" in *Some Contemporaries;* facsimile of manuscript for unpublished poem "Show Us the Sea," p. 185.

B 54 McCULLOUGH'S BRIEF LIVES
1980

McCullough's | Brief | Lives | [rule] Selected 'Eye on Books' Interviews | By David W. McCullough | Book-of-the-Month Club, Inc. | New York

1980.

Interview, pp. 51–52, was previously published as "David McCullough's Eye on Books" (see D 224). Republished in McCullough's *People, Books & Book People* (New York: Harmony Books, [1981]).

B 55 RICHARD EBERHART: A CELEBRATION
1980

[2-page title] *Richard Eberhart: A Celebration* | [left] edited by: Sydney Lea | Jay Parini | M. Robin Barone | designed by: Kate Emlen | [right: photo of Eberhart]

Middlebury, Vt.: New England Review/Kenyon Hill Publications, 1980. Wrappers.

Untitled prose tribute by Dickey, p. [11]. Previously unpublished.

B 56 THE CALL OF THE WILD . . .
1981

[line of decorations] | THE CALL OF | THE WILD, | WHITE FANG, | and | Other Stories | [decoration] | Jack London | Edited by ANDREW SINCLAIR | Introduction by JAMES DICKEY | [penguin] | PENGUIN BOOKS | [line of decorations]

New York, 1981. Wrappers.

"Introduction," pp. 7–16, was previously unpublished. Collected as "Blood Zero" in *Night Hurdling*.

B 57 F. SCOTT FITZGERALD POEMS 1911–1940
1981

F. Scott Fitzgerald | POEMS | 1911–1940 | Edited by Matthew J. Bruccoli | Foreword by James Dickey | [device] | Bruccoli Clark | Bloomfield Hills, Michigan & Columbia, South Carolina | 1981

Copyright page: 'First Printing'.

Essay: "F. Scott Fitzgerald's Poetry: The Unreflecting Shield," pp. xi–xv, was previously unpublished. Collected as "The Unreflecting Shield" in *Night Hurdling*.

Note: Also limited issue of 100 numbered and signed copies with a tipped-in certificate of limitation.

B 58 THE GREAT AMERICAN WRITERS' COOKBOOK
1981

The | Great | American | Writers' | Cookbook | Edited by | Dean Faulkner Wells | *Introduction by Craig Claiborne* | [logo] | YOKNAPATAWPHA PRESS | Oxford, Mississippi

1981. Comb binding.

"Dickey's Off-Trail Deer-Liver Slumgullion," p. 97. Previously unpublished.

B 59 MSS SPRING 1981
1981

[black rule] | [gray] MSS | [black] [rule] | [drawing] | [rule] | [gray] SPRING 1981 | [black] [rule] | [rule] | EDITED BY JOHN GARDNER AND L. M. ROSENBERG | [rule] | PRESS WORKS PUBLISHING, INC. | Dallas, Texas

Poem "From Time" was previously unpublished; poem "Deborah as Scion" ("With Rose at Cemetery" and "In Lace and Whale Bone") was previously published in *Scion*.

B 60 WRITERS AT WORK
1981

Writers at Work | The *Paris Review* Interviews | FIFTH SERIES | *Edited by George Plimpton* | *Introduction by* | *Francine du Plessix Gray* | [device] | THE VIKING PRESS NEW YORK

1981.

Published simultaneously in wrappers by Penguin Books (New York).

Interview with Franklin Ashley, pp. 199–229; includes facsimile of revised typescript of "Falling." Interview and facsimile were previously published as "James Dickey: The Art of Poetry XX" (see D 193).

B 61 CONTEMPORARY SOURCES
1982

Contemporary | *Sources* | [rule] | Readings from | *"Writer's Workshop"* | [rule] | *with an introduction by* | *William Price Fox* | Holt, Rinehart and Winston | New York Chicago San Francisco Philadelphia Montreal Toronto | London Sydney Tokyo Mexico City Rio de Janeiro Madrid

1982. Copyright page: '2 . . . 059 . . . 1'. Wrappers.

Quotes Dickey, pp. 128–129. Previously unpublished. Also partly quoted in *"Writer's Workshop" Study Guide,* ed. Beth Littlejohn, Rebecca Parke, and Charles Israel (New York: Holt, Rinehart & Winston, 1982), p. 39.

B 62 JAMES DICKEY A BIBLIOGRAPHY
1982

JAMES DICKEY | A BIBLIOGRAPHY | of his Books, Pamphlets, and Broadsides | *by* STUART WRIGHT | PRESSWORKS | Dallas, Texas

1982.

Untitled foreword, p. vii. Previously unpublished.

B 63 CONTEMPORARY AUTHORS
1983

[script] Contemporary | Authors | [roman] A Bio-Bibliographical Guide to | Current Writers in Fiction, General Nonfiction, | Poetry, Journalism, Drama, Motion Pictures, | Television, and Other Fields | ANN EVORY | LINDA METZGER | Editors | PETER M. GAREFFA | DEBORAH A. STRAUB | Associate Editors | NEW REVISION SERIES | [script] volume 10 | *GALE RESEARCH COMPANY • BOOK TOWER • DETROIT, MICHIGAN 48226*

1983.

Interview with Mary Bruccoli, pp. 137–140. Previously unpublished.

B 64 DICTIONARY OF LITERARY BIOGRAPHY
YEARBOOK: 1982
1983

DICTIONARY OF LITERARY BIOGRAPHY | YEARBOOK: 1982 | Edited by | Richard Ziegfeld | Associate Editors: | Jean W. Ross | Lynne C. Zeigler | A Bruccoli Clark Book | Gale Research Company • Book Tower • Detroit, Michigan 48226 | 1983

Interview, pp. 142–147, was previously unpublished. Text includes facsimile of corrected proof for "The G. I. Can of Beets, . . . ," p. 142. Collected in *The Voiced Connections of James Dickey*.

B 65 FOR REYNOLDS PRICE
1983

[within single-rules frame] [red] For | REYNOLDS PRICE | [black] *1 February 1983* | [red decorated rule] | [black] FRED CHAPPELL | JAMES DICKEY | ANNE TYLER | EUDORA WELTY | PRIVATELY PRINTED

Winston-Salem, N.C.: Palæmon Press, 1983. Wrappers. 150 copies.

Essay: "Reynolds Price: A Tribute," pp. [6–8]. Previously unpublished.

Locations: MJB; ScU.

B 66 INTERVIEWS WITH CONTEMPORARY WRITERS
1983

Interviews | with | Contemporary Writers | Second Series, 1972–1982 | Edited by L. S. Dembo | THE UNIVERSITY OF WISCONSIN PRESS

1983.

Interview with David L. Arnett, pp. 74–88. Previously published as "An Interview with James Dickey" (see D 184). Collected in *The Voiced Connections of James Dickey*.

B 67 OSIRIS AT THE ROLLER DERBY
1983

Osiris | at the | Roller | Derby | J. Edgar Simmons | *With a foreword by JAMES DICKEY | and an afterword by Jes Simmons* | [printing press] | CEDARS-HOUSE PRESS | 406 W. 28 STREET | BRYAN, TEXAS 77801

1983. Dust jacket over unprinted wrappers.

"Foreword," pp. v–vii, was previously unpublished. Collected as "Devastation in the Arroyo" in *Night Hurdling.*

Locations: JRB; MJB.

B 68 OYSTERING
1983

OYSTERING | [rule] | A WAY OF LIFE | JACK LEIGH | FOREWORD BY JAMES DICKEY | [rule] | CAROLINA ART ASSOCIATION

Charleston, S.C., 1983.

"Foreword," unpaged. Previously unpublished.

B 69 READINGS FOR WRITING
1983

READINGS | FOR WRITING | [pink rule] | [pink] Elizabeth Cowan | [black] Texas A & M University | Scott, Foresman and Company Glenview, Illinois | [pink rule] | Dallas, Tex. Oakland, N.J. Palo Alto, Calif. | Tucker, Ga. London, England

1983. Copyright page: '1 . . . 6-KPF-8 . . . 2'.

Interview with Cowan, pp. 117–119, was previously unpublished; also reprints "How to Enjoy Poetry."

B 70 SOUTH CAROLINA BUSINESS
1983

[white] 1983 Volume 3 Five Dollars | [yellow rule] | [white] SOUTH CARO-LINA | BusinesS | *PRESERVE ECONOMIC FREEDOM TO ADVANCE HU-MAN PROGRESS* | [yellow rule] | [color map of South Carolina] [white] *SOUTH CAROLINA* 2002. | *WHAT THE WORLD* | *IS COMING TO!*

Columbia: South Carolina Chamber of Commerce. Wrappers; cover title.

William W. Starr, "An Interview with James Dickey," pp. 39–41. Previously unpublished. Collected in *The Voiced Connections of James Dickey.*

Locations: JRB; MJB.

B 71 THE IMAGINATION AS GLORY
   1984

The Imagination | as Glory: The Poetry of | James Dickey | *Edited and with an Introduction by* | Bruce Weigl and T. R. Hummer | University of Illinois Press | *Urbana and Chicago*

1984.

Essays: "The Energized Man," pp. 163–164, is a first book appearance; "The Imagination of Glory," pp. 166–173, was previously unpublished.

B 72 A SOUTHERN RENASCENCE MAN
   1984

[two-page title with photo of Warren] A SOUTHERN RENASCENCE MAN | VIEWS OF | ROBERT PENN | WARREN | [decoration] *by Thomas L. Connelly,* | *Louis D. Rubin, Jr., Madison Jones,* | *Harold Bloom, and James Dickey* | Edited by WALTER B. EDGAR | Louisiana State University Press | Baton Rouge and London

1984.

Essay: "Warren's Poetry: A Reading and Commentary," pp. 81–93. Previously unpublished.

B 73 DICTIONARY OF LITERARY BIOGRAPHY
   YEARBOOK: 1984
   1985

Dictionary of Literary Biography | Yearbook: 1984 | Edited by | Jean W. Ross | A Bruccoli Clark Book | Gale Research Company • Book Tower • Detroit Michigan 48226

1985.

Poem: "To Be Done in Winter by Those Surviving Truman Capote," p. 171. Precedes publication in *Proceedings of the American Academy and Institute of Arts and Letters* (see C 323).

B 74 45 CONTEMPORARY POEMS
1985

45 | CONTEMPORARY | POEMS | The Creative Process | Edited by | Alberta T. Turner | Cleveland State University | [ship logo] | Longman | New York & London

1985. Copyright page: 'Printing: 9 8 7 6 5 4 3 2 1'.

Poem "Deborah Burning a Doll Made of House-Wood," pp. 44–45, was previously collected; interview with Dickey, pp. 45–47, was previously unpublished.

B 75 A GUIDE TO THE MODERN LITERARY MANUSCRIPTS
COLLECTION
1985

A GUIDE | TO | THE MODERN LITERARY MANUSCRIPTS COLLECTION | IN | THE SPECIAL COLLECTIONS | OF | THE WASHINGTON UNIVERSITY LIBRARIES | DECEMBER 1985 | WASHINGTON UNIVERSITY LIBRARIES

St. Louis, Mo. Wrappers; comb binding.

Facsimile of Dickey drafts, following p. 74. Previously unpublished.

B 76 IMAGES OF THE SOUTHERN WRITER
1985

Images of the Southern Writer | Photographs by Mark Morrow | [device] | The University of Georgia Press   Athens

1985. Copyright page: '89 . . . 85 5 . . . 1'.

Quotes Dickey, p. 16. Previously unpublished.

B 77 SINGULAR VOICES
1985

[script] Singular | Voices | [roman] AMERICAN | POETRY | TODAY | Edited by | STEPHEN BERG | [device] AVON | PUBLISHERS OF BARD, CAMELOT, DISCUS AND FLARE BOOKS

1985. Copyright page: 'First Avon Printing, March 1985'.

Essay "Concerning the Book *Puella* and Two of Its Poems," pp. 35–37, was previously unpublished; poem "Deborah as Scion (I & II)," pp. 31–34, was previously published in *Scion* and in B 59.

B 78 CONVERSATIONS WITH SOUTH CAROLINA POETS
1986

[rule] CONVERSATIONS | [rule] | *With South Carolina Poets* | [rule] | by | GAYLE R. SWANSON and WILLIAM B. THESING | *With a Foreword by James Dickey* | John F. Blair, Publisher | Winston-Salem, North Carolina

1986.

"Foreword," pp. xi-xii. Previously unpublished.

B 79 LAND OF SUPERIOR MIRAGES
1986

Adrien Stoutenburg | LAND OF SUPERIOR MIRAGES | New and Selected Poems | *edited by* DAVID R. SLAVITT | *with a foreword by* JAMES DICKEY | THE JOHNS HOPKINS UNIVERSITY PRESS | *Baltimore and London*

1986.

"Foreword," pp. ix–xi. Previously unpublished.

B 80 THE WRITER AS CELEBRITY
1986

THE | *WRITER* | *AS* | *CELEBRITY* | *INTIMATE INTERVIEWS* | *Maralyn Lois Polak* | M. Evans and Company, Inc. New York

1986. Copyright page: '9 . . . 1'.

Interview, " 'Have a Beer with Your Soul,' " pp. 46–50, was previously published as "James Dickey: 'Have a Beer with Your Soul' " (see D 230).

B 81 THE COMPLETE SHORT STORIES OF THOMAS WOLFE
1987

[decorated rule] | THE COMPLETE | SHORT STORIES OF | THOMAS WOLFE | [decorated rule] | *Edited by Francis E. Skipp* | FOREWORD BY JAMES DICKEY | CHARLES SCRIBNER'S SONS | *New York*

1987. Copyright page: '*First Edition*'.

'Foreword,' pp. ix–xv. Previously unpublished.

Note: Dickey's introduction was inserted as 12 xerographic leaves in the wrappered proof copies.

B82 DICTIONARY OF LITERARY BIOGRAPHY
YEARBOOK: 1986
1987

Dictionary of Literary Biography | Yearbook: 1986 | Edited by | J. M. Brook | A Bruccoli Clark Layman Book | Gale Research Company • Book Tower • Detroit, Michigan 48226

1987.

Dickey statement on Robert Penn Warren, p. 36. Previously unpublished.

B83 FROM THE GREEN HORSESHOE
1987

From the Green Horseshoe | Poems by James Dickey's Students | University of South Carolina Press

1987. Published in cloth and wrappers.

Essay: "From the Green Horseshoe," pp. ix–x. Previously unpublished.

Note: An excerpt from this introduction appeared in the Fall 1987 University of South Carolina Press catalogue, preceding publication of the book.

B84 SELECTED READINGS
1987

SELECTED READINGS | SPRING, 1987 | DOUBLEDAY & COMPANY, INC.

Wrappers.

Prepublication excerpt from *Alnilam*, pp. 19–33.

Locations: JRB; MJB.

B 85 TOWARD THE YEAR 2000
1987

BELLSOUTH CORPORATION | [white on navy] Toward the Year 2000: | Perspectives on the Information Age | [navy, black, red, and blue illustration] | [black] 1986 Annual Report | [red rule]

Atlanta, 1987. Wrappers; cover title.

Statement by Dickey, p. 12. Previously unpublished.

B 86 TRAVELS THROUGH NORTH & SOUTH CAROLINA, . . .
1988

TRAVELS | [decorative rule] | THROUGH | NORTH & SOUTH CAROLINA, | GEORGIA, | EAST & WEST FLORIDA, | THE CHEROKEE COUNTRY, THE EXTENSIVE | TERRITORIES OF THE MUSCOGULGES, | OR CREEK CONFEDERACY, AND THE | COUNTRY OF THE CHACTAWS | BY WILLIAM BARTRAM | [decorative rule] | INTRODUCTION BY JAMES DICKEY | [penguin] | PENGUIN BOOKS

New York, 1988. Wrappers.

Essay: "Cerulean Ixea, The Exuberant Fields, Gnaphalium, The Absolute Crocodile and the Wondrous Machine," pp. vii–xi. Previously unpublished.

B 87 TELL IT TO THE KING
1988

[two-page title] TELL IT TO THE KING | *LARRY KING* | *with Peter Occhiogrosso* | *G. P. PUTNAM'S SONS • NEW YORK*

1988. Copyright page: '1 . . . 10'.

Statements, p. 244. Previously unpublished.

B 88 POETRY'S CATBIRD SEAT
1988

Poetry's Catbird Seat | [tapered rule] | THE CONSULTANTSHIP IN POETRY |
IN THE ENGLISH LANGUAGE AT THE | LIBRARY OF CONGRESS, 1937–
1987 | *William McGuire* | LIBRARY OF CONGRESS • WASHINGTON | 1988

Quotes Dickey passim. Previously unpublished.

B 89 SOUTH CAROLINA: THE NATURAL HERITAGE
1989

Stephen H. Bennett, Robert C. Clark, and Thomas M. Poland, *South Carolina:
The Natural Heritage*. Columbia: University of South Carolina Press, 1989.

Foreword by Dickey.

Note: An excerpt from the foreword appeared in the Fall 1989 University of
South Carolina Press catalogue preceding publication of the book.

B 90 DICTIONARY OF LITERARY BIOGRAPHY
DOCUMENTARY SERIES
1989

*Dictionary of Literary Biography Documentary Series, Vol. 7: Modern Ameri-
can Poets*, ed. Karen L. Rood. Detroit, New York, Fort Lauderdale, London:
Bruccoli Clark Layman/Gale Research, 1989.

Includes previously unpublished material by Dickey and facsimiles manuscripts, pp. 3–126.

C. First Appearances in Journals and Newspapers, Excluding Interviews and Articles Quoting Dickey

First publication in journals and newspapers of material by Dickey, arranged chronologically. This section includes poetry, essays, reviews, letters, prepublication excerpts from books, and statements by Dickey. (Items that simply report rather than directly quote his opinions—his choices for best books of the year, for example—appear in Section D.) Only substantive revisions between first newspaper/journal publication and later book publication are noted. Poems or other material reprinted in articles or interviews are not listed. Some works that first appeared in A entries were shortly thereafter republished in journals; these items are not recorded in Section C, but are instead noted in Section A—if they are likely to cause confusion (see A 40). Journal titles, newspaper headlines, and newspaper section/page designations have been styled.

C 1

"Christmas Shopping, 1947," *Gadfly* [Vanderbilt University], 3 (Winter 1947), 59.

Poem. As Jim Dickey. Collected in *Veteran Birth*.

C 2

"Sea Island," *Gadfly*, 3 (Spring 1948), 104.

Poem. Collected in *Veteran Birth*.

C 3

"King Crab and Rattler," *Gadfly*, 3 (Spring 1948), 104–105.

Poem. Collected in *Veteran Birth*.

C 4

"Whittern and the Kite," *Gadfly*, 4 (Summer 1949), 26.

Poem. As James L. Dickey. Collected in *Veteran Birth*.

C 5

"The Shark at the Window," *Sewanee Review*, 59 (April–June 1951), 290–291.

Poem. As James L. Dickey. See AA 4.

C 6

"Of Holy War," *Poetry*, 79 (October 1951), 24.

Poem. As James L. Dickey.

C 7

"A Too-Sure Hand: Clarksville Man Competent Stylist," *Houston Post*, 12 April 1953, sec. 7, p. 7.

Review of *The Last Husband and Other Stories* by William Humphrey. As James L. Dickey.

C 8

"Her Present Phase: Jean Stafford's Inventive Stories," *Houston Post,* 17 May 1953, sec. 7, p. 7.

Review of *Children Are Bored on Sunday* by Stafford. As James L. Dickey.

C 9

"Two Poems," *Poetry,* 82 (June 1953), 137–139.

"The Child in Armor" and "The Anniversary." As James L. Dickey.

C 10

"Collection Includes Aiken's Early Work," *Houston Post,* 18 October 1953, sec. 6, p. 5.

Review of *Collected Poems* by Conrad Aiken. As James L. Dickey.

C 11

"Sacheverell Sitwell Collects His Essays," *Houston Post,* 8 November 1953, sec. 6, p. 5.

Review of *Selected Works* by Sitwell. As James L. Dickey.

C 12

"Jean Giono Writes of Plague Summer in Southern France," *Houston Post,* 17 January 1954, sec. 6, p. 2.

Review of *The Horseman on the Roof* by Giono. As James L. Dickey.

C 13

"M. Ayme Tosses a Whodunit," *Houston Post,* 7 February 1954, sec. 7, p. 7.

Review of *The Secret Stream* by Marcel Ayme. As James L. Dickey.

C 14

"International Magazine Presents Good Cross Section," *Houston Post,* 14 February 1954, sec. 7, p. 7.

Review of *Botteghe Oscure XII,* ed. Marguerite Caetani.

C 15

"Business as a Way of Life: Hotel Proprietor Is Hero of Herbert Gold's Second Novel," *Houston Post*, 21 February 1954, sec. 5, p. 4.

Review of *The Prospect Before Us* by Gold. As James L. Dickey.

C 16

"Welsh and Cajun Folk Portrayed," *Houston Post*, 16 May 1954, sec. 5, p. 4.

Review of *Under Milk Wood* by Dylan Thomas. As James L. Dickey.

C 17

"Third Book of Stories," *Houston Post*, 6 June 1954, sec. 5, p. 4.

Review of *The Widows of Thornton* by Peter Taylor. As James L. Dickey.

C 18

"Verve and Invention in Hawkes' Two Novels," *Houston Post*, 6 June 1954, sec. 5, p. 4.

Review of *The Goose on the Grave* (containing *The Owl* and *The Goose on the Grave*) by John Hawkes. As James L. Dickey.

C 19

"The Ground of Killing," *Sewanee Review*, 62 (October 1954), 623–624.

Poem.

C 20

"The Sprinter's Mother," *Shenandoah*, 6 (Spring 1955), 17–18.

Poem.

C 21

"The Angel of the Maze," *Poetry*, 86 (June 1955), 147–153.

Poem. First part is titled "The Maze"; second part is titled "The Angel" (not the same as B 24).

C 22

"The Confrontation of the Hero (April, 1945)," *Sewanee Review*, 63 (July–September 1955), 461–464.

Poem. As James L. Dickey.

C 23

"The Vigils," *Beloit Poetry Journal*, 6 (Fall 1955), 21–23.

Poem.

C 24

"Some of All of It," *Sewanee Review*, 64 (April–June 1956), 324–348.

Review of *Figures of a Double World* by Thomas McGrath; *The Gentle Weight Lifter* by David Ignatow (see A 5, A 11); *Want My Shepherd* by Howard O. Sackler; *The Moral Circus* by Edwin Honig; *Dry Sun, Dry Wind* by David Wagoner; *Book of Moments* by Kenneth Burke (see A 11); *The Poems of Gene Derwood* (see A 11); *The Salt Garden* by Howard Nemerov (see A 5, A 11); *The Nightfishing* by W. S. Graham (see A 11); and *Selected Poems* by Randall Jarrell (see A 5, A 11). As James L. Dickey.

C 25

"The Flight," *Beloit Poetry Journal*, 6 (Summer 1956), 16–19.

Poem.

C 26

"Five Poets," *Poetry*, 89 (November 1956), 110–117.

Review of *The Scattered Causes* by Samuel French Morse (see A 11); *Antennas of Silence* by Ernest Sandeen; *Friday's Child* by Wilfred Watson; *Delta Return* by Charles Bell; and *An American Takes a Walk* by Reed Whittemore (see A 11).

C 27

"The Father's Body," *Poetry*, 89 (December 1956), 145–149.

Poem.

C 28

"An Exchange on 'Delta Return,' " *Poetry*, 89 (March 1957), 391–392.

Letters from Rolfe Humpries and Dickey about Dickey's review of Charles Bell's *Delta Return*. See C 26.

C 29

"The Swimmer," *Partisan Review*, 24 (Spring 1957), 244–246.

Poem.

C 30

"The First Morning of Cancer," *Poetry*, 90 (May 1957), 97–102.

Poem.

C 31

"To Be Edward Thomas," *Boland Poetry Journal Chapbook*, no. 5 (Summer 1957), 10–15.

Poem.

C 32

"From Babel to Byzantium," *Sewanee Review*, 65 (July–September 1957), 508–530.

Review of *Howl* by Allen Ginsberg (see A 5, A 11); *In the Winter of Cities* by Tennessee Williams; *Poems* by Marcia Nardi; *Men and Tin Kettles* by Richard Lyons; *The Battlement* by Donald F. Drummond (see A 5—"The Winters Approach," A 11); *Some Trees* by John Ashbery (see A 11); *Changes of Garments* by Neil Weiss; *Other Knowledge* by Leonore G. Marshall; *The Center Is Everywhere* by E. L. Mayo; *Green Armor on Green Ground* by Rolfe Humphries (see A 11); *Moon's Farm* by Herbert Read (see A 11); *Poets of Today III* (Lee Anderson, Spencer Brown, Joseph Langland); and *Villa Narcisse* by Katherine Hoskins (see A 11). Concluding remarks appear in A 5 as part of "Toward a Solitary Joy."

C 33

"The Sprinter's Sleep," *Yale Review*, 47 (September 1957), 72.

Poem. Collected in *Into the Stone*.

C 34

"The Work of Art," *Hudson Review*, 10 (Autumn 1957), 400–402.

Poem.

C 35

"The Red Bow," *Sewanee Review,* 65 (October–December 1957), 627–634.

Poem.

C 36

"A Beginning Poet, Aged Sixty-Five," *Quarterly Review of Literature,* 9 (Winter 1958), 272–273.

Poem.

C 37

"The Cypresses," *Quarterly Review of Literature,* 9 (Winter 1958), 268–270.

Poem.

C 38

"Poem," *Quarterly Review of Literature,* 9 (Winter 1958), 270–271.

Collected in *Into the Stone.*

C 39

"In the Presence of Anthologies," *Sewanee Review,* 66 (April–June 1958), 294–314.

Review of *The New Poets of England and America,* ed. Donald Hall, Robert Pack, and Louis Simpson (see A 5, A 11—"In the Presence of Anthologies"); *Mavericks,* ed. Howard Sergeant and Dannie Abse; *A Case of Samples* by Kingsley Amis (see A 5—"New Poets of England and America I," A 11—"In the Presence of Anthologies"); *Poets of Today IV* (George Garrett, Theodore Holmes, Robert Wallace); *Letter From a Distant Land* by Philip Booth (see A 5, A 11); *The Hawk in the Rain* by Ted Hughes (see A 11); *For Some Stringed Instrument* by Peter Kane Dufault; *When We Were Here Together* by Kenneth Patchen (see A 5, A 11); *Declensions of a Refrain* by Arthur Gregor; *The Strange Islands* by Thomas Merton; *Time Without Number* by Daniel Berrigan; *Poems* by Richmond Lattimore; *In Time Like Air* by May Sarton (see A 11); *Poems 1947–1957* by William Jay Smith (see A 11); *Promises* by Robert Penn Warren (see A 11); *Great Praises* by Richard Eberhart (see A 5, A 11); *Collected Poems* by Edwin Muir (see A 11); and *Selected Poems* by Lawrence Durrell (see A 11). Concluding remarks appear in A 5 as "The Second Birth."

C 40

"Genesis," *Commentary*, 25 (May 1958), 427.

Poem.

C 41

"Joel Cahill Dead," *Beloit Poetry Journal*, 8 (Summer 1958), 18–19.

Poem.

C 42

"Dover: Believing in Kings," *Poetry*, 92 (August 1958), 283–290.

Poem. Collected in *Drowning With Others; Poems 1957–1967*.

C 43

"The Falls," *Impetus*, no. 3 (Winter 1959), 3–4.

Poem.

C 44

"The Other," *Yale Review*, 48 (March 1959), 348–400.

Poem. Collected in *Into the Stone; Poems 1957–1967*.

C 45

"A Gold-Mine of Consciousness," *Poetry*, 94 (April 1959), 41–44.

Review of *Sheepfold Hill* by Conrad Aiken (see A 11).

C 46

"The Vegetable King," *Sewanee Review*, 67 (April–June 1959), 278–280.

Poem. Collected in *Into the Stone; Poems 1957–1967*.

C 47

"Five Poets," *Poetry*, 94 (May 1959), 117–123.

Review of *The Sum* by Alan Stephens; *A Local Habitation* by Ellen Kay (see A 5—"The Winters Approach," A 11); *A Book of Kinds* by Margaret Tongue (see A 11); *Passage After Midnight* by William Pillin; and *The Death of Venus* by Harold Witt (see A 5, A 11).

C 48

"The Jewel," *Saturday Review*, 42 (6 June 1959), 38.

Poem. Collected in *Into the Stone; Poems 1957–1967*.

C 49

"The Game," *Poetry*, 94 (July 1959), 211–212.

Poem. Collected in *Into the Stone*.

C 50

"The Landfall," *Poetry*, 94 (July 1959), 213–215.

Poem. Collected in *Into the Stone*.

C 51

"The Signs," *Poetry*, 94 (July 1959), 215–218.

Poem. Collected in *Into the Stone*.

C 52

"The Enclosure," *Poetry*, 94 (July 1959), 218–220.

Poem. Collected in *Into the Stone; Poems 1957–1967*.

C 53

"The Performance," *Poetry*, 94 (July 1959), 220–221.

Poem. Collected in *Into the Stone; Poems 1957–1967*.

C 54

"The String," *Poetry*, 94 (July 1959), 222–223.

Poem. Collected in *Into the Stone; Poems 1957–1967*.

C 55

"Below the Lighthouse," *Poetry*, 94 (July 1959), 223–225.

Poem. Collected as "On the Hill Below the Lighthouse" in *Into the Stone; Poems 1957–1967*.

C 56

"Into the Stone," *Poetry*, 94 (July 1959), 225–226.

Poem. Collected in *Into the Stone; Poems 1957–1967*.

C 57

"The Human Power," *Sewanee Review*, 67 (July–September 1959), 497–519.

Review of *Shadow and Wall* by Tania van Zyl; *Certain Poems* by John Edward Hardy; *The Wilderness and Other Poems* by Louis O. Coxe; *Poems* by Emma Swan (see A 11); *The Night of the Hammer* by Ned O'Gorman (see A 5); *Third Day Lucky* by Robin Skelton; *First Poems* and *The Country of a Thousand Years of Peace and Other Poems* by James Merrill (see A 11); *The Dark Sister* by Winfield Townley Scott (see A 11); *Plays and Poems 1948–58* by Elder Olson (see A 5, A 11); *95 Poems* by E. E. Cummings (see A 5, A 11); and *The Odyssey: A Modern Sequel* by Nikos Kazantzakis (see A 11).

C 58

"Awaiting the Swimmer," *Kenyon Review*, 21 (Autumn 1959), 609–610.

Poem. Collected in *Into the Stone; Poems 1957–1967*.

C 59

"Orpheus Before Hades," *New Yorker*, 35 (5 December 1959), 52.

Poem. Collected in *Into the Stone*.

C 60

"The Call," *Hudson Review*, 12 (Winter 1959–1960), 560.

Poem. Collected in *Into the Stone* and as the first part of "The Owl King" in *Drowning with Others; Poems 1957–1967; The Owl King*. See C 107.

C 61

"Reading *Genesis* to a Blind Child," *Wormwood Review*, 1, no. 1 (1960), unpaged.

Poem.

C 62

"A Child's Room," *Quarterly Review of Literature*, 10 (Winter 1960), 247–248.

Poem.

C 63

"The Wedding," *Quarterly Review of Literature,* 10 (Winter 1960), 248–249.
Poem. Collected in *Into the Stone; Poems 1957–1967.*

C 64

"Near Darien," *Quarterly Review of Literature,* 10 (Winter 1960), 249–251.
Poem. Collected in *Into the Stone; Poems 1957–1967.*

C 65

"The Scratch," *Quarterly Review of Literature,* 10 (Winter 1960), 251–253.
Poem. Collected in *Drowning with Others.*

C 66

"Uncle," *Quarterly Review of Literature,* 10 (Winter 1960), 253–254.
Poem. Collected in *Into the Stone.*

C 67

"The Island," *Sewanee Review,* 68 (January–March 1960), 89–90.
Poem. Collected in *Drowning with Others.*

C 68

"Sleeping Out at Easter," *Virginia Quarterly Review,* 36 (Spring 1960), 218–219.
Poem. Collected in *Into the Stone; Poems 1957–1967.*

C 69

"The Prodigal," *Poetry Northwest,* 1 (Spring–Summer 1960), 10–13.
Poem.

C 70

"To a Beginning Poet, Aged Sixty," *Atlantic Monthly,* 205 (May 1960), 69.
Poem. Collected as "To Landrum Guy, Beginning to Write at Sixty" in *Drowning with Others.*

C71

"The Underground Stream," *New Yorker*, 36 (21 May 1960), 42.

Poem. Collected in *Into the Stone; Poems 1957–1967*.

C72

"Walking on Water," *New Yorker*, 36 (18 June 1960), 44.

Poem. Collected in *Into the Stone; Poems 1957–1967*.

C73

"Trees and Cattle," *New Yorker*, 36 (16 July 1960), 34.

Poem. Collected in *Into the Stone; Poems 1957–1967*.

C74

"A Birth," *New Yorker*, 36 (13 August 1960), 30.

Poem. Collected in *Drowning with Others; Poems 1957–1967*. See AA 2.

C75

"Between Two Prisoners," *Yale Review*, 50 (Autumn 1960), 86–88.

Poem. Collected in *Drowning with Others; Poems 1957–1967*.

C76

"Drowning with Others," *Partisan Review*, 27 (Fall 1960), 636–637.

Poem. Collected in *Drowning with Others; Poems 1957–1967*.

C77

"Mindoro, 1944," *Paris Review*, 6 (Autumn–Winter 1960), [122–123].

Poem. Collected in *Into the Stone*.

C78

"The Suspect in Poetry or Everyman as Detective," *Sewanee Review*, 68 (October–December 1960), 660–674.

Review of *The Sense of Movement* by Thom Gunn (see A 5, A 11); *Portrait of Your Niece and Other Poems* by Carol Hall; *The Clever Body* by Melvin Walker LaFollette; *A Lattice for Momos* by R. G. Everson; *Guy Fawkes Night and Other Poems* by John Press; *Apples From Shinar* by Hyam Plutzik; *The*

Crooked Lines of God by Brother Antoninus (see A 5, A 11); *The Crow and the Heart* by Hayden Carruth (see A 5, A 11); and *The Prodigal Son* by James Kirkup (see A 11). Concluding remarks appear in A 5 as part of "Toward a Solitary Joy."

C 79

"Autumn," *New Yorker,* 36 (29 October 1960), 42.

Poem. Collected in *Drowning with Others.*

C 80

"Listening to Foxhounds," *New Yorker,* 36 (26 November 1960), 48.

Poem. Collected in *Drowning with Others; Poems 1957–1967.*

C 81

"Antipolis," *Poetry,* 97 (December 1960), 153–154.

Poem. Collected in *Drowning with Others.*

C 82

"A View of Fujiyama After the War," *Poetry,* 97 (December 1960), 154–156.

Poem. Collected in *Drowning with Others.*

C 83

"Inside the River," *Poetry,* 97 (December 1960), 156–157.

Poem. Collected in *Drowning with Others; Poems 1957–1967.*

C 84

"The Magus," *New Yorker,* 36 (24 December 1960), 30.

Poem. Collected in *Drowning with Others; Poems 1957–1967.*

C 85

"The Change," *Kenyon Review,* 23 (Winter 1961), 71.

Poem. Collected in *Drowning with Others.*

C 86

"Hunting Civil War Relics at Nimblewill Creek," *Sewanee Review,* 69 (January–March 1961), 139–141.

Poem. Collected in *Drowning with Others; Poems 1957–1967.*

C 87

"Five First Books," *Poetry,* 97 (February 1961), 316–320.

Review of *Myths and Texts* by Gary Snyder (see A 5); *The Year of the Green Wave* by Bruce Cutler; *Bone Thoughts* by George Starbuck; *To Bedlam and Part Way Back* by Anne Sexton (see A 5, A 11); and *What a Kingdom It Was* by Galway Kinnell (see A 5, A 11).

C 88

"The Summons," *Virginia Quarterly Review,* 37 (Spring 1961), 222–223.

Poem. Collected in *Drowning with Others; Poems 1957–1967.*

C 89

"Fog Envelops the Animals," *Virginia Quarterly Review,* 37 (Spring 1961), 224–225.

Poem. Collected in *Drowning with Others; Poems 1957–1967.*

C 90

"Via Appia," *Choice: A Magazine of Poetry and Graphics,* 1 (Spring 1961), 50–51.

Poem.

C 91

"The Twin Falls," *Choice: A Magazine of Poetry and Graphics,* 1 (Spring 1961), 52.

Poem. Collected in *Drowning with Others.*

C 92

"Facing Africa," *Encounter,* 16 (April 1961), 41.

Poem. Collected in *Drowning with Others; Poems 1957–1967.*

C 93

"The Death and Keys of the Censor," *Sewanee Review,* 69 (April–June 1961), 318–332.

Review of *The New American Poetry 1945–1960,* ed. Donald M. Allen (see A 5—"The Grove Press New American Poets (1960)," A 11—"In the Presence

of Anthologies"); *The Maximus Poems* by Charles Olson (see A 5, A 11);
Madonna of the Cello by Robert Bagg; *Say Pardon* by David Ignatow (see A 5,
A 11); *Wonderstrand Revisited* by Charles H. Philbrick; *First Poems* by Lewis
Turco (see A 11); *The Drunk in The Furnace* by W. S. Merwin (see A 5, A 11);
Outlanders by Theodore Weiss (see A 11); *Poems 1930–1960* by Josephine
Miles (see A 11); and *New and Selected Poems* by Howard Nemerov (see A 5,
A 11).

C 94

Letters between Brother Antoninus and Dickey, *Sewanee Review,* 69 (April–
June 1961), 351–354.

Exchange concerning Dickey's review of Brother Antoninus's *The Crooked
Lines of God.* See C 78, C 96.

C 95

"In the Tree House at Night," *New Yorker,* 37 (24 June 1961), 30.

Poem. Collected in *Drowning with Others; Poems 1957–1967.*

C 96

Letters between Brother Antoninus and Dickey, *Sewanee Review,* 69 (July–
September 1961), 510–513.

Exchange concerning Dickey's review of Brother Antoninus's *The Crooked
Lines of God.* See C 78, C 94.

C 97

"Confession Is Not Enough," *New York Times Book Review,* 9 July 1961, p. 14.

Review of *Kaddish* by Allen Ginsberg (see A 5, A 11); *The Maximus Poems* and
The Distances by Charles Olson; and *Mountain, Fire, Thornbush* by Harvey
Shapiro.

C 98

"The Lifeguard," *New Yorker,* 37 (5 August 1961), 24.

Poem. Collected in *Drowning with Others; Poems 1957–1967.*

C 99

"The Salt Marsh," *New Yorker,* 37 (16 September 1961), 46.

Poem. Collected in *Drowning with Others; Poems 1957–1967.*

C 100

"Letter to Jane Esty," *Mutiny*, 4 (Fall–Winter 1961–1962), 5.

Dickey's response to attacks on his review "Confession Is Not Enough." See C 97.

C 101

"In the Lupanar at Pompeii," *Kenyon Review*, 23 (Autumn 1961), 631–633.

Poem. Collected in *Drowning with Others; Poems 1957–1967*.

C 102

"Correspondences and Essences," *Virginia Quarterly Review*, 37 (Autumn 1961), 635–640.

Review of *The Many Islands* by William Goodreau; *Apollonian Poems* by Arthur Freeman; *Poems and Translations* by Thomas Kinsella; *Halfway* by Maxine W. Kumin; *Abraham's Knife* by George Garrett; *Journey to a Known Place* by Hayden Carruth (see A 5, A 11); *West of Your City* by William Stafford (see A 5, A 11); and *I Am! Says the Lamb* and *Words for the Wind* by Theodore Roethke (see A 5, A 11).

C 103

"The Movement of Fish," *New Yorker*, 37 (7 October 1961), 58.

Poem. Collected in *Drowning with Others; Poems 1957–1967*.

C 104

"In the Mountain Tent," *New Yorker*, 37 (28 October 1961), 54.

Poem. Collected in *Drowning with Others; Poems 1957–1967*.

C 105

"The Heaven of Animals," *New Yorker*, 37 (18 November 1961), 48.

Poem. Collected in *Drowning with Others; Poems 1957–1967*. See AA 12.

C 106

"For the Nightly Ascent of the Hunter Orion over a Forest Clearing," *New Yorker*, 37 (2 December 1961), 58.

Poem. Collected in *Drowning with Others; Poems 1957–1967*.

C 107

"The Owl King," *Hudson Review,* 14 (Winter 1961–1962), 550–556.

Poem. First part is titled "The Owl King"; second part is titled "The Blind Child's Story." Collected as the second and third parts of "The Owl King" in *Drowning with Others; Poems 1957–1967; The Owl King.* See C 60.

C 108

"Armor," *Hudson Review,* 14 (Winter 1961–1962), 557–558.

Poem. Collected in *Drowning with Others; Poems 1957–1967.*

C 109

"Toward a Solitary Joy," *Hudson Review,* 14 (Winter 1961–1962), 607–613.

Review of *Skeleton of Light* by Thomas Vance; *The Bluebells and Other Verse* by John Masefield; *The Gardener* by John Hall Wheelock; *Poets of Today VIII* (Albert Herzing, John M. Ridland, David R. Slavitt); *The Lovemaker* by Robert Mezey (see A 5); *The Royal Tiger's Face* by Marvin Solomon; *The Nets* by Paul Blackburn; *Eighty-Five Poems* and *Solstices* by Louis MacNeice (see A 11); *Weep Before God* by John Wain; *In the Stoneworks* by John Ciardi; and *Versions from Fyodor Tyutchev* by Charles Tomlinson (see A 11). Introductory remarks appear in A 5 as part of "Toward a Solitary Joy."

C 110

"Adam in Winter," *Choice: A Magazine of Poetry and Graphics,* 2 (1962), 14–15.

Poem.

C 111

"The Hospital Window," *Poetry,* 99 (January 1962), 236–237.

Poem. Collected in *Drowning with Others; Poems 1957–1967.*

C 112

"A Dog Sleeping on My Feet," *Poetry,* 99 (January 1962), 238–239.

Poem. Collected in *Drowning with Others; Poems 1957–1967.*

C 113

"After the Night Hunt," *Poetry,* 99 (January 1962), 239–240.

Poem. See B 44.

C 114

"The Gamecocks," *Poetry*, 99 (January 1962), 240–242.

Poem.

C 115

"Under Oaks," *New York Times*, 1 January 1962, p. 22.

Poem. See B 22.

C 116

"Fence Wire," *New Yorker*, 38 (24 February 1962), 36.

Poem. Collected in *Helmets; Poems 1957–1967*.

C 117

"A Note on the Poetry of John Logan," *Sewanee Review*, 70 (April–June 1962), 257–260.

Review of *Ghosts of the Heart* by Logan (see A 5, A 11).

C 118

"By Canoe Through the Fir Forest," *New Yorker*, 38 (16 June 1962), 32.

Poem. Collected as first part of "On the Coosawattee" in *Helmets; Poems 1957–1967*. See B 4, C 126, C 127.

C 119

"The Step," *Literary Review*, 5 (Summer 1962), 474–475.

Poem.

C 120

"Springer Mountain," *Virginia Quarterly Review*, 38 (Summer 1962), 436–441.

Poem. Collected in *Helmets; Poems 1957–1967*.

C 121

"The Stillness at the Center of the Target," *Sewanee Review*, 70 (July–September 1962), 484–503.

Review of *The Unfinished Man* by Nissim Ezekiel; *The Astronomy of Love* by John Stallworthy; *Knowledge of the Evening* by John Frederick Nims (see A

11); *The Tree Witch* by Peter Viereck; *Advice to a Prophet* by Richard Wilbur (see A 11); *The Opening of the Field* by Robert Duncan (see A 11); *Medusa in Gramercy Park* by Horace Gregory (see A 11); *The Screens and Other Poems* by I. A. Richards (see A 11); *Collected Poems* by Yvor Winters (see A 11); and *A Marianne Moore Reader* (see A 11).

C 122

"A Letter," *Sewanee Review,* 70 (July–September 1962), 416–417.

Poem. Collected in *Poems 1957–1967*. See B 4.

C 123

"At the Home for Unwed Mothers," *Quarterly Review of Literature,* 12 (Fall–Winter 1962), 55–56.

Poem.

C 124

"A Sound Through the Floor," *Quarterly Review of Literature,* 12 (Fall–Winter 1962), 57–59.

Poem.

C 125

"On Discovering That My Hand Shakes," *Quarterly Review of Literature,* 12 (Fall–Winter 1962), 59–60.

Poem.

C 126

"Below Ellijay," *Poetry,* 101 (October–November 1962), 27–28.

Poem. Collected as the second part of "On the Coosawattee" in *Helmets; Poems 1957–1967*. See C 118, C 127.

C 127

"On the Inundation of the Coosawattee Valley," *Yale Review,* 52 (December 1962), 234–235.

Poem. Collected under the title "The Inundation" as the third part of "On the Coosawattee" in *Helmets; Poems 1957–1967*. See C 118, C 126.

C 128

"Poems of North and South Georgia," *New Yorker,* 38 (1 December 1962), 60–61.

Poems. "At Darien Bridge, Georgia" (collected as "At Darien Bridge"), "In the Marble Quarry," "The Dusk of Horses" (see B 4), "The Beholders," and "The Poisoned Man." Collected in *Helmets; Poems 1957–1967.*

C 129

"James Dickey: Two Poems," *Mutiny,* no. 12 (1963), 96–98.

"Walking the Fire Line" and "The Courtship."

C 130

"Paestum," *Shenandoah,* 14 (Winter 1963), 7–10.

Poem.

C 131

"Under Buzzards," *Granta* [Queen's College, Cambridge University], 67 (2 March 1963), 9.

Poem. Different from C 229.

C 132

"Dialogues with Themselves," *New York Times Book Review,* 28 April 1963, p. 50.

Review of *Children Passing* by Richard Emil Braun; *All My Pretty Ones* by Anne Sexton (see A 5); and *Arrivals and Departures* by Charles Gullans.

C 133

"Kudzu," *New Yorker,* 39 (18 May 1963), 44.

Poem. Collected in *Helmets; Poems 1957–1967.*

C 134

"The Scarred Girl," *New Yorker,* 39 (1 June 1963), 36.

Poem. Collected in *Helmets; Poems 1957–1967.*

C 135

"Drinking from a Helmet," *Sewanee Review*, 71 (July–September 1963), 451–457.

Poem. Collected in *Helmets; Poems 1957–1967*.

C 136

"The Being," *Poetry*, 102 (August 1963), 281–284.

Poem. Collected in *Helmets; Poems 1957–1967*.

C 137

"Why in London the Blind Are Saviors," *Poetry*, 102 (August 1963), 284–286.

Poem.

C 138

"A Folk-Singer of the Thirties," *Poetry*, 102 (August 1963), 286–291.

Poem. Collected in *Helmets; Poems 1957–1967*.

C 139

"Bums, On Waking," *New Yorker*, 39 (7 September 1963), 34.

Poem. Collected in *Helmets; Poems 1957–1967*.

C 140

"Goodbye to Serpents," *New Yorker*, 39 (21 September 1963), 47.

Poem. Collected in *Helmets; Poems 1957–1967*.

C 141

"Horses and Prisoners," *Hudson Review*, 16 (Autumn 1963), 384–385.

Poem. Collected in *Helmets; Poems 1957–1967*.

C 142

"Blowgun and Rattlesnake," *Texas Quarterly*, 7 (Autumn 1963), 158–160.

Poem.

C 143

"In the Child's Night," *Virginia Quarterly Review*, 39 (Autumn 1963), 590–591.

Poem. Collected in *Helmets*. See AA 8.

C 144

"Ways and Means," *Shenandoah*, 15 (Autumn 1963), 56–61.

Review of *Movie-Going* by John Hollander; *Manhattan Pastures* by Sandra Hochman; *A Paper Horse* by Robert Watson; *Naked as the Glass* by Jean Burden; and *The Collected Later Poems* by William Carlos Williams.

C 145

"Cherrylog Road," *New Yorker*, 39 (12 October 1963), 51.

Poem. Collected in *Helmets; Poems 1957–1967*. In collections the female protagonist's name is changed from Charlotte Holbrook to Doris Holbrook.

C 146

"Breath," *New Yorker*, 39 (9 November 1963), 48.

Poem. Collected in *Helmets*.

C 147

"That Language of the Brain," *Poetry*, 103 (December 1963), 187–190.

Review of *The Morning Song of Lord Zero* by Conrad Aiken (see A 11).

C 148

"The Driver," *New Yorker*, 39 (7 December 1963), 54.

Poem. Collected in *Helmets; Poems 1957–1967*.

C 149

"The Many Ways of Speaking in Verse," *New York Times Book Review*, 22 December 1963, p. 4.

Review of *The Wheel of Summer* by Joseph Langland; *The Nesting Ground* by David Wagoner; *The Selected Poems of John Malcolm Brinnin; Caged in an Animal's Mind* by Stanley Burnshaw; *The Moving Target* by W. S. Merwin; and *The City of Satisfactions* by Daniel Hoffman.

C 150

"The Ice Skin," *New Yorker*, 39 (28 December 1963), 37.

Poem. Collected in *Helmets; Poems 1957–1967*.

C 151

"The Leap," *North American Review*, n.s. 1, no. 4 (1964), 31.

Poem. Collected in *Poems 1957–1967*.

C 152

"Mary Sheffield," *Shenandoah*, 15 (Winter 1964), 52–53.

Poem. Collected in *Poems 1957–1967*.

C 153

"Fox Blood," *Quarterly Review of Literature*, 13 (Winter–Spring 1964), 37–38.

Poem. Collected in *Buckdancer's Choice; Poems 1957–1967*.

C 154

"For the Linden Moth," *Quarterly Review of Literature*, 13 (Winter–Spring 1964), 38–40.

Poem.

C 155

"The Rafters," *Quarterly Review of Literature*, 13 (Winter–Spring 1964), 40–42.

Poem.

C 156

"Winter Trout," *Paris Review*, 8 (Winter–Spring 1964), [98–99].

Poem. Collected in *Helmets; Poems 1957–1967*.

C 157

"First and Last Things," *Poetry*, 103 (February 1964), 316–324.

Review of *The Hawk and the Lizard* by Gene Frumkin; *The Imaged Word* by Rolf Fjelde; *Blind Man's Holiday* by R. G. Everson; *Final Solutions* by Frederick Seidel; *Naked as the Glass* by Jean Burden; *New Poems* by Robert Graves (see A 11); *Affinities* by Vernon Watkins (see A 11); *The Beginning and the End* by Robinson Jeffers (see A 11); *Collected Poems* by Ralph Hodgson (see A 11); *The Collected Later Poems* by William Carlos Williams (see A 11); and *Charles Baudelaire: The Flowers of Evil,* ed. Marthiel and Jackson Mathews.

C 158

"Reincarnation," *New Yorker,* 40 (7 March 1964), 51.

Poem. Collected in *Buckdancer's Choice* and as "Reincarnation (I)" in *Poems 1957–1967.*

C 159

"The Second Sleep," *Kenyon Review,* 26 (Spring 1964), 302–303.

Poem. Collected as first part of "Fathers and Sons" in *Buckdancer's Choice; Poems 1957–1967.* See C 183.

C 160

"Your Next-Door Neighbor's Poems," *Sewanee Review,* 72 (April–June 1964), 307–321.

Review of *Countermoves* by Charles Edward Eaton; *Imperatives* by Anthony Ostroff; *The Beginning and the End* by Robinson Jeffers; *Poems 1951–1961* by Robert Hazel; *A Harlot's Hire* by Allen Grossman; *The Rank Obstinacy of Things* by Paul Roche; *Guarded by Women* by Robert Pack; *Selected Poems* by Anne Ridler; *Collected Verse Plays* by Richard Eberhart; and *Sun-Stone* by Octavio Paz.

C 161

"The Firebombing," *Poetry,* 104 (May 1964), 63–72.

Poem. Collected in *Two Poems of the Air; Buckdancer's Choice; Poems 1957–1967.*

C 162

"Them, Crying," *New Yorker,* 40 (9 May 1964), 42.

Poem. Collected in *Buckdancer's Choice; Poems 1957–1967.*

C 163

"The Escape," *New Yorker,* 40 (18 July 1964), 30.

Poem. Collected in *Buckdancer's Choice; Poems 1957–1967.*

C 164

"Angina," *New Yorker,* 40 (15 August 1964), 30.

Poem. Collected in *Buckdancer's Choice; Poems 1957–1967.*

C 165

"The War Wound," *New Yorker,* 40 (12 September 1964), 54.

Poem. Collected in *Buckdancer's Choice; Poems 1957–1967.*

C 166

"Pursuit from Under," *Hudson Review,* 17 (Autumn 1964), 412–414.

Poem. Collected in *Buckdancer's Choice; Poems 1957–1967.*

C 167

"Faces Seen Once," *Hudson Review,* 17 (Autumn 1964), 414–416.

Poem. Collected in *Buckdancer's Choice; Poems 1957–1967.*

C 168

"The Common Grave," *New Yorker,* 40 (24 October 1964), 54.

Poem. Collected in *Buckdancer's Choice; Poems 1957–1967.*

C 169

"Theodore Roethke," *Poetry,* 105 (November 1964), 119–122.

Review of *Sequences, Sometimes Metaphysical* by Roethke (see A 11—second part of Roethke essay).

C 170

"Children Reading," *New York Times Book Review,* 1 November 1964, pt. 2, p. 1.

Poem.

C 171

"Sled Burial: Dream Ceremony," *Southern Review,* n.s. 1 (January 1965), 125–126.

Poem. Collected as "Sled Burial, Dream Ceremony" in *Buckdancer's Choice; Poems 1957–1967*.

C 172

"Barnstorming for Poetry," *New York Times Book Review*, 3 January 1965, pp. 1, 22–23.

Essay. Collected in *Babel to Byzantium*.

C 173

"The Shark's Parlor," *New Yorker*, 40 (30 January 1965), 32–33.

Poem. Collected in *Buckdancer's Choice; Poems 1957–1967*.

C 174

"Two Open Letters Concerning the Critic's Role," *Sewanee Review*, 73 (January–March 1965), 176–178.

Letters between Charles Edward Eaton and Dickey.

C 175

"The Night Pool," *Virginia Quarterly Review*, 41 (Spring 1965), 231–232.

Poem. Collected in *Buckdancer's Choice; Poems 1957–1967*.

C 176

"Gamecock," *Virginia Quarterly Review*, 41 (Spring 1965), 232–233.

Poem. Collected in *Buckdancer's Choice; Poems 1957–1967*.

C 177

"The Head-Aim," *Virginia Quarterly Review*, 41 (Spring 1965), 233–234.

Poem. Collected in *Poems 1957–1967*. See AA 1.

C 178

"The Fiend," *Partisan Review*, 32 (Spring 1965), 206–209.

Poem. Collected in *Buckdancer's Choice; Poems 1957–1967*.

C 179

"Reality's Shifting Stages: Reviews by Five Hands," *Kenyon Review*, 27 (Spring 1965), 378–384.

Includes Dickey's review of *Arms of Light* by Clair McAllister, pp. 382–384.

C 180

"Dust," *The Bulletin* [Sydney, Australia], 8 May 1965, p. 55.

Poem. Collected in *Buckdancer's Choice; Poems 1957–1967*.

C 181

"Sustainment," *Yale Review*, 54 (June 1965), 547–548.

Poem. Collected in *Poems 1957–1967*. See B 8.

C 182

"The Celebration," *Harper's Magazine*, 230 (June 1965), 50.

Poem. Collected in *Buckdancer's Choice; Poems 1957–1967*.

C 183

"The Aura," *New Yorker*, 41 (5 June 1965), 38.

Poem. Collected as the second part of "Fathers and Sons" in *Buckdancer's Choice; Poems 1957–1967*. See C 159.

C 184

"An Old Family Custom," *New York Times Book Review*, 6 June 1965, pp. 1, 16.

Essay.

C 185

"Buckdancer's Choice," *New Yorker*, 41 (19 June 1965), 36.

Poem. Collected in *Buckdancer's Choice; Poems 1957–1967*. See AA 5.

C 186

"Mangham," *Kenyon Review*, 27 (Summer 1965), 476–477.

Poem. Collected in *Buckdancer's Choice; Poems 1957–1967*.

C 187

"Deer Among Cattle," *Shenandoah*, 16 (Summer 1965), 78.

Poem. Collected in *Poems 1957–1967*.

C 188

"Slave Quarters," *New Yorker*, 41 (14 August 1965), 28–29.

Poem. Revised and collected in *Buckdancer's Choice; Poems 1957–1967*.

C 189

"False Youth: Summer," *Harper's Magazine*, 231 (September 1965), 115.

Poem. Collected as first part of "False Youth: Two Seasons" in *Poems 1957–1967* (see C 196); collected as "Summer: Porch-Wings" in *False Youth: Four Seasons*. See B 8.

C 190

"Hedge Life," *New Yorker*, 41 (4 September 1965), 34.

Poem. Collected in *Poems 1957–1967*.

C 191

"Coming Back to America," *New Yorker*, 41 (18 September 1965), 57.

Poem. Collected in *Poems 1957–1967*.

C 192

"The Birthday Dream," *Nation*, 201 (27 September 1965), 170.

Poem. Collected in *Poems 1957–1967; False Youth: Four Seasons*.

C 193

"Orientations," *American Scholar*, 34 (Autumn 1965), 646, 648, 650, 656, 658.

Review of *The Lost World* by Randall Jarrell; *77 Dream Songs* by John Berryman (see A 11); *To What Strangers, What Welcome* by J. V. Cunningham (see A 11); *Selected Poems* by Louis Simpson (see A 11); *The Wreck of the Thresher and Other Poems* by William Meredith (see A 11); *A Roof of Tiger Lilies* by Donald Hall; *To Build a Fire* by Melville Cane; and *Roots and Branches* by Robert Duncan (see A 11).

C 194

"The Language of Poetry," *New York Times Book Review*, 7 November 1965, p. 6.

Review of poetry anthologies for children: *Sprints and Distances*, ed. Lillian Morrison; *This Land Is Mine*, ed. Al Hines; *The Earth Is the Lord's*, ed. Helen

Plotz; *A Book of Love Poems,* ed. William Cole; *Read Me a Poem,* ed. Ellen Lewis Buell; *Poems to Be Read Aloud,* ed. Ann McFerran; *In a Spring Garden,* ed. Richard Lewis; *The Golden Journey,* ed. Louise Bogan and William Jay Smith; *A Child's Calendar* by John Updike; *In the Woods, in the Meadow, in the Sky* by Aileen Fisher; *8 A.M. Shadows* by Patricia Hubbell; *Poe,* ed. Dwight Macdonald; *Emerson,* ed. J. Donald Adams; and *The Green Roads* by Edward Thomas.

C 195

"Poems of the Sixties—4," *Times Literary Supplement,* 25 November 1965, p. 1069.

"Seeking the Chosen" by Dickey; other poems by Louis Simpson, John Berryman, and John Ashbery.

C 196

"False Youth: Winter," *New Yorker,* 42 (26 February 1966), 44.

Poem. Collected as the second part of "False Youth: Two Seasons" in *Poems 1957–1967* (see C 189); collected as "Winter: Thumb-Fire" in *False Youth: Four Seasons.*

C 197

"Adultery," *Nation,* 202 (28 February 1966), 252.

Poem. Collected in *Poems 1957–1967.*

C 198

"For the Last Wolverine," *Atlantic Monthly,* 217 (June 1966), 70–71.

Poem. Collected in *Poems 1957–1967.*

C 199

"The Bee," *Harper's Magazine,* 232 (June 1966), 80–81.

Poem. Collected in *Poems 1957–1967.*

C 200

"Work and Play," *New York Times Book Review,* 5 June 1966, pp. 1, 60–62.

Statement by Dickey, p. 1.

C 201

"Encounter in the Cage Country," *New Yorker*, 42 (11 June 1966), 34.

Poem. Collected in *Poems 1957–1967*.

C 202

"The Sheep-Child," *Atlantic Monthly*, 218 (August 1966), 86.

Poem. Collected as "The Sheep Child" in *Poems 1957–1967*.

C 203

"The Flash," *Transatlantic Review*, no. 22 (Autumn 1966), 59.

Poem. Collected in *Poems 1957–1967*. See AA 1, C 216.

C 204

"Turning Away," *Hudson Review*, 19 (Autumn 1966), 361–368.

Poem. Collected in *Eye-Beaters*.

C 205

"Robert Frost, Man and Myth," *Atlantic Monthly*, 218 (November 1966), 53–56.

Essay and review of *Robert Frost: The Early Years* by Lawrance Thompson. Collected as "Robert Frost" in *Babel to Byzantium*.

C 206

"Wallace Stevens' Fine Letters," *Washington Sunday Star*, 13 November 1966, p. D3.

Review of *Letters of Wallace Stevens*, ed. Holly Stevens.

C 207

"What the Angels Missed," *New York Times Book Review*, 25 December 1966, pp. 1, 16.

Review of *Tell Me, Tell Me: Granite, Steel, and Other Topics* by Marianne Moore (see A 11).

C 208

"Sun," *New Yorker*, 42 (28 January 1967), 32.

Poem. Collected in *Poems 1957–1967.*

C 209

"Falling," *New Yorker,* 42 (11 February 1967), 38–40.

Poem. Collected in *Poems 1957–1967.*

C 210

"Snakebite," *New Yorker,* 43 (25 February 1967), 44.

Poem. Collected in *Poems 1957–1967.*

C 211

"Power and Light," *New Yorker,* 43 (11 March 1967), 60–61.

Poem. Collected in *Poems 1957–1967.*

C 212

"May Day Sermon to the Women of Gilmer County by a Lady Preacher Leaving the Baptist Church," *Atlantic Monthly,* 219 (April 1967), 90–97.

Poem. Collected as "May Day Sermon to the Women of Gilmer County, Georgia, by a Woman Preacher Leaving the Baptist Church" in *Poems 1957–1967.*

C 213

"Dark Ones," *Saturday Evening Post,* 240 (8 April 1967), 72.

Poem. Collected in *Poems 1957–1967.* See B 14.

C 214

"Of Mind and Soul," *New York Times Book Review,* 18 June 1967, pp. 10, 12.

Review of *Rubrics for a Revolution* by John L'Heureux and *Excursions: New and Selected Poems* by Katherine Hoskins (See A 11).

C 214a

"Computerized Rape and the Vale of Soul-Making," *University of South Carolina Magazine,* 4 (Winter 1968), 6–9.

Text of Dickey's 1968 University of South Carolina commencement address. Collected in *Night Hurdling.*

C 215

"Comments to Accompany *Poems: 1957–1967*," *Barat Review*, 3 (January 1968), 9–15.

Discussions of "Faces Seen Once," "At Darien Bridge," "Cherrylog Road," "Encounter in the Cage Country" (recycled in A 16—"*Falling*"), "Sun," "The Sheep Child" (recycled in A 16—"*Falling*"), "Adultery," and "Power and Light."

C 216

"James Dickey: Worksheets," *Malahat Review*, no. 7 (July 1968), 113–117.

Poem. Five successive versions of "The Flash." See AA 1, C 203.

C 217

"Victory," *Atlantic Monthly,* 222 (August 1968), 48–50.

Poem. Collected in *Eye-Beaters*.

C 218

"The Lord in the Air," *New Yorker*, 44 (19 October 1968), 56.

Poem. Collected in *Eye-Beaters*.

C 219

"The Eye-Beaters," *Harper's Magazine*, 237 (November 1968), 134–136.

Poem. Collected in *Eye-Beaters*.

C 220

"The Greatest American Poet," *Atlantic Monthly,* 222 (November 1968), 53–58.

Review of *The Glass House* by Allan Seager and memoir of Seager. Collected as "The Greatest American Poet: Theodore Roethke" in *Sorties*.

C 221

"A Poet Witnesses a Bold Mission," *Life,* 65 (1 November 1968), 26.

Essay. See B 31.

C 222

["For the First Manned Moon Orbit,"] *Life,* 66 (10 January 1969), 22a, 22c–22d.

Untitled poem. Collected as "For the First Manned Moon Orbit," the first part of "Apollo," in *Eye-Beaters*. See C 234.

C 223

"Knock," *New Yorker*, 44 (25 January 1969), 92.

Poem. Collected in *Eye-Beaters*. See AA 3.

C 224

"The Place," *New Yorker*, 45 (1 March 1969), 40.

Poem. Collected in *Eye-Beaters*.

C 225

"Madness," *New Yorker*, 45 (26 April 1969), 40.

Poem. Collected in *Eye-Beaters*. See B 19.

C 226

"Living There," *Harper's Magazine*, 238 (May 1969), 52–53.

Poem. Collected as the first part of "Two Poems of Going Home" in *Eye-Beaters*. See C 237.

C 227

"The Poet of Secret Lives and Misspent Opportunities," *New York Times Book Review*, 18 May 1969, pp. 1, 10.

Review of *Edwin Arlington Robinson: The Life of Poetry* by Louis O. Coxe. Collected as "Edwin Arlington Robinson" in *Sorties*.

C 228

"Blood," *Poetry*, 114 (June 1969), 149–150.

Poem. Collected in *Eye-Beaters*.

C 229

"Diabetes," *Poetry*, 114 (June 1969), 151–155.

Two-part poem containing "Sugar" and "Under Buzzards" (see C 131). Collected in *Eye-Beaters*.

C 230

"Venom," *Poetry,* 114 (June 1969), 156–157.

Poem. Collected in *Eye-Beaters.*

C 231

"The Cancer Match," *Poetry,* 114 (June 1969), 158–159.

Poem. Collected in *Eye-Beaters.*

C 232

"Pine: Taste, Touch and Sight," *Poetry,* 114 (June 1969), 160–162.

Poem. Collected as third, fourth, and fifth parts of "Pine" in *Eye-Beaters.* See C 233.

C 233

"Pine," *New Yorker,* 45 (28 June 1969), 89.

Two-part poem containing "Sound" and "Smell." Collected without titles as first and second parts of "Pine" in *Eye-Beaters.* See C 232.

C 234

"The Moon Ground," *Life,* 67 (4 July 1969), 16c.

Poem. Collected as second part of "Apollo" in *Eye-Beaters.* See C 222.

C 235

"Messages," *New Yorker,* 45 (2 August 1969), 30.

Two-part poem containing "Butterflies" and "Giving a Son to the Sea." Collected in *Eye-Beaters.*

C 236

Statement on arts in Atlanta, *DeKalb Literary Arts Journal,* 4 (Fall 1969), v.

C 237

"Looking for the Buckhead Boys," *Atlantic Monthly,* 224(October 1969), 53–56.

Poem. Collected as the second part of "Two Poems of Going Home" in *Eye-Beaters.* See C 226.

C 238

"Root-light, or the Lawyer's Daughter," *New Yorker,* 45 (8 November 1969), 52.

Poem. Collected in *Strength of Fields.*

C 239

"Drums Where I Live," *New Yorker,* 45 (29 November 1969), 56.

Poem. Collected as the second part of "Two Poems of the Military" in *Strength of Fields.* See C 241.

C 240

"At Mercy Manor," *Atlantic Monthly,* 224 (December 1969), 75–76.

Poem. Collected as "Mercy" in *Eye-Beaters.*

C 241

"Haunting the Maneuvers," *Harper's Magazine,* 240 (January 1970), 95.

Poem. Collected as the first part of "Two Poems of the Military" in *Strength of Fields.* See B 25, C 239.

C 242

"Two Days in September," *Atlantic Monthly,* 225 *(February 1970),* 78–108.

Prepublication excerpt from *Deliverance.*

C 243

Irene Stokvis Land, ed., "First Novelists," *Library Journal,* 95 (1 February 1970), 516–522.

Statements by thirty-four first novelists; statement by Dickey, p. 517.

C 244

"Camden Town," *Virginia Quarterly Review,* 46 (Spring 1970), 242–243.

Poem. Collected as the first part of "Two Poems of Flight-Sleep" in *Strength of Fields.* See C 260.

C 245

Excerpts from *Deliverance, Literary Guild Magazine,* April 1970, pp. [2]–5.

Probably precedes book publication.

C 246

"James Dickey Tells About *Deliverance*," *Literary Guild Magazine*, April 1970, pp. 6–7.

Essay.

C 247

"The Process of Writing a Novel," *Writer*, 83 (June 1970), 12–13.

Excerpt from a speech given at a March 1970 session of the National Book Awards. Speech quoted in Edwin Tribble, "National Book Awards as a Time for Stocktaking," *Washington Sunday Star*, 8 March 1970, p. F7; Martha Mac-Gregor, "The Week in Books," *New York Post*, 21 March 1970, p. 37; "NBA Week: A Little Heat, A Little Light," *Publishers Weekly*, 197 (23 March 1970), 24–29.

C 248

"Exchanges," *Harvard Bulletin*, 72 (6 July 1970), 36–39.

Poem. Reprinted in *Atlantic Monthly*, 226 (September 1970), 63–67. Collected in *Exchanges; Strength of Fields*.

C 249

"The Poet Tries to Make a Kind of Order: A 'Self-Interview' with James Dickey," *Mademoiselle*, 71 (September 1970), 142–143, 209–210, 212.

Prepublication excerpt from the "*Falling*" section of *Self-Interviews*.

C 250

"The High Cost of Fame: Reflections on the Bitch-Goddess by Nine Authors Who Have Scored with Her," *Playboy*, 18 (January 1971), 123–127.

Statement by Dickey, p. 124.

C 251

"Listening to America," *New York Times Book Review*, 14 March 1971, pp. 2, 37.

Review of *Listening to America: A Traveler Rediscovers His Country* by Bill Moyers.

C 252

"Female Sexuality, What It Is—And Isn't. Answers From . . . ," *Mademoiselle,* 73 (July 1971), 108–117.

Brief essays by twelve writers; essay by Dickey, p. 108. Collected as "Complicity" in *Night Hurdling.*

C 253

"For the Death of Vince Lombardi," *Esquire,* 76 (September 1971), 142.

Poem. Collected as "For the Death of Lombardi" in *Strength of Fields.* See B 26.

C 254

"Kamikaze" in "Four New Poems by Yevgeny Yevtushenko," *Playboy,* 18 (October 1971), 152.

Dickey adaptation of Yevtushenko poem. See B 27.

C 255

"False Youth: Autumn: Clothes of the Age," *Atlantic,* 228 (November 1971), 67.

Poem. Collected in *Strength of Fields; False Youth: Four Seasons.* See B 33.

C 256

"The Rain Guitar," *New Yorker,* 47 (8 January 1972), 36.

Poem. Collected in *Strength of Fields.*

C 257

"There in Body and Spirit, but Not in Imagination," *New York Times Book Review,* 6 February 1972, pp. 7, 22.

Review of *The Donner Party* by George Keithley.

C 258

Review of *In the Terrified Radiance* by Stanley Burnshaw, *New York Times Book Review,* 24 September 1972, p. 4.

C 259

"James Dickey on the Journals and Diaries of W.N.P. Barbellion (Bruce Cummings)," *Mademoiselle,* 76 (January 1973), 133–134.

Essay. Collected as "Imagination and Pain" in *Night Hurdling*.

C 260

"Reunioning Dialogue," *Atlantic Monthly*, 231 (January 1973), 46–49.

Poem. Collected as the second part of "Two Poems of Flight-Sleep" in *Strength of Fields*. See C 244.

C 261

"Remnant Water," *New Yorker*, 49 (10 March 1973), 36.

Poem. Collected in *Strength of Fields*.

C 262

Michael Dempsy, "*Deliverance* | Boorman: Dickey in the Woods," *Cinema*, 8 (Spring 1973), 10–17.

Article; quotes briefly from Dickey's *Deliverance* screenplay.

C 263

"A Look into Your Future . . . Life Style," *Today's Health*, 51 (April 1973), 54, 65.

Essay.

C 264

"Camping," *New York Times Book Review*, 10 June 1973, pp. 6, 22.

Essay. Collected as "The Grass Mountain Kid: Family Camping Exposed" in *Night Hurdling*.

C 265

"Delights of the Edge," *Mademoiselle*, 79 (June 1974), 118–119.

Essay. Collected in *Night Hurdling*.

C 266

"Blowjob on a Rattlesnake," *Esquire*, 82 (October 1974), 177–178, 368.

Essay. Collected as "The Enemy from Eden" in *Enemy from Eden; Night Hurdling*.

C 267

"Jericho The South Beheld," *Southern Living,* 9 (October 1974), 1A–16A.

Prepublication excerpts and paintings from *Jericho.*

C 268

"Small Visions from a Timeless Place," *Playboy,* 21 (October 1974), 152–154, 220–221.

Prepublication excerpts from *Jericho.*

C 269

"What's Right with America," *Ladies Home Journal,* 92 (October 1975), 68–69.

Statements by Dickey and others.

C 270

Review of *Memoirs and Opinions 1926–1974* by Allen Tate, *New Republic,* 173 (4 October 1975), 22–24. See C 280.

C 271

"Cahill Is Blind," *Esquire,* 85 (February 1976), 67–69, 139–144, 146.

Prepublication excerpt from *Alnilam.*

C 272

Ralph Tyler, "Literary Figures Offer Plots and Quips," *New York Times,* 1 August 1976, D1, D13, D16.

Statements by Dickey and others on possible plots for sequel to *Gone With the Wind* by Margaret Mitchell.

C 273

"James Dickey's Glory," *Esquire,* 86 (October 1976), 81.

Essay. Collected as "Night Hurdling" in *Night Hurdling.* See B 45.

C 274

"Seeds of Man," *New York Times Book Review,* 3 October 1976, pp. 2–3.

Review of *Seeds of Man: An Experience Lived and Dreamed* by Woody Guthrie.

C 275

"Authors' Authors," *New York Times Book Review,* 5 December 1976, pp. 4, 102–105.

Statements by Dickey and others about books they liked that year. Dickey chose *Dreamthorp* by Alexander Smith, *The O'Hara Concern* by Matthew J. Bruccoli, and *A Prince of Our Disorder* by John E. Mack.

C 276

"The Strength of Fields," *Washington Post Special Supplement—The Carter Presidency,* 20 January 1977, p. 3.

Inaugural poem. Also noted in *New York Times,* 21 January 1977, p. B6. Reprinted in *Strength of Fields* (poem). Collected in *Strength of Fields* (collection). See AA 11, B 41.

C 277

"Poet James Dickey on Carter and the Born-Again South," *U.S. News and World Report,* 82 (18 April 1977), 67.

Essay.

C 278

"Frantic to Overtake Himself," *New York Times Book Review,* 18 September 1977, pp. 7, 44.

Review of *Jack: A Biography of Jack London* by Andrew Sinclair.

C 279

"God's Images," *Southern Living,* 12 (October 1977), 113–120.

Prepublication excerpts and etchings from *God's Images.*

C 280

"A Man Deeply Rooted in His Culture," *The State* [Columbia, S.C.], 11 December 1977, p. E4.

Dickey's remarks on Allen Tate drawn from a conversation with William W. Starr and Dickey's review of Tate's *Memoirs and Opinions 1926–1974* (see C 270).

C 281

Facsimile of questionnaire with comment and signature by Dickey, *Poets on Stage* (New York: SOME, 1978), p. 101.

On copyright page: '*Poets on Stage* is a special issue of *SOME* magazine. . . .'

Published in cloth (200 copies) and in wrappers (800 copies).

C 282

"Books Southerners Recommend," *Southern Living,* 13 (January 1978), 158–159.

Dickey recommends *Permanent Errors* by Reynolds Price, *Lancelot* by Walker Percy, and *Collected Stories* by Peter Taylor.

C 283

"James Dickey Chooses His Favorite Poetry Books," *Bookviews,* 1 (February 1978), 18–19.

Dickey discusses these poetry collections: *The New Oxford Book of English Verse,* ed. Helen Gardner; *The New Oxford Book of American Verse,* ed. Richard Ellmann; *Complete Poems* by Randall Jarrell; *Collected Poems: 1919–1976* by Allen Tate; *Selected Poems, 1923–1975* by Robert Penn Warren; *Notebook* by Robert Lowell; *In Mediterranean Air* by Ann Stanford; *Weather of Six Mornings* by Jane Cooper; *Gates* by Muriel Rukeyser; *Collected Poems* by Howard Nemerov; *Poems* by R. P. Blackmur; and *Collected Poems* by James Wright.

C 284

"Pursuing the Grey Soul," *Weekend Magazine,* 28 (30 June 1978), 20–21.

Essay. Collected as "In Pursuit of the Grey Soul" in *In Pursuit of the Grey Soul* and as "A Hand-Line: In Pursuit of the Grey Soul" in *Night Hurdling.*

C 285

"Compassionate Classicist," *New York Times Book Review,* 10 December 1978, pp. 14, 56–57.

Review of *This Blessed Earth* and *Afternoon: Amagansett Beach* by John Hall Wheelock.

C 286

"Water-Magic in Sunlight: The Voyage of the Needle," *GQ: Gentleman's Quarterly,* 48 (Winter 1978–1979), 146.

Poem. Collected as "The Voyage of the Needle" in *Strength of Fields.*

C 287

"The Energized Man," *Billy Goat,* 2 (1979), 1–3.

Essay. See B 71.

C 288

"Introductory Remarks to a Reading: Eighth Annual Walt Whitman Festival, Camden, New Jersey, 4 May 1977," *Mickle Street Review,* no. 1 (1979), 3–6.

Speech.

C 289

"Far-Out Sounds," *Next,* Preview Issue (1979), 110–111.

Article including lists by Dickey and eight others of music they would send into space for the edification of extraterrestrials. Dickey chose *Water Music Suite,* George Frederic Handel; "Royal Garden Blues," as played by Bix Beiderbecke; Overture to *Rienzi,* Richard Wagner; *Concerto for Orchestra,* Bela Bartok; "Duellin' Banjos," as recorded by Eric Weissberg and Steve Mandel; *Horn Concerto in D Major,* Wolfgang Amadeus Mozart; and "Ragtime Annie," as recorded by Doc and Merle Watson.

C 290

"Selling His Soul to the Devil by Day . . . and Buying It Back by Night," *TV Guide,* 27 (14 July 1979), 18–20.

Essay.

C 291

"Works in Progress," *New York Times Book Review,* 15 July 1979, pp. 1, 14–16, 20.

Includes statement by Dickey on *Alnilam,* p. 15.

C 292

William Meredith, "Consultants' Choice: Books of Verse Selected by Eight Former Poetry Consultants and the Present Consultant," *Quarterly Journal of the Library of Congress,* 36 (Fall 1979), 377–384.

Includes Dickey's statement on *Collected Poems* by Murial Rukeyser, p. 382.

C 293

"The Geek of Poetry," *New York Times Book Review*, 23 December 1979, pp. 9, 17–18.

Review of *Letters of Vachel Lindsay*, ed. Marc Chenetier. Collected in *Night Hurdling*.

C 294

"Is Regional Writing Dead? Nine Authors and Editors Reply," *The Student* [Wake Forest University], Spring 1980, pp. 29–36.

Responses to questionnaire; statement by Dickey, p. 32.

C 295

"Purgation," *Kenyon Review*, n.s. 2 (Spring 1980), 28–29.

A substantially revised version of the poem that first appeared in *Head-Deep* and was subsequently collected in *Strength of Fields*. The revised version is collected in *Night Hurdling*.

C 296

"The Surround," *Atlantic Monthly*, 246 (July 1980), 58.

Poem. Collected in *Puella*.

C 297

"Robert Penn Warren's Courage," *Saturday Review*, 7 (August 1980), 56–57.

Review of *Being Here: Poetry 1977–1980* by Warren. Collected as "The Weathered Hand and Silent Space" in *Night Hurdling*.

C 298

"The Eagle's Mile," *Hastings Constitutional Law Quarterly*, 8 (Fall 1980), 1–3.

Poem. Collected in *Night Hurdling*. See AA 9.

C 299

"Poets Laureate," *Time*, 116 (6 October 1980), 9.

Letter.

C 300

"Open Letter to the Open World About Verlin Cassill," *December: A Magazine of the Arts and Opinion,* 23, nos. 1/2 (1981), 143–144.

Prose tribute to R. V. Cassill.

C 301

"Five Poems from *Puella,*" *Poetry,* 137 (March 1981), 313–320.

"Deborah Burning a Doll Made of House-Wood," "Deborah, Moon, Mirror, Right Hand Rising," "Veer-Voices: Two Sisters Under Crows," "Heraldic: Deborah and Horse in Morning Forest," and "Springhouse, Menses, Held Apple, House and Beyond."

C 302

"The Lyric Beasts," *Paris Review,* 23 (Spring 1981), [165–166].

Poem. Collected in *Puella.*

C 303

"Why I Live Where I Live," *Esquire,* 95 (April 1981), 62–64.

Essay. Collected as "The Starry Place Between the Antlers" in *The Starry Place Between the Antlers; Night Hurdling.*

C 304

"Seductive Summer Nights (Excellently Bright, or Shell Roads)," *Harper's Bazaar,* no. 3235 (June 1981), 81–82.

Essay. Collected as "Excellently Bright, or Shell Roads" in *Night Hurdling.*

C 305

"Tapestry and Sail," *Lone Star Review,* 3 (July/August 1981), 4.

Poem. Collected in *Puella.*

C 306

"Backward to Byzantium—and Babel: Afterword to the New Ecco Edition," *Antaeus,* no. 43 (Autumn 1981), 125–129.

Essay. Collected as "Afterword to *Babel to Byzantium*" in *Night Hurdling.* See A 11.1.e.

C 307

Janet Larsen McHughes, "From Manuscript to Performance Script: The Evolution of a Poem," *Literature in Performance*, 2 (November 1981), 26–49.

Article; facsimiles Dickey's drafts of "Sleeping Out at Easter," prints excerpts from performance scripts and Cheryl Ness Genette's score for McHughes's musical adaptation of the poem, quotes from McHughes's previously unpublished conversation with Dickey, and contains an afterword by Dickey.

C 308

"Six Poems," *Kenyon Review,* n.s. 4 (Winter 1982), 1–8.

"Deborah in Mountain Sound: Bell, Glacier, Rose," "Ray-Flowers I," "Ray-Flowers II," "Doorstep, Lightning, Waif-Dreaming," "Deborah in Ancient Lingerie, in Thin Oak Over Creek," and "The Lode." Collected in *Puella.*

C 309

"How to Enjoy Poetry," published as an advertisement by the International Paper Company (February 1982) and noted in the following magazines and newspapers: *New York Times Science Times, Newsweek, People, Psychology Today, Scholastic Magazine, Time* (student edition).

C 310

"Deborah and Dierdre as Drunk Bridesmaids Foot-Racing at Daybreak," *Graham House Review,* No. 6 (Spring 1982), 5–6.

Poem. Collected in *Puella.*

C 311

"Summons," *Graham House Review,* no. 6 (Spring 1982), 7–8.

Poem. Collected in *Puella.* See A 46.

C 312

"Why Men Drive," *Playboy Guide: Electronic Equipment,* Spring/Summer 1982, pp. 59–62.

Essay. Collected as "Body, Backstretch, and the Outside Man" in *Night Hurdling.*

C 313

"False Youth: Spring: The Olympian," *Amicus Journal,* 4 (Summer 1982), 27.

Poem. Collected in *False Youth: Four Seasons*.

C314

Lee Bartlett and Hugh Witemeyer, "Ezra Pound and James Dickey: A Correspondence and a Kinship," *Paideuma*, 11 (Fall 1982), 290–312.

Article; prints letters between Pound and Dickey.

C315

"Sand," *Clockwatch Review*, 2, no. 1 (1983), 15.

Poem.

C316

"Crystal," *Clockwatch Review*, 2, no. 1 (1983), 16.

Poem.

C317

"For Richard Hugo," *Corona*, 3 (1983), 16–17.

Prose tribute.

C318

"Dear Mr. Chernofsky," *AB Bookman's Weekly*, 71 (17 January 1983), 358.

Letter.

C319

"Points to Ponder," *Reader's Digest*, 122 (March 1983), 33.

Statement by Dickey quoted from *The Sunday Show* with Connie Goldman, National Public Radio.

C320

"The Poetics of Dress," *Esquire*, 99 (March 1983), 100–103.

Essay.

C321

"James Dickey with Others: Five Poems," *American Poetry Review*, 12 (March/April 1983), 3–4.

Three of these poems—"Heads" (with Lucien Becker), "Attempted Departure" (with André du Bouchet), and "Lakes of Värmland" (with André Frénaud)— are reprinted from *Värmland*. "Farmers" (with André Frénaud), and "Craters" (with Michel Leiris) are collected in *Night Hurdling*.

C 322

"The G.I. Can of Beets, the Fox in the Wave, and the Hammers Over Open Ground," *South Atlantic Review*, 48 (May 1983), 1–16.

Essay (originally speech delivered at the 1982 South Atlantic Modern Language Association meeting). Collected in *Night Hurdling*.

C 323

"Truman Capote, 1924–1984," *Proceedings of the American Academy and Institute of Arts and Letters*, ser. 2, no. 35 (1984), 69–75.

Essay and poem—"To Be Done in Winter by Those Surviving Truman Capote." Both reprinted with new introductory comments by Dickey in "Proceedings: Truman Capote," *Paris Review*, 97 (Fall 1985), 184–190. See B 73.

C 324

"Blind Snow, Warm Water," *Partisan Review*, 51 (50th-Anniversary Issue, 1984), 526–528.

Prepublication excerpt from *Alnilam*.

C 325

Dannye Romine, "Words to Remember: How Mothers Influenced 6 Budding Writers," *Charlotte Observer*, 13 May 1984, p. F10.

Statements by Dickey and five other writers.

C 326

"On the Flight of an Arrow," *Goodlife*, June/July 1984, p. 68.

Essay.

C 327

Tom Jenks, "In the Works," *Esquire*, 102 (August 1984), 113–116.

Statements from 53 writers, including Dickey, p. 114.

C 328

"The Casual Brilliance of Stephen Crane," *Washington Post Book World,* 19 August 1984, pp. 1, 9.

Review of *Stephen Crane: Prose and Poetry,* ed. J. C. Levenson.

C 329

Michiko Kakutani, "Some Thoughts on Capote," *New York Times,* 26 August 1984, sec. 1, p. 42.

Statements by William Shawn, John Knowles, George Plimpton, and Dickey.

C 330

"Peter Davison's Unblinking Eye," *Boston Globe,* 30 December 1984, pp. 1, 14.

Review of *Praying Wrong: New and Selected Poems, 1957–1984* by Davison.

C 331

"Air," *Verse* [The Citadel, Charleston, S.C.], 2nd issue (1985), 3.

Poem.

C 332

"The Nightmare Cat of Paradise," *New York Times Book Review,* 27 January 1985, p. 16.

Review of *Cry of the Panther: Quest of a Species* by James P. McMullen.

C 333

"Cobra," *New York Quarterly,* no. 27 (Summer 1985), 26.

Poem.

C 334

"Cosmic Deliverance," *Halley's Comet* (Commemorative Issue), 1986, pp. 8–9.

Essay.

C 335

"The Worlds of a Cosmic Castaway," *New York Times Book Review,* 2 February 1986, p. 8.

Review of *Collected Poems 1948–1984* by Derek Walcott.

C 336

"Spring-Shock," *Paris Review,* 100 (Summer/Fall 1986), 66–67.

Poem.

C 337

R. H. [Rust Hills], "Don't Everybody Talk at Once," *Esquire,* 106 (August 1986), 99–100, 102–104.

Survey of writers; Dickey statements passim.

C 338

Review of *The Wolfpen Poems* by James Still, *Los Angeles Times Book Review,* 7 December 1986, pp. 1, 16.

C 339

"From the Low Country: Five Poems by James Dickey," *Southern Magazine,* 1 (January 1987), 47–49.

"Two Women," "Daybreak," "Vessels," "Wetlands Bridge," and "Tomb Stone."

C 340

"Eagles," *American Poetry Review,* 16 (March/April 1987), 56.

Poem.

C 341

"Broomstraws," *Helicon Nine,* no. 17/18 (Spring 1987), 112–134.

Prepublication excerpt from *Alnilam.*

C 342

"The Captains," *Esquire,* 107 (April 1987), 176–178, 181–[182], [185]–186.

Prepublication excerpt from *Alnilam.*

C 342a

"The Poet Speaks," *Portfolio* [University of South Carolina], 7 (Summer 1987), 23.

Letter.

C 343

"Treasured Places," *Life*, 10 (July 1987), 35–42, 44.

Essays by Colin Fletcher, Galen Rowell, Edward Abbey, Barry Lopez, Tom Robbins, Edward Hoagland, Peter Matthiessen, and Dickey, p. 42.

C 344

"The Little More," *Poetry*, 150 (July 1987), 208–210.

Poem.

C 345

Gordon Van Ness, " 'When Memory Stands Without Sleep': James Dickey's War Years," *James Dickey Newsletter*, 4 (Fall 1987), 2–13.

Article; quotes from unpublished letters by Dickey, from unpublished TS "History of the 418th NFS" by Dickey, and from unpublished interview with Dickey by Van Ness.

C 346

"James Dickey: Ten Poems," *American Poetry Review*, 17 (March/April 1988), 36–38.

"Weeds," "The One," "The Three," "Basics" ("Level" and "Simplex"), "Night Bird," "Sleepers," "Snow Thickets," "Sea," "Expanses," and "Moon Flock."

C 347

William W. Starr, "James Dickey Speaks in Yet Another Voice," *The State*, 17 April 1988, p. F5.

Prepublication excerpts from *Wayfarer: A Voice from the Southern Mountains*.

C 348

"Daughter." *Southpoint*, 1 (November 1989), 88.

Poem.

D. First Appearances in Journals and Newspapers of Interviews and Articles Quoting Dickey

First publication in journals and newspapers of interviews and articles including *previously unpublished* quotations from Dickey, arranged chronologically.

This section is necessarily incomplete. Since the mid-1960s, Dickey has made many public appearances, during which he has granted hundreds of interviews and has been the subject of hundreds of articles quoting him. Moreover, as one of the most prominent writers in the United States, he has responded to requests for statements on a wide range of subjects. Every effort has been made to record these journal and newspaper appearances, but no doubt many of them remain undiscovered.

Newspaper and journal reports quoting from Dickey's public addresses (for example, his 1966 National Book Award speech) are not listed in Section D, but are instead noted in the entries for the first substantial publication of the addresses (either Section A or Section C). Journal titles, newspaper headlines, and newspaper section/page designations have been styled.

D 1

Betsy Hopkins Lochridge, "Literary Scene: Writers Differ on Prospects for '60s," *Atlanta Journal and Constitution,* 27 December 1959, p. E2.

Article; quotes Dickey.

D 2

Betsy Fancher, "Editor's Shelf: Poet Must Be Tough, Fanatical," *Atlanta Journal and Constitution,* 18 September 1960, p. E2.

Interview.

D 3

Dee Dee Carpenter, "Poet Dickey Wins Audiences' Praise," *Western Round-Up* [Western College, Oxford, Ohio], 6 December 1962.

Article; quotes Dickey.

D 4

Frank Daniel, "Successful Atlanta Poet Turns to the Novel," *Atlanta Journal and Constitution,* 30 August 1964, p. C1.

Interview.

D 5

Lawrence Lock, "James Dickey Stresses Value of Detail in Poetry," *Milwaukee Sentinel,* 19 July 1965, p. 14.

Article; quotes Dickey.

D 6

"Poet Dickey to Speak at Coffee Hour," *Campus Times* [University of Rochester], 9 November 1965, p. 3.

303

Article; quotes Dickey.

D7

"An Interview with James Dickey," *Eclipse* [San Fernando Valley State College], no. 5 (1965–1966), 5–20.

Collected in *The Voiced Connections of James Dickey*.

D8

"Leaves in February: Resident Poet Dickey to Teach at Wisconsin," [*San Fernando*] *Valley State Daily Sundial,* 14 January 1966, p. 3.

Interview.

D9

Loren Loverde and Betsy Edelson, "An Interview with James Dickey," *Quixote,* 1 (March 1966), 64–67.

D10

Robert Cromie, "Meet James Dickey, a King-Sized Poet," *Chicago Tribune,* 15 March 1966, sec. 2, p. 2.

Interview.

D11

Leslie Cross, "Wisconsin's and America's Poet of the Year, James Dickey, Talks of His Life and Craft," *Milwaukee Journal,* 20 March 1966, sec. 5, p. 4.

Interview.

D12

"Poet Urges Aspiring Writers 'To Be Daring, Go for Broke,' " *Racine Journal-Times,* 22 March 1966, p. A5.

Interview.

D13

"1966 NBA Awards Ceremonies at Philharmonic Hall," *Publishers Weekly,* 189 (28 March 1966), 28–39.

Article; quotes from a Dickey interview, p. 34.

D 14

"James Dickey Writer-in-Residence Wins National Book Award," *Wisconsin Alumnus*, 67 (April 1966), 8.

Article; quotes Dickey.

D 15

Carey Roberts, "How James Dickey Views Poetry," *Atlanta Journal and Constitution Magazine*, 17 April 1966, pp. 16, 18.

Interview.

D 16

Paul O'Neil, "The Unlikeliest Poet," *Life*, 61 (22 July 1966), 68–70, 72–74, 77–79.

Article; quotes Dickey. See B 15.

D 17

"Behind the Scenes in McLean," *The McLean [Va.] Scene*, 3 (September 1966), 9.

Article; quotes Dickey.

D 18

Leroy F. Aarons, "New Library Consultant: Ex-Adman Dickey: Don't Just Work for Oblivion," *Washington Post,* 10 September 1966, p. D6.

Interview.

D 19

Nan Robertson, "New National Poetry Consultant Can Also Talk a Nonstop Prose: James Dickey Speaks on Art, Life and LSD to Press at Library of Congress," *New York Times,* 10 September 1966, p. 11.

Interview.

D 20

David Holmberg, "New Poetry Consultant Is a Man of Action," *Washington Daily News,* 10 September 1966, p. 6.

Interview.

D21

Kenneth Ikenberry, "Library 'Missionary': Poet to Spread Word on Joys of Culture," *Washington Sunday Star,* 11 September 1966, p. D21.

Interview.

D22

"The New Nostalgia," *St. Louis Post-Dispatch,* 13 September 1966, p. C2.

Brief editorial; quotes Dickey.

D23

"For Poetry," *Newark Evening News,* 17 September 1966, p. 4.

Brief editorial; quotes Dickey.

D24

Carolyn Kizer and James Boatwright, "A Conversation with James Dickey," *Shenandoah,* 18 (Autumn 1966), 3–28.

Interview. Collected as "In Virginia" in *Night Hurdling.* See B 32.

D25

James R. Dickenson, " 'Yevtushenko Is Many Things to Many People,' " *National Observer,* 5 (28 November 1966), 5.

Article; quotes Dickey.

D26

"Things Happen: An Interview with Dickey," *Wisconsin Review,* 2 (December 1966), 2, 4–6.

Collected in *The Voiced Connections of James Dickey.*

D27

Ann Bradley, "Poet Says Getting Married Best Thing in His Life," *Washington Sunday Star,* 19 February 1967, p. H2.

Interview.

D28

"Dickey a Delight," *The Statesman* [State University of New York—Stony Brook], 22 February 1967, p. 6.

Article; quotes Dickey.

D 29

Phil Casey, " 'Dazzlingly Simple' Poetry Is Predicted for the Future," *Washington Post,* 25 April 1967, p. A9.

Article; quotes Dickey.

D 30

Milton Berliner, "Poetry for People: Obscure and Confessional Poetry on Way Out, Says Consultant," *Washington Daily News,* 26 April 1967, p. 63.

Article; quotes Dickey.

D 31

Carol Shumate, "Literary Critic Calls Quality of Poet Rare," *The Skiff* [Texas Christian University], 16 May 1967, p. 1.

Article; quotes Dickey.

D 32

Gary Ormond Cohen, "The Poet," *Vanderbilt Alumnus,* 53 (September–October 1967), 14, 16–17.

Article; quotes Dickey.

D 33

Jean G. Lawlor, "The Poetry," *Vanderbilt Alumnus,* 53 (September–October 1967), 15, 18–19.

Article; quotes Dickey.

D 34

Bruce Pennington and Robert B. Shaw, "Silhouette: James Dickey," *Harvard Crimson,* 9 November 1967, p. 2.

Interview.

D 35

Nancy Malone, "Poet with Power: James Dickey," *Read,* 17 (15 November 1967), 10–12.

Interview. Collected in *The Voiced Connections of James Dickey.*

D 36

Olivia Skinner, "A Muscular Exponent of Poetry: James Dickey, Former Football Player, Reads His Verse in Appearance Here," *St. Louis Post-Dispatch,* 15 November 1967, p. F2.

Interview.

D 37

"Poet Built Like A Rugby Forward," *New Zealand Herald* [Auckland], 11 March 1968.

Article; quotes Dickey.

D 38

John Dorsey, "Overfilling the Image of a Poet," *Baltimore Sun,* 17 March 1968, pp. D1, D3.

Interview.

D 39

Francis Roberts, "James Dickey: An Interview," *Per/Se* [Stanford, Calif.], 3 (Spring 1968), 8–12.

Collected in *The Voiced Connections of James Dickey.*

D 40

Carol Buck, "The 'Poetry-Thing' with James Dickey," *Poetry Australia,* 21 (April 1968), 4–6.

Interview.

D 41

Suzanne Hardy, "Poet James Dickey to Speak at USC," *The State and Columbia Record* [Columbia, S.C.], 19 May 1968, p. A13.

Article; quotes Dickey.

D 42

"Poet Dickey Will Speak at USC Commencement," *Florence [S.C.] Morning News,* 19 May 1968.

Article; quotes Dickey. Edited and retitled versions of this article have also been noted in the *Greenville [S.C.] News,* 19 May 1968, and in the *Loudoun Times-Mirror* [Leesville, Va.], 30 May 1968.

D43

Thomas P. Mayer, "Largest USC Commencement Class Told 'See More . . . Respond More,' " *Columbia [S.C.] Record,* 1 June 1968, pp. A1, A2.

Article; quotes Dickey.

D44

Jay A. Gross, "Graduates Hear Poet on 'New Awareness,' " *The State and Columbia Record,* 2 June 1968, p. B1.

Article; quotes Dickey.

D45

Suzanne Hardy, "James Dickey and Family Come to Carolina," *The State and Columbia Record,* 2 June 1968, p. E3.

Article; quotes Dickey.

D46

H. C. Neal, "Versatile Georgia Poet to Lecture at Convention," *Oklahoma City Daily Oklahoman,* 18 June 1968, p. N1.

Interview.

D47

Reba Collins, "Dickey to Speak at Convention: Pickin', Singin', Writer Leads Colorful Life," *The Vistette* [Central State College, Edmond, Okla.], 20 June 1968, p. 1.

Interview.

D48

"The University of Colorado Writers' Conference," *University of Colorado Bulletin,* 68 (26 June 1968), 2.

Article; quotes Dickey.

D49

Steve Brawer, "The How and Why of Writing: Workshop Instructors Talk About Creativity: James Dickey," *Colorado Daily* [University of Colorado, Boulder], 2 August 1968, pp. 1, 2, 4.

Interview.

D 50

Entry canceled.

D 51

Eddie Chin, " 'Successor' to Frost Joins English Faculty," *The Gamecock* [University of South Carolina], 27 September 1968, p. 5

Article; quotes Dickey.

D 52

Ann Carter, "At Tech Seminar: Poet Dickey Reads Some of His Works," *Atlanta Journal,* 9 October 1968, p. B3.

Article; quotes Dickey.

D 53

Barbara Joye, "Tech Poet," *The Great Speckled Bird* [Atlanta], 1 (14 October 1968), 12.

Article; quotes Dickey.

D 54

Reg Murphy, "The Biggest Man in Campus Rhyme," *Atlanta Constitution,* 2 November 1968, p. 4.

Article; quotes Dickey.

D 55

Robert McHugh, "All Things Considered: USC Poet James Dickey Deposes Old Word Gods," *Columbia Record,* 30 November 1968, pp. C1, C3.

Interview.

D 56

"The Poet as Journalist," *Time,* 92 (13 December 1968), 75.

Interview.

D 57

Alice Youmans, "ODK Backs 'Student Power' at Province Conference Here," *The Gamecock,* 4 March 1969, p. 1.

Article; quotes Dickey.

D58

John Pennington, " 'Such a Homecoming,' " *Atlanta Journal,* 1 April 1969, p. A12.

Article; quotes Dickey.

D59

John Pennington, "The Great Walk: What Frail Prose Can Soar So High?" *Atlanta Journal,* 18 July 1969, p. A4.

Article; quotes Dickey.

D60

Lee Simowitz, "Dickey Tires of 'That' Label: Speaking as Poet Who's In He Deplores U.S. Thing," *Atlanta Constitution,* 7 April 1969, p. 6.

Interview.

D61

" 'I Like Quite a Lot of Bad Poetry.' Druid Interviews: James Dickey," *Druid* [London], Fall 1969, pp. 4–10.

D62

"Atlanta Poet's Day: Dickey to Speak at DeKalb," *Atlanta Journal and Constitution,* 9 November 1969, p. D17.

Article; quotes Dickey.

D63

Harry S. Pease, "Cheers Hail Apollo Trio," *Milwaukee Journal,* 9 November 1969, sec. 1, pp. 1, 18.

Article; quotes Dickey.

D64

Dorothy Nix, "Poet Dickey Sees Survival as Central," *Atlanta Journal,* 19 November 1969, p. E18.

Interview.

D 65

Mary Hollingsworth, "Four Writers at DeKalb," *DeKalb Literary Arts Journal,* 4, no. 4 (1970), 40–45, 47.

Article; quotes Dickey.

D 66

Sam Hopkins and Richard Miles, "A New Decade: Problems, Hopes and Plans," *Atlanta Journal and Constitution,* 1 January 1970, pp. A1, A18.

Article; quotes Dickey.

D 67

Thomas Humber, "Well-Known Poet Publishes Novel," *Atlanta,* 9 (March 1970), 66.

Review of *Deliverance;* quotes Dickey.

D 68

Katharine Davis Fishman, "When the Book People Honor Their Own," *New York Times Book Review,* 1 March 1970, pp. 8, 36–38.

Article; quotes Dickey.

D 69

Henry Raymont, "Technology Is Called a Threat to Man," *New York Times,* 4 March 1970, p. 41.

Article; quotes Dickey.

D 70

Keith Coulbourn, "James Dickey: The Poetic Gadfly," *Atlanta Journal and Constitution Magazine,* 15 March 1970, pp. 6–7, 38–41, 43.

Interview.

D 71

Jo Woestendiek, "It's Difficult for a Poet to Write a Novel," *Houston Chronicle Zest,* 15 March 1970, p. 34.

Interview.

D72

"Poet Dickey Autographs First Novel for McNair," *Columbia Record,* 18 March 1970, p. B1.

Article; quotes Dickey. Syndicated by AP.

D73

"Poet Pleads for South Carolina River," *Washington Post,* 19 March 1970, p. C6.

Article; quotes Dickey. Syndicated by AP. Also noted under various titles in *Charleston [S.C.] News and Courier,* 18 March 1970; *Greenville News,* 18 March 1970; *Charlotte Observer,* 18 March 1970; *Johnson City [Tenn.] Press-Chronicle,* 19 March 1970.

D74

William McPherson, "Most Serious Kind of Game," *Washington Post,* 21 March 1970, p. C10.

Review of *Deliverance;* quotes Dickey. Also noted in *Columbia Record,* 28 March 1970.

D75

"First Dickey Novel May Be Best Seller," *Charleston [S.C.] Evening Post,* 21 March 1970, p. B1.

Article; quotes Dickey. Syndicated by UPI.

D76

Walter Clemons, "James Dickey, Novelist," *New York Times Book Review,* 22 March 1970, p. 20.

Interview.

D77

Leonard Sanders, "Poet Dickey Now Novelist," *Fort Worth Star Telegram,* 22 March 1970, p. G7.

Article; quotes Dickey.

D78

Howard Maniloff, "Our Man Dickey's Been Around: Rooted in Georgia, His Fictional Violence Could Happen 'Anywhere,' " *Charlotte Observer,* 29 March 1970, p. F6.

Interview.

D79

Sam Hopkins, "Poet Dickey Coy About Movie Take," *Atlanta Constitution,* 31 March 1970, p. C6.

Article; quotes Dickey.

D80

Cherie Hart-Green, "Pen-Manship," *Women's Wear Daily,* 9 April 1970, p. 44.

Interview.

D81

Gene Shalit, "The Book Shelf," *Cleveland Press Showtime,* 10 April 1970, p. 16.

Column item; quotes Dickey.

D82

Hollie I. West, "Author Hits 'McCarthyism,' " *Washington Post,* 17 April 1970, p. C9.

Article; quotes Philip M. Stern, Art Buchwald, and Dickey.

D83

" 'Everyone's Notion of a Poet,' " *Time,* 95 (20 April 1970), 92.

Article; quotes Dickey.

D84

"Enduring or Endangering? Pornography in Print Is Questioned: Six Authors Have Answers," *Richmond News Leader,* 28 April 1970, p. 14.

Article; quotes Dickey.

D85

Pat Bryant, "Poet Discusses His First Novel," *Richmond Times-Dispatch,* 28 April 1970, p. A8.

Interview.

D 86

Anne Ball, "Pale or Glowing? Word Portrait's Intensity Must Vary, 5 Writers Say," *Richmond News Leader,* 29 April 1970, p. 35.

Article; quotes Dickey.

D 87

Betty Parker Ashton, "Authors Discuss Sex, Violence," *Richmond Times-Dispatch,* 29 April 1970, p. A10.

Article; quotes Dickey.

D 88

Maurice Duke, "Book and Author Dinner Speakers Gave Richmonders Rare Evening," *Richmond Times-Dispatch,* 3 May 1970, p. P5.

Article; quotes Dickey.

D 89

John Barkham, "Poet Hits Jackpot with First Novel," *Newport News Daily Press New Dominion Magazine,* 24 May 1970, p. 17.

Interview. Syndicated.

D 90

Rob Wood, "Dickey: Novel May Be Last: 'Poetry Is Best Language,' " *Charleston News and Courier,* 31 May 1970, p. A14.

Interview. Syndicated by AP. Also noted under various titles in *Durham [N.C.] Morning Herald,* 31 May 1970; *The State,* 3 June 1970; *The Morning Call* [Allentown, Pa.], 4 June 1970; *Pensacola News-Journal,* 7 June 1970.

D 91

L. E., "Dickey Best Seller Resulted After Poet Was Victim of Urge," *Durham Morning Herald,* 14 June 1970, p. D5.

Review of *Deliverance;* quotes Dickey.

D 92

Charles Fellenbaum, "Dickey Delivers," *The Gamecock,* 17 June 1970, pp. 1, 5.

Interview.

D 93

"Catch Up With . . . James Dickey," *Mademoiselle,* 71 (July 1970), 22.

Review of *Deliverance;* quotes Dickey.

D 94

Henry Raymont, "3 Book Clubs Pick Paul Horgan Novel," *New York Times,* 31 July 1970, sec. 12, p. 1.

Article; quotes Dickey.

D 95

"Esquire Names Dickey Its 1st Poetry Editor," *The State,* 3 December 1970, p. B5.

Article; quotes Dickey.

D 96

Harold T. P. Hayes, "Editor's Note," *Esquire,* 75 (January 1971), 8, 162.

Column item; quotes Dickey.

D 97

Licia Drinnon, "Dickey Addresses Graduation, Receives Honorary Degree," *Times and Challenge* [Wesleyan College, Macon, Ga.], 14 January 1971, pp. 1, 8.

Article; quotes Dickey.

D 98

John Logue, "James Dickey Describes His Life and Works as He 'Moves Toward Hercules,' " *Southern Living,* 6 (February 1971), 44–49, 60, 65.

Interview. Collected in *The Voiced Connections of James Dickey.*

D 99

"Wesleyan Creates an Experience," *Atlanta Constitution,* 15 February 1971, p. A6.

Article; quotes Dickey.

D 100

Lynda Norton, "Just for 'Spite,'" *Charleston Evening Post,* 19 March 1971, p. D1.

Interview with Maxine Dickey; quotes James Dickey.

D 101

Margaret W. Garrett, "Artists on Campus Preserve Freedom," *Charleston Evening Post,* 19 March 1971, p. B1.

Article; quotes Dickey.

D 102

Jack Leland, "James Dickey: Credibility Is Good," *Charleston Evening Post,* 19 March 1971, p. B1.

Interview.

D 103

Robert P. Stockton, "Dickey: 'The Poet Sells It Like It Is,'" *Charleston News and Courier,* 19 March 1971, p. B1.

Interview.

D 104

"201st Founder's Day Held," *Charleston News and Courier,* 20 March 1971, p. B1.

Article; quotes Dickey.

D 105

"Dickey: Provide Encounters Between Artist, Layman," *The State,* 20 March 1971, A9.

Article; quotes Dickey.

D 106

"Dickey Says Art 'Personal Discovery,'" *Columbia Record,* 20 March 1971, p. A5.

Article; quotes Dickey.

D 107

"Wide Poetry Variety His Aim," *Phoenix Republic,* 4 April 1971, p. N9.

Article; quotes Dickey.

D 108

Chris Shearouse, "Poet in N.O.: Dickey's Trouble Is NOT Writing," *New Orleans States-Item,* 23 April 1971, p. 12.

Interview.

D 109

Geoffrey Norman, "The Stuff of Poetry," *Playboy,* 18 (May 1971), 148–149, 230, 232, 234, 236, 238, 240, 242.

Article; quotes Dickey.

D 110

"Dickey Is Awarded Honorary Degree at Wesleyan's 132nd Commencement," *Wesleyan College Now,* 1 (June 1971), [3].

Article; quotes Dickey.

D 111

"Two S.C. Authors Draw Crowd Here," *The State,* 19 June 1971, p. B3.

Article; quotes Dickey.

D 111a

William D. McDonald, "Poet James Dickey Goes Hollywood," *The State,* 27 June 1971, pp. E1, E9.

Interview.

D 112

Sara Lindau, "James Dickey to Appear on Buckley Firing Line," *Wilmington [N.C.] News,* 23 August 1971.

Article; quotes Dickey.

D 113

"Buckley's Firing Line: Dickey Voices Views on U.S. Spirit," *Columbia Record,* 25 August 1971, p. A4.

Article; quotes Dickey.

D 114

Phil Casey, "Massive Magicman," *Washington Post*, 20 November 1971, p. E1.

Interview.

D 115

"Poet Dickey Wins Award for Novel," *The State*, 30 November 1971, p. B1.

Article; quotes Dickey. Syndicated by UPI.

D 116

Albin Krebs, "Notes on People," *New York Times*, 1 December 1971, sec. 1, p. 53.

Column item; quotes Dickey.

D 117

Caroline Cross, "James Dickey," *Broken Ink*, 2, no. 2 (1972), 37–40.

Interview.

D 118

Gabriel Moore, "Conversation with James Dickey," *New South*, 27 (Winter 1972), 66–70.

Interview.

D 119

Tom Burke, "Conversation with, um, Jon Voight," *Esquire*, 77 (January 1972), 116–119, 150, 155–158.

Article; quotes Dickey.

D 120

"4,000 in South Carolina Charmed by Yevtushenko," *New York Times*, 26 January 1972, p. 30.

Article; quotes Dickey.

D 120a

Bob Craft, "Standing Ovation Given Russian Poet," *The Gamecock*, 26 January 1972, pp. 1, 5.

Article; quotes Dickey.

D 121

Michael Putney, "A Russian Writer's Garden Party," *National Observer*, 12 February 1972, p. 6.

Article; quotes Dickey.

D 122

David McClellan, "James Dickey Contemplates Life, Literature in New Book," *Johnson City [Tenn.] Press Chronicle*, 19 February 1972.

Review of *Sorties;* quotes conversation with Dickey.

D 123

Roger Ebert, "What Kind of Playmate Is Burt?" *New York Times*, 26 March 1972, p. D13.

Interview with Burt Reynolds, who briefly quotes Dickey.

D 124

William Packard, "Craft Interview with James Dickey," *New York Quarterly*, no. 10 (Spring 1972), 16–35.

Collected as "In New York" in *Night Hurdling*. See B35.

D 125

Robert Wilson, " 'Writing Becomes Habit of Mind," Dickey Says," *Greenville News*, 9 April 1972, p. A6.

Interview.

D 126

Bill McDonald, "Honorary Members Tapped," *The State*, 17 April 1972, p. B1.

Column item; quotes Dickey.

D 127

John Chancellor and Edwin Newman, moderators, "Why Is the Moon So 'Boring'?" *National Observer*, 11 (6 May 1972), 22.

Excerpts from an NBC television panel discussion with Norman Mailer, Arthur C. Clarke, Alan B. Shepherd, Jr., Chancellor, Newman, and Dickey.

D128

"Being a Celebrity: Taxing but Better than Obscurity," *Florence [S.C.] Morning News,* 21 May 1972, p. D1.

Excerpts from Dickey interview.

D129

Dew James, " 'First Generation Suburban' Looks at Environment," *Florence Morning News,* 21 May 1972, p. D1.

Article; quotes Dickey.

D130

"James Dickey Recites Poetry, Reads Novel," *The Dartmouth,* 26 May 1972, pp. 1, 5.

Article; quotes Dickey.

D131

Phyllis Meras, "James Dickey, Poet, Now Screen Writer-Actor, Talks of New Film," *Martha's Vineyard Gazette,* 28 July 1972, p. A1.

Interview.

D132

" 'The Best People I Have Ever Known, and Also the Worst, Were Poets': A Talk with James Dickey," *Mademoiselle,* 75 (August 1972), 282–283, 417–420.

Interview. Collected as "In Mademoiselle" in *Night Hurdling.*

D133

Phil Thomas, "Dickey a Poet First, Many Things Second," *Houston Post,* 23 August 1972, p. AA12.

Article; quotes Dickey.

D134

N. Michael Niflis, "A Special Kind of Fantasy: James Dickey on the Razor's Edge," *Southwest Review,* 57 (Autumn 1972), 311–317.

Article; quotes conversation with Dickey.

D 135

Tom Parks, "James Dickey Interview: 'I Will Always Have to Go with the Word,'" *Horizon* [South Carolina Council of Teachers of English], October 1972, pp. 2, 16–19.

D 136

Betsy Fancher, "Deliverance from Babel," *Georgia,* 16 (October 1972), 30–32, 47.

Interview.

D 137

Richard Maschal, "The 'Deliverance' of James Dickey: The South's Foremost Living Poet Is Happy with His Movie and Himself," *Charlotte Observer,* 8 October 1972, pp. D1, D4.

Interview. Syndicated by Knight. Also noted under various titles in *Detroit Free Press,* 5 November 1972, and *Miami Herald,* 31 December 1972.

D 138

Jerry LeBlanc, "The Deliverance of James Dickey," *New York Sunday News Magazine,* 29 October 1972, pp. 30–32, 40.

Interview. Distributed by the Sunday Group. Also noted under different titles in *Milwaukee Journal Magazine,* 29 October 1972, and *Chicago Tribune Magazine,* 29 October 1972.

D 138a

"American Poet Ezra Pound Dies," *The State,* 2 November 1972, pp. A1, A7.

Article; quotes Dickey.

D 139

"Short, Rare Appearance May Be His Last: Poet James Dickey Reads at State College," *Worcester [Mass.] Evening Gazette,* 9 November 1972, p. 31.

Article; quotes Dickey.

D 140

"The End of the Great Adventure," *Time,* 100 (18 December 1972), 46–49, 55.

Article; quotes Dickey.

D141

"James Dickey," *Columbia College Criterion* [Columbia, S.C.], Winter 1973, pp. 6–8.

Interview.

D142

William Heyen and Peter Marchant, "A Conversation with James Dickey," *Southern Review*, n.s. 9 (January 1973), 135–156.

Collected as "In Louisiana" in *Night Hurdling*.

D143

Max Kvidera, "Fashion Talks: Poet James Dickey Woos Muse in Blue Jeans," *New York Daily News Record*, 23 January 1973, pp. 1, 18, 20.

Article; quotes Dickey.

D143a

" 'Deliverance' Producers Sued," *The Gamecock*, 1 February 1973, p. 2.

Article; quotes Dickey.

D144

Melanie J. Kennison, "New Banner Interview: James Dickey," *New Banner*, 1 (4 and 18 February 1973), 4–6.

D145

Bill McDonald, " 'Deliverance' Superb," *The State*, 9 February 1973, p. B1.

Column item; quotes Dickey.

D45a

Bill McDonald, "Night Lights," *The State*, 18 February 1973, p. E2.

Column item; quotes Dickey.

D146

Kay Tucker, "The 'Deliverance' Story: He Had Plot in 5 Minutes, Took 8 Years to Do Book," *Charlotte News*, 26 February 1973, p. A1, A3.

Article; quotes Dickey.

D 147

Joe McNulty, "James Dickey: A Portrait of the Artist as a Good Ole Boy,"
Greensboro [N.C.] Daily News Cavalcade, 11 March 1973, pp. D1, D11.

Interview.

D 148

Jack Creech, " 'It's Like a Blind Man in a Dark Room, Hunting a Black Dog . . .
There Is No Answer,' " *Watauga Democrat* [Boone, N.C.], 12 March 1973, pp.
A1, A2.

Article; quotes Dickey.

D 149

"Dickey's Style Distinct During Poetry Reading," *The Gamecock,* 12 April
1973, p. 2.

Article; quotes Dickey.

D 150

Neville Patterson, "Poet Feels Guilt for River Tragedies," *Columbia Record,* 13
April 1973, pp. A9, A10.

Article; quotes Dickey.

D 151

Glenn Helgeland, "James Dickey, The Archer's Author," *Archery World,* 22
(April/May 1973), 34–37.

Interview. Collected in *The Voiced Connections of James Dickey.*

D 152

Laura Chambless, "The Many Faces of James Dickey," *Tampa Tribune-Times,*
13 May 1973, p. C3.

Interview.

D 153

Daryl Stephenson, "Author of Best-Seller Is Festival Lecturer," *Bristol [Va.]
Herald Courier,* 2 August 1973, p. B1.

Interview.

D 154

"Chattooga Death Toll Upsets James Dickey," *Atlanta Constitution*, 14 August 1973, p. B4.

Article; quotes Dickey. Syndicated by AP. Also noted under different title in *The State*, 14 August 1973.

D 155

"Names in the News: Chattooga Deaths Sadden Dickey," *Atlanta Journal*, 14 August 1973, p. B1.

Column item; quotes Dickey.

D 156

Ruth Heimbuecher, "It's Verse for their Health: Poets 'Live in Hell,' Bard Dickey Declares," *Pittsburgh Press*, 4 October 1973, p. 23.

Article; quotes Dickey.

D 157

Donald Miller, "Dickey Talk at Forum Fills House," *Pittsburgh Post-Gazette*, 4 October 1973, p. 8.

Article; quotes Dickey.

D 158

Bunky Flagep, "River Holds Death for Many Who Run It," *Los Angeles Times*, 28 October 1973, sec. 5, pp. 10–12.

Article; quotes Dickey. Syndicated by Knight.

D 159

Geoffrey Norman, "*Playboy* Interview: James Dickey," *Playboy*, 20 (November 1973), 81–82, 86, 89, 92, 94, 212–216.

Collected in *The Voiced Connections of James Dickey*.

D 159a

Marshall Swanson, " 'Big Jim Dickey Is Back in Town,' " *The Gamecock*, 29 November 1973, p. 4.

Article; quotes Dickey.

D 159b

"Reflections on James Dickey," *The Drury Mirror* [Drury College, Springfield, Mo.], 30 November 1973, p. 5.

Article; quotes Dickey.

D 160

Jerry Bledsoe, "What Will Save Us From Boredom?" *Esquire*, 80 (December 1973), 227–233.

Article; quotes Dickey.

D 161

"People, Etc.," *Memphis Commercial Appeal Mid-South Magazine*, 2 December 1973, p. 77.

Column item; quotes Dickey.

D 162

"Who Is Reading What in S.C.?" *The State*, 23 December 1973, p. E4.

Survey. Dickey chose *A Second Flowering* by Malcolm Cowley; *The Foxfire Book;* poems by Robert Penn Warren; and *The Southern Country Cookbook.*

D 163

Robert H. Moore, "The Last Months at Harper's: Willie Morris in Conversation," *Mississippi Review,* 3 (1974), 121–130.

Article; quotes Dickey in footnote.

D 164

Andrew Sabel, "James Dickey: The Man, the Writer," *The Pittsburgher*, First Quarter 1974, pp. 20–24.

Interview.

D 165

David Havird, "Novelist Styron Pays Social Visit," *The Gamecock,* 28 January 1974, pp. 4, 7.

Article; quotes William Styron and Dickey.

D 165a

JDL [John Logue], "Books About the South," *Southern Living,* 9 (February 1974), 184, 186.

Article; quotes Hubert Shuptrine and Dickey.

D 166

Jonathan White, "An Interview with James Dickey: 'Poetry Is the Center of the Creative Wheel for Me,' " *Myrtle Beach [S.C.] Journal American,* 18 February 1974, p. 2.

D 167

Henry Mitchell, "Dickey, Friend of Bears and Byron," *Washington Post Style,* 19 March 1974, pp. B1, B2.

Interview.

D 168

Marcia Kass, "Dickey Captivates, Delights Audience," *The Diamondback* [University of Maryland], 21 March 1974, p. 10.

Article; quotes Dickey.

D 168a

Marcia Kass, "A Two-Fisted Poet," *Argus/Dimension* [University of Maryland], 29 March 1974, p. 3.

Interview.

D 169

"Poetry, Politics, Peonies: Flower Festival Opens," *Anderson [S.C.] Independent,* 26 July 1974, p. A1.

Article; quotes Dickey.

D 170

Jerry Cassidy, "What the Poetry Editor of *Esquire* Is Like: Interview with James Dickey," *Writer's Digest,* 54 (October 1974), 16–20.

D 171

Charlotte Phelan, " 'Jericho' Unusual Joint Effort," *Houston Post,* 4 October 1974, p. D2.

Article; quotes Dickey.

D 172

Bobbie Calhoun, "Sales of Nostalgic 'Jericho' Soaring," *Charlotte Observer,* 18 October 1974, pp. C1, C2.

Article; quotes Dickey.

D 173

Bob Talbert, "Poet, Artist Blend Talents for Major Literary Coup," *Toledo [Ohio] Blade,* 20 October 1974.

Article; quotes Dickey.

D 173a

Ken Webb, "New Book Has Focus on 'Timeless South,' " *The State,* 20 October 1974, p. B10.

Article; quotes Dickey.

D 173b

Monte Basgall, "James Dickey Down Home," *Richmond Times-Dispatch,* 25 October 1974, p. D1.

Article; quotes Dickey.

D 174

Jan Rothleitner, "Dickey Shares Perspective," *The State,* 21 November 1974, p. C3.

Article; quotes Dickey.

D 175

"Poet James Dickey: Now He's the 'Top Cat,' " *National Observer,* 4 December 1974, p. 24.

Interview.

D 176

"Dinner Meeting of the Institute November 20, 1974—*Far Tortuga* A Reading by Peter Matthiessen," *Proceedings of the American Academy and Institute of Arts and Letters*, 2nd ser., no. 25 (1975), 62.

Introduction by Jacques Barzun quotes Dickey.

D 177

"Interview: James Dickey," *Unmuzzled Ox*, 3, no. 2 (1975), 74–85.

Collected in *The Voiced Connections of James Dickey*.

D 178

"Poet Says Columbia Zoo Is a Major Part of Life," *Rock Hill [S.C.] Herald*, 7 January 1975.

Article; quotes Dickey.

D 179

D Ke Wright and Ed Clark, "James Dickey: A Man for All Seasons," *The Lance* [University of South Carolina—Lancaster], 4 (Spring 1975), 8–11.

Interview.

D 180

"USC Poet to Take Leave of Absence," *The Gamecock*, 17 April 1975, pp. 1, 4.

Article; quotes Dickey.

D 181

Jerry Kosicki, "James Dickey Reads Poetry Tonight," *The Carroll News* [John Carroll University], 25 April 1975, p. 3.

Article; quotes Dickey.

D 182

Ann Waldron, "James Dickey Said He Was the Finest Critical Literary Intellect He Ever Met, With a Mind Like a 'Laser Beam,' " *Houston Chronicle Zest*, 1 June 1975, p. 12.

Article; quotes Dickey on Monroe Spears.

D 183

"Neglected Books of the Twentieth Century," *Antaeus*, 18 (Summer 1975), 133–136.

Authors' survey; Dickey chose *The Journal of a Disappointed Man* by W.N.P. Barbellion.

D 184

David L. Arnett, "An Interview with James Dickey," *Contemporary Literature*, 16 (Summer 1975), 286–300.

Collected in *The Voiced Connections of James Dickey*. See B 66.

D 185

P. R. Bellury, "James Dickey," *Buckhead Atlanta*, 18 August 1975, pp. 1, 8.

Article; quotes Dickey.

D 185a

"People," *Time*, 106 (29 September 1975), 46.

Column item; quotes Dickey.

D 186

Dan Gleason, "James Dickey: One Man Who Reached the Top by Telling the Truth," *In the Know*, 1 (December 1975), 34–37.

Interview.

D 187

L. L. Simms, "Interview with James Dickey," *Copula* [San Francisco State University Poetry Center], 1st issue [c. 1976], 41–46.

Collected in *The Voiced Connections of James Dickey*.

D 188

Vince Clemente, "John Hall Wheelock: Poet of Death & Honeysuckle," *Long Pond Review*, January 1976, pp. 10–18.

Article; quotes Dickey.

D 189

Thomas Scheye, "Dickey Poems Arrest Time," *Brooklandville [Md.] News American,* 9 March 1976, p. A9.

Article; quotes Dickey.

D 190

Isaac Rehert, "Dickey Sort of Missed at First, But Then Hit Mark," *Brook-landville [Md.] Sun,* 11 March 1976, p. B1.

Article; quotes Dickey.

D 191

"Trash Will Come—You Have to Take the Chance," *US News and World Report,* 80 (15 March 1976), 55–56.

Interview.

D 192

Michael Wentzel, "James Dickey Pours on the Plain Talk, Turns It Into Art," *Baltimore Evening Sun,* 22 March 1976, p. B1.

Interview.

D 193

Franklin Ashley, "James Dickey: The Art of Poetry XX," *Paris Review,* 17 (Spring 1976), [52–53], 54–88.

Interview and facsimile of typescript page of "Falling." See B 60.

D 194

William W. Starr, "Business World Fascinating to Dickey," *The State,* 12 April 1976, p. B1.

Interview.

D 195

Stephen Cassal, "Robbed Poet Meets Dickey," *Florida Flambeau* [Florida State University], 23 April 1976, p. 5

Article; quotes Dickey.

D 196

Doug Gardner, " 'Deliverance' Author Is 'Hooked' on Film," *Augusta [Ga.] Chronicle,* 5 May 1976.

Interview.

D 197

Cecil Smith, "Poet's TV Version: Dickey Delivers 'Call of the Wild,' " *Los Angeles Times,* 5 May 1976, sec. 4, pp. 1, 22.

Interview. Syndicated. Also noted under different title in *Greenville News,* 22 May 1976.

D 198

Thomas Lask, "Long Poem by Dickey Due in Fall," *New York Times,* 11 June 1976, p. C24.

Article; quotes Dickey.

D 199

Robert L. King, "Y'all Dassn't Judge a Man by the Southrin Way He Talks," *Cherry Hill [N.J.] Courier-Post,* 8 July 1976, pp. 1, 6.

Article; quotes Dickey.

D 200

Merry Bateman, "Poet in Residence: James Dickey Returns," *The Gamecock,* 16 September 1976, p. 3.

Interview.

D 201

Dottie Ashley, " 'Zodiac' Puts James Dickey Back in Literary Spotlight," *Columbia Record,* 30 September 1976, p. B6.

Interview.

D 202

Carole Ashkinaze, "What's Your Secret Desire?" *Atlanta Journal and Constitution,* 23 October 1976, p. B6.

Article; quotes Dickey.

D 203

William W. Starr, "Assignment: Books," *The State,* 14 November 1976.

Column item; quotes Dickey.

D 204

Bill Collins, "South Doomed, Dickey Tells Reporters at HPC," *Winston-Salem Journal,* 19 November 1976, p. 13.

Article; quotes Dickey.

D 205

"People in the News: The South Is the Future, Says USC's James Dickey," *Aiken [S.C.] Standard,* 19 November 1976, p. 3.

Column item; quotes Dickey.

D 206

Dottie Ashley, "Dickey the Robert Frost of Carter Administration?" *Columbia Record,* 6 December 1976, p. A1.

Article; quotes Dickey.

D 207

"Dickey Expects Carter Bid to Read Inaugural Poetry," *Atlanta Journal,* 7 December 1976, p. A3.

Article; quotes Dickey. Syndicated by UPI. Also noted under different title in *The State,* 8 December 1976.

D 208

Nan Robertson, "How Writers Navigate Their Sea of Books," *New York Times,* 27 December 1976, p. C10.

Article; quotes Dickey.

D 209

William W. Starr, "Dickey Says Marriage to Open 'A New Life,' " *The State,* 31 December 1976, p. B1.

Interview.

D210

Dottie Ashley, "Writer Seemed Nervous at Wedding," *Columbia Record,* 31 December 1976, p. 2.

Article; quotes Dickey.

D211

"James Dickey Marries Former Student," *Chattanooga News-Free Press,* 31 December 1976.

Article; quotes Dickey.

D212

"Dickey to Preview His Inaugural Poem," *Myrtle Beach [S.C.] Sun-News,* 14 January 1977.

Article; quotes Dickey.

D213

Franklin Ashley, "Happy: For Newly Widowed Poet James Dickey, Deliverance Is a Bride Named Debbie," *People,* 7 (17 January 1977), [28, 30].

Article; quotes Dickey.

D214

Donna Landry, "A Deliverance for Carter," *Washington Post,* 19 January 1977, pp. B1, B3.

Interview. Syndicated. Also noted under various titles in *Raleigh [N.C.] Times,* 20 January 1977, and *The State,* 20 January 1977.

D215

Celestine Sibley, "Capital Tidies Up, Chips Ice as Dickey Recites," *Atlanta Constitution,* 20 January 1977, p. A9.

Article; quotes Dickey.

D216

Jane Shealy and Mark J. Lundgren, "Mr. Dickey Goes to Washington," *The Gamecock,* 20 January 1977, p. 3.

Interview.

D 217

Peter Behr, "Carter Will Draw Strength from Fields of Home, Southern Poet-Friend Says," *Baltimore Sun,* 21 January 1977, p. A6.

Interview.

D 218

Roger Simon, "Jimbo Dickey Now Unofficial Laureate," *New Orleans Times-Picayune,* 21 January 1977, sec. 1, p. 15.

Article; quotes Dickey.

D 219

Pete Axthelm, "A Voice of the South," *Newsweek,* 89 (31 January 1977), 25.

Article; quotes Dickey.

D 220

Samuel Moon Hudson, "Dickey Delivers His Poetry, Debbie Runs Interference," *Dallas Times Herald,* 7 February 1977, pp. C1, C4.

Interview.

D 221

"Poet Predicts Southern Customs Will Gain National Acceptance," *The Daily Texan* [University of Texas, Austin], 24 March 1977, p. 2.

Interview.

D 222

George Christian, "Lord, Jimbo! James Dickey and the Expansive Imagination," *Houston Chronicle,* 27 March 1977, p. 12.

Interview.

D 223

Jim Townsend, "Dickey," *Charlotte,* 9 (March/April 1977), 22–24.

Interview. Collected in *The Voiced Connections of James Dickey.*

D 224

"David McCullough's Eye on Books," *Book-of-the-Month-Club News,* Special Spring 1977, pp. 6, 24, 26.

Interviews with Christopher Isherwood, Marshall Efron and Alfa-Betty Olsen, and Dickey. See B 54.

D 225

W. C. Barnwell, "James Dickey on Yeats: An Interview," *Southern Review,* 13 (Spring 1977), 311–316.

Collected in *The Voiced Connections of James Dickey.*

D 226

Dan Frazier, "Dickey Discusses Southern Tradition," *Fort Worth Star Telegram,* 28 April 1977, p. B1.

Interview.

D 227

Laura Egbert, "Writer Ruled by Words," *The Daily Skiff* [Texas Christian University], 29 April 1977, p. 1.

Article; quotes Dickey.

D 228

Clare Colquitt, "James Dickey, 'First a Poet,' Will Take a Whirl at Diplomacy," *TCU Monthly,* 8 (May 1977).

Article; quotes Dickey.

D 229

Blaine Harden, "The Top Cat and Big Deal Among Poets," *Washington Sunday Times Advertiser,* 8 May 1977, pp. E1, E4.

Interview.

D 230

Maralyn Lois Polak, "James Dickey: 'Have a Beer with Your Soul,' " *Philadelphia Inquirer,* 19 June 1977, pp. 7–8.

Interview. See B 80.

D 231

Phil Patton, "Interview: James Dickey," *Sky,* 6 (July 1977), 26–27, 42, 44–45.

D 232

"The Southern Ideal: Anybody but Farrah," *Atlanta Constitution*, 3 August 1977, p. B3.

Article; quotes Dickey.

D 233

William W. Starr, "Declarations from Dickey," *The State*, 28 August 1977, pp. E1, E2.

Interview.

D 234

William W. Starr, "A 'Great, Tragic, Caring Poet,' " *The State*, 14 September 1977, p. A3.

Article; quotes Dickey on death of Robert Lowell.

D 235

Joseph Cuomo, "An Interview with James Dickey," *A Shout in the Street*, no. 3 (Fall 1977), 9–12.

D 236

Young Dawkins, "James Dickey and the Heavenly Music," *Hilton Head [S.C.] Quarterly*, 1 (Fall 1977), 8–12.

Interview.

D 237

Diana Loercher, "Georgia Poet Who Cast Carter as a Mythical Hero," *Christian Science Monitor*, 5 October 1977, p. 19.

Interview. Syndicated. Also noted under different titles in *Hickory [N.C.] Daily Record*, 12 October 1977 and *Washington Post*, 19 October 1977.

D 238

Dolly Darr, "James Dickey: Always the Poet," *Spartanburg [S.C.] Herald-Journal*, 5 November 1977, p. B1.

Interview.

D 239

Elizabeth Cleland, " 'Poet's Role Is Eternal,' Dickey Says," *Washington Star,* 24 November 1977, pp. A1, A25.

Interview.

D 239a

"Dickey Presents Book of Poetry to Mrs. Carter," *The State,* 24 November 1977, p. B12.

Article; quotes Dickey. Syndicated by UPI.

D 240

Caroline Harkleroad, "James Dickey: A Poet—First, Last, and Always," *The Atlantan,* 26 November 1977, p. 16.

Article; quotes Dickey.

D 241

"James Dickey Initiated," *Pi Kappa Alpha Newsletter* [Vanderbilt University Sigma Chapter], 2, no. 1 (1978), 1.

Article; quotes Dickey.

D 242

Rachelle Delaney, "Words—Music: Poet Dickey Doesn't Know Which Has Been More Important to Him," *Florida Times-Union/Jacksonville Journal,* 19 February 1978, pp. I1, I7.

Interview.

D 243

"Dickey Fans Crowd Finale," *Sherman [Tex.] Democrat,* 1 March 1978, sec. 1, p. 12.

Article; quotes Dickey.

D 244

Jasmine McGee, "Eccentric Poet Wears Four Watches on the Same Arm," *Sherman Democrat,* 5 March 1978, sec. 3, p. 3.

Article; quotes Dickey.

D245

Coyte White, "Audience Captivated by Dickey," *Myrtle Beach Sun-News,* 11 March 1978, pp. A1, A2.

Article; quotes Dickey.

D246

Geoffrey Himes, "I Think Continually of Those Who Were Truly Great," *Columbia [Md.] Flier,* 16 March 1978, p. 50.

Article; quotes Dickey.

D247

Leslie Laurence, "Dickey: No Red-Hot Flashes of Genius," *Jacksonville [Fla.] Journal,* 24 March 1978, p. 15.

Interview.

D248

Twyla Dell, "Dickey, Gardner: 'Impromptu Trialogue,'" *Broadside* [George Mason University], 27 March 1978, pp. 15–16.

Article; quotes John Gardner and Dickey.

D248a

Grace Zibart, "Will the South Lose Its Flavor?" *Vanderbilt Today* [Vanderbilt University], April 1978, pp. 3–4.

Article; quotes Dickey.

D249

Leslie Laurence, "Colorful Banners, Poet James Dickey Opens Arts Festival," *Jacksonville Journal,* 7 April 1978, p. 22.

Article; quotes Dickey.

D250

Ann Hyman, "Poet Has 'Triangular Eyes,'" *Florida Times-Union* [Jacksonville], 7 April 1978, pp. A1, A19.

Interview.

D 251

Douglas Swanson, "James Dickey: Holding Forth as a Southerner," *Sun Herald* [Biloxi, Gulfport, Ocean Springs, Pascagoula, Miss.], 16 April 1978, p. A2.

Interview.

D 252

"James Dickey at Work on Guitar Book," *Bruccoli Clark News*, 1 (May 1978), 3.

Article; quotes Dickey.

D 253

"Manuscript Edition of Dickey's *Zodiac*," *Bruccoli Clark News*, 1 (May 1978), 3.

Article; quotes Dickey.

D 254

Blaine Harden, "A Sun Day Beginning: Songs, Dance at Dawn," *Washington Post*, 4 May 1978, pp. C1, C4.

Article; quotes Dickey.

D 255

Roxanne Bilyeu, "Teaching at George Mason University: James Dickey Brings Deliverance to Campus," *The Globe* [George Mason University], 11 May 1978, pp. 15, 19.

Article; quotes Dickey.

D 256

W. G. Neville III, "Dickey: Southern Reflections," *Statesboro [Ga.] Herald*, 26 May 1978.

Interview.

D 257

Caroline Bernd, "James Dickey: Man of Many Talents Wants to Be Remembered as Poet," *Savannah Morning News*, 26 May 1978, p. C1.

Article; quotes Dickey.

D 258

Mike Norris, "Dickey Laments Decline in Students' Writing," *Newport News Daily Press,* 19 September 1978.

Article; quotes Dickey.

D 259

Earl Turner, "An Interview with . . . James Dickey," *Vetletter* [University of South Carolina], 2 (October 1978), 2.

Collected in *The Voiced Connections of James Dickey.*

D 260

Jane Shealy, "A Southerner Preoccupied with Time," *Carolina Reporter* [University of South Carolina], 12 October 1978, p. 12.

Interview.

D 261

Sandra Greenberg, "Looking for That Impossible Image: An Interview with James Dickey," *Subject to Change* [Washington University], 5 (26 October 1978), 21, 31.

D 262

Jon Anderson, "Poetry's Survival Kit Filled by Friends at Dinner, Auction," *Chicago Tribune,* 25 November 1978, sec. 1, p. 15.

Article; quotes Dickey.

D 263

William W. Starr, "Assignment Books," *The State,* 10 December 1978, p. E4.

Column item; quotes Dickey.

D 264

USC News [University of South Carolina], 26 January 1979, pp. 1–4.

Article on USC Visiting Writers Series; quotes Dickey.

D 265

Peggy Friedmann and Betty Bedell, "A Conversation with James Dickey," *Kalliope,* 1 (February 1979), 30–35.

Collected in *The Voiced Connections of James Dickey*.

D 266

"Writers to Share Talents at USC," *The State*, 4 February 1979, pp. E1, E2.
Article; quotes Dickey.

D 267

William W. Starr, "Literary Giant Allen Tate Dies," *The State*, 10 February
1979, p. A15.
Article; quotes Dickey.

D 268

William W. Starr, "Optimism Is Reflected in Poet's Life, Writing," *The State*, 1
March 1979, p. B18.
Interview with Richard Wilbur; quotes Dickey.

D 269

Mark Chevalier, "Wilbur Electrifies Crowd," *The Gamecock*, 2 March 1979,
p. 11.
Article; quotes Richard Wilbur and Dickey.

D 270

Elizabeth Slater, "Dickey Sustains Suspense at Norwich Film Discussion,"
Barre-Montpelier [Vt.] Times Argus, 21 April 1979, p. 9.
Article; quotes Dickey.

D 271

Roger Mann, " 'Deliverance' Writer a Production in Himself," *Burlington [Vt.]
Free Press*, 25 April 1979, pp. D1, D6.
Interview.

D 272

Eddie Sue Judy, "Spectre of 'Deliverance' Still Haunts Dickey," *Lewiston [Id.]
Morning Tribune*, 27 April 1979, p. A17.
Interview.

D 273

"Dickey on Pound: Influential, but Not the Greatest," *Lewiston Morning Tribune,* 29 April 1979.

Article; quotes Dickey.

D 274

"Angler's Art Defined in Dickey's 'Piscine Reverie,' " *Bruccoli Clark News,* 1 (May 1979), 3.

Article; quotes Dickey.

D 275

"USC Honors Poet," *Columbia Record,* 16 May 1979, p. B7.

Article; quotes Dickey.

D 276

Robert Kirsch, "Reviews: Evil of Necessity," *Los Angeles Times,* 28 May 1979, sec. 4, pp. 1, 13.

Article; quotes Dickey.

D 276a

"He Was Very Nice, Easy-Going," *The State,* 13 June 1979, p. D5.

Article; quotes Dickey on John Wayne.

D 277

Michiko Kakutani, "Publishing: Maas, Dickey, and Gill," *New York Times* [late edition], 21 September 1979, p. C23.

Article; quotes Dickey.

D 278

William W. Starr, "James Dickey," *The State Magazine,* 23 September 1979, pp. 10–11.

Interview.

D 279

Rhonda Owens, "James Dickey Keeps Flame of Romanticism Alive," *Arkansas Democrat* [Little Rock], 8 October 1979, p. B3.

Article; quotes Dickey.

D 280

Mike Trimble, "Dickey at UALR: A Poet Talks About 'Glorious Drudgery,'"
Arkansas Gazette [Little Rock], 14 October 1979, pp. F1, F15.

Interview.

D 281

"Dickey Displays His Down-to-Earth Personality," *Forum* [University of Arkansas, Little Rock], 15 October 1979, p. 7.

Article; quotes Dickey.

D 282

Sheldon Kelly, "James Dickey—'Poet of Survival and Hope,'" *Reader's Digest*,
115 (November 1979), 112–115.

Article; quotes Dickey.

D 283

Sid Stapleton, "James Dickey: Impressions of a Life in Progress," *Southern
World*, 1 (November/December 1979), 24–26.

Interview.

D 283a

Chris Tucker, "An Interview with James Dickey," *Lone Star Book Review*, 1
(December 1979), 5, 25.

D 284

Dean Honeycutt, "A Legendary Poet: Dickey, Like His Writing, Is Real," *The
Breeze* [James Madison University], 4 December 1979, p. 12.

Interview.

D 285

Ron McFarland, "An Interview with James Dickey," *Slackwater Review*, 3
(Winter 1979–1980), 17–33.

Collected in *The Voiced Connections of James Dickey*.

D 286

Skip Eisiminger, "A Year With James Dickey," *Pembroke Magazine,* no. 12 (1980), 161–166.

Article; quotes Dickey.

D 287

George Redman, "James Dickey: The Teacher Beheld," *Spectator Magazine,* 1 (Winter 1980), 24–27, 45.

Article; quotes Dickey.

D 288

L. M. Rosenberg, "James Dickey: Experiments with Language," *Chicago Tribune Book World,* 27 January 1980, pp. 1, 4.

Review of *Strength of Fields;* quotes Dickey.

D 289

Ann Marie Matonak, "Pilgrimage," *Talon* [United States Air Force Academy], 25 (February 1980), 23.

Article; briefly quotes Dickey.

D 290

Michelle Green, "Southern Laureate of Literature," *Atlanta Constitution,* 18 February 1980, pp. B1, B3.

Interview.

D 291

Joe Cumming, Jr., "If There Is No New Dickey, We Will Have to Invent Him," *Atlanta Journal and Constitution,* 2 March 1980, p. E5.

Article; quotes Dickey.

D 292

William W. Starr, "James Dickey Gets Air Force Tribute," *The State,* 10 March 1980, p. B16.

Article; quotes Dickey.

D 293

Will Lester, "James Dickey's Poetry, Wit: Reading Has Something for Every-one," *Columbia Record,* 13 March 1980, p. B2.

Article; quotes Dickey.

D 294

William W. Starr, "Assignment Books," *The State Magazine,* 30 March 1980, p. 10.

Article; quotes Dickey.

D 295

Robert M. Eich, "What Do the Famous Folk Do?" *Easy Living,* 7 (Spring 1980), 3–5.

Article; quotes Dickey.

D 295a

"Transition," *Newsweek,* 95 (7 April 1980), 74.

Column item; quotes Dickey on the death of James Wright.

D 296

John O. Meekins, "Writer James Dickey Meets an Old Friend Here," *Columbus [Ga.] Citizen-Journal,* 28 April 1980.

Article; quotes Dickey.

D 297

Frank Zoretich, "Dickey's Seattle 'Deliverance,' " *Seattle Post-Intelligencer,* 22 June 1980, p. F10.

Interview.

D 298

Bruce Joel Hillman, "The Hunter in Poetry," *Country Gentleman,* 130 (Summer 1980), 28–31.

Interview.

D 299

Jim Tharpe, "James Dickey: His 'Deliverance' Turned into an Industry—One That Threatens a River He Admires," *Greenville News,* 7 August 1980, pp. A1, A10.

Interview.

D 300

Dave Precht, "Why James Dickey Plays the Game," *Southern Outdoors,* 28 (September 1980), 92–93.

Interview.

D 301

Anna Stewart, "Party: Styron, Updike, Bacall and Mailer Join in a Romp at Roseland," *People,* 14 (10 November 1980), 144, 147.

Article; briefly quotes Dickey.

D 301a

William Childress, "A Visit with James Dickey," *St. Louis Post-Dispatch,* 4 December 1980, pp. G1, G3.

Interview.

D 302

Bruce Joel Hillman, "The Voices of James Dickey," *Writer's Yearbook 1981,* 52 (1981), 28–33.

Interview. Collected as "At Home: The Voices of James Dickey" in *Night Hurdling.*

D 303

Bill Meyers, "From McCann-Erickson to America's Poet Laureate," *Adweek,* January 1981, pp. 10–11.

Interview.

D 304

David Morrison, "The Wilderness of Heaven," *Atlanta Weekly,* 1 February 1981, pp. 10–13, 17, 22–23.

Article; quotes Dickey.

D 305

Nell Williams, "Poetry Domineering Force in James Dickey's Works," *Oxford Eagle* [University of Mississippi], 16 February 1981, p. 10.

Interview.

D 306

Betty Price, "James Dickey Exudes a Southern-Soft Manner: 'Deliverance' Author Prefers Dixie's Casualness," *Fort Myers [Fla.] News-Press,* 26 March 1981, p. D1.

Interview.

D 307

"Poetry of James Dickey Stuns, Amuses and Haunts Rosse Hall Audience," *Kenyon College Alumni Review,* Spring 1981, p. 1.

Article; quotes Dickey.

D 308

Christopher S. Smith, "Dickey Enthralls 300 with Poems, Tales," *The Chronicle* [Duke University], 7 April 1981, pp. 1, 6.

Article; quotes Dickey.

D 309

Ed Hodges, "Discipline Required: Poet James Dickey Has Advice for Young Writers," *Durham Morning Herald,* 12 April 1981, p. D3.

Interview.

D 310

Diane Norman, "James Dickey—Poet," *Beaufort [S.C.] Gazette Lowcountry Leisure,* 1 May 1981, pp. 6–7.

Article; quotes Dickey.

D 311

Herbert Mitgang, "Writers Go Public, for Love Rather Than Lucre," *New York Times,* 27 May 1981, p. C20.

Article; quotes Dickey.

D312

Deb Richardson-Moore, "Dickey Cues Pupils in on Love of Poetry," *Greenville News,* 25 July 1981, p. A7.

Interview.

D313

Paul Christensen, "Ritual Magic: An Interview with James Dickey," *Lone Star Review,* 3 (July/August 1981), 3–4.

Collected as "In Texas" in *Night Hurdling.*

D314

Dannye Romine, "Bad Boy Writer Provides More Pastry, Less Puff," *Charlotte Observer,* 2 August 1981, pp. E1, E6.

Article; quotes Dickey.

D315

Rosanna Hall, "James Dickey Calls Bynner an Interesting Man," *Santa Fe New Mexican,* 9 August 1981, p. D1.

Interview.

D316

Tom Jacobs, " 'Subterranean Audience for It': Poet Dickey Has the Prestige But Lacks Pretension," *Albuquerque Journal,* 16 August 1981, pp. D1, D3.

Interview.

D317

Peter Eichstaedt, "Dickey Drawls Poetry, Draws Laughs," *Santa Fe New Mexican,* 24 August 1981, pp. A1, A9.

Article; quotes Dickey.

D318

Minda McGonagle, "Poetry Key to Private 'Self,' " *Santa Fe New Mexican,* 23 August 1981, p. A2.

Interview.

D319

Wally Gordon, "First Person," *Albuquerque Journal,* 25 August 1981, p. B1.

Column item; quotes Dickey.

D320

Bruce Woodford, "A Lot of Dickey and a Little Bynner," *Santa Fe Reporter,* 27 August 1981, pp. 25, 28.

Article; quotes Dickey.

D321

Peter O'Boyle, III, "Incognito: Movie Star Slips Quietly In, Out of Town— Almost," *The State,* 18 September 1981, pp. C1, C6.

Article on Robert Redford; quotes Dickey.

D322

Jim Jenkins, "Gentle Soul, Dickey Charms with Poetry," *Greensboro [N.C.] Daily News,* 17 October 1981, p. A14.

Article; quotes Dickey.

D323

Eric Ries, "The Predatory Writer: Novelist, Poet James Dickey Stalks the Southern Experience," *High Point [N.C.] Enterprise,* 18 October 1981, p. C12.

Article; quotes Dickey.

D324

Bill McDonald, "Trivia Quiz," *The State,* 1 November 1981, p. E1.

Column item; quotes Dickey.

D325

Michael Blowen, "James Dickey Starts a New Chapter," *Boston Globe Magazine,* 13 December 1981, pp. 12–13, 46, 50–51, 65.

Interview.

D326

Mark Dolan, "James Dickey: The Poet Is Trying to Shake His Adventurer-

Writer Image," *Florida Times-Union/Jacksonville Journal*, 27 December 1981, p. G6.

Interview.

D327

Cynthia Thompson, "Rapidly Changing Technology Affecting Man's Psychology," *Press and Banner and Abbeville [S.C.] Medium*, 30 December 1981.

Article; quotes Dickey. Released through University of South Carolina News Bureau. Also noted under various titles in *Greer [S.C.] Citizen*, 30 December 1981; *Gaffney [S.C.] Ledger*, 31 December 1981; *Columbia [S.C.] Star Reporter*, 7 January 1982.

D328

William W. Starr, " 'One Last Word' on 'Deliverance,' " *The State*, 24 January 1982, p. B10.

Interview.

D329

Pat LaMee, "Resident Artists Anticipate 'Explosion' of Ideas," *Little Sentinel* [Orlando, Fla.?], 11 February 1982, p. 4.

Article; quotes Dickey.

D330

Dan Casale, "ACA Artists Outline Goals of May Residency: 'Slow Release Genius,' " *Pelican* [Orlando, Fla.?], 14 February 1982, p. 8.

Article; quotes Dickey.

D330a

William W. Starr, "Dickey Praises Warren's Poetry," *The State*, 28 February 1982, p. C13.

Article; quotes Dickey.

D331

Ed Montini, "James Dickey: Carolina Poet Makes Contact with Writings," *Arizona Republic*, 11 April 1982, pp. F1, F2.

Interview.

D332

Rick Nichols, "James Dickey, Major Poet and Man of Gusto," *Philadelphia Inquirer,* 16 April 1982, pp. D1, D3.

Interview.

D333

Michele Ross, "Dickey: The Atlanta-Born Poet Wants People to Read His Work and Judge Him by That, Nothing Else," *Atlanta Journal Lifestyle,* 27 April 1982, pp. B1, B5.

Interview.

D334

Terry Roberts, "Getting to the Gold: James Dickey," *Arts Journal,* 7 (May 1982), 12–14.

Interview. Collected as "In North Carolina" in *Night Hurdling.*

D335

L. Elisabeth Beattie, "James Dickey Rides Again," *Carolina Lifestyle,* 1 (May 1982), 42–46.

Interview. Collected in *The Voiced Connections of James Dickey.*

D336

Sara Roen, "Dickey Tells About Turning His Outrageous Ideas into Poetry," *Little Sentinel* [Orlando, Fla?], 9 May 1982, p. 8.

Article; quotes Dickey.

D337

Ed Hayes, "James Dickey, Always the Poet," *Orlando Sentinel,* 15 May 1982, pp. F1, F10.

Interview.

D338

James Cervantes, "A Conversation with James Dickey," *Scottsdale [Ariz.] Progress Sunday Magazine,* 15 May 1982, p. 5.

Interview.

D339

Dannye Romine, "What Some Carolina Writers Are Reading," *Charlotte Observer*, 22 August 1982, p. F6.

Boxed short articles; quotes Dickey's choices of *Testimonies* by Patrick O'Brien; poetry by John Montague and Mary Oliver; *Byron in Italy* and *Alexander Pope: The Education of a Genius* by Peter Quennell; *Collected Essays of George Orwell;* and Leon Edel's 5-volume biography of Henry James.

D340

Dolly Langdon, "James Dickey's Wife, Deborah, Says Deliverance Is Escape from Her Poet Husband's Shadow," *People,* 18 (30 August 1982), 37–38, 41.

Article; quotes Dickey.

D341

Leslie Bennetts, "Singing and Dancing Debuts, of Sorts," *New York Times,* 14 October 1982, p. C18.

Article; quotes Dickey.

D342

Hank Nuwer, "James Dickey: Still Going for Broke," *Dynamic Years,* November–December 1982, pp. 56, 58–60.

Interview.

D343

Deirdre Donavan, "Dickey: Into the Soul of a Writer, Poet," *Georgetown [S.C.] Times,* 4 November 1982, p. B3.

Interview.

D343a

Margaret Corvini, "Women Have 'What' as Good as Men," *The State,* 1 December 1982, p. B1.

Article; quotes Dickey.

D343b

"Who's Gonna Win Today? Some Columbia Folks Make Their Choices," *The State,* 30 January 1983, p. C2.

Column item; quotes Dickey's Super Bowl prediction.

D344

Dannye Romine, "Honoring, Analyzing, Dissecting, Inspecting James Dickey at 60," *Charlotte Observer,* 13 February 1983, pp. F1, F7.

Article; quotes Dickey.

D345

Lanette Causey, "James Dickey: A Conversation with the Poet," *Denton [Tex.] Record-Chronicle,* 28 February 1983, p. A10.

Interview.

D346

William Mullen, "Altered States of America: Why Drug Use Is Growing," *Chicago Tribune,* 13 March 1983, sec. 2, pp. 1–2.

Article; quotes Dickey.

D347

Laura Haynes, "James Dickey: Poet Finds Sports Pages Memorable," *Orange [Tex.] Leader,* 20 March 1983, pp. D1, D3.

Interview.

D348

Don Belt, "Chattooga River Country: Wild Water, Proud People," *National Geographic,* 163 (April 1983), 458–476.

Article; quotes Dickey.

D349

Eve Oakley, "James Dickey: Mixing Poetry with a Yen for Action," *Fayetteville [Ark.] Observer,* 18 April 1983, p. A7.

Interview.

D350

Jim Files, "Dickey Goes for Broke," *TWN** [Glenwood Springs, Colo.], 20 July 1983, p. 24.

Article; quotes Dickey.

D351

Anita H. Rosenau, "Author of 'Deliverance' Shares Talent," *Snowmass Sun* [Snowmass Village, Colo.], 29 July 1983, p. 19.

Article; quotes Dickey.

D352

Leslie Bates, "Recovering the Cosmos: Poet James Dickey at 60," *City Paper* [Washington, D.C.], 3 (28 October–3 November 1983), 1, 7, 9.

Interview. Collected in *The Voiced Connections of James Dickey*.

D353

Foxy Gwynne, "Something Foxy: James Dickey, Poet Laureate, in Westchester," *Bedford/Lewisboro [N.Y.] Ledger,* 9 November 1983.

Article; quotes Dickey.

D354

John Monk, "In Search of a Palmetto Poet: Job of Poet Laureate Is Vacant, Waiting in South Carolina," *Charlotte Observer,* 31 December 1983, pp. A1, A4.

Article; quotes Dickey.

D355

William W. Starr, "Committee Goes in Search of . . . A Poet Laureate," *The State,* 18 January 1984, p. B1

Article; quotes Dickey.

D356

Thomas Fox, "James Dickey: On the Road," *Memphis Commercial Appeal,* 18 March 1984, p. H3.

Interview.

D357

David Pryor, "Dickey Visits ASC: Daughter Inspired Poet's Latest Work," *Decatur [Ala.] Daily,* 24 March 1984, pp. 1, 3.

Interview.

D358

Darlene Keeton, "Dickey, Huie Talk of 'Literary Art' at ASC." *Athens [Ala.] News Courier*, 25 March 1984, p. A3.

Article; quotes William Bradford Huie and Dickey.

D359

"Canoeing Isn't Like Movie, Dickey Says," *The State*, 25 March 1984, p. C4.

Article; quotes Dickey.

D360

Karen Middleton, "The Writing Life—Authors Dickey and Huie Talk of 'Loneliest' Struggle," *Huntsville [Ala.] Times*, 26 March 1984, p. B6.

Article; quotes William Bradford Huie and Dickey.

D360a

Chris Handal, "Dickey, Kuhne Partnership Merges Photos, Poems," *The Gamecock*, 28 March 1984, p. 8.

Article; quotes Sharon Anglin Kuhne and Dickey.

D361

Bettye Givens, "Interview with James Dickey," *Texas Review*, 5 (Spring/Summer 1984), 73–85.

Collected in *The Voiced Connections of James Dickey*.

D362

Phil Ward, "A Man Dressed Like Burt Reynolds," *Baton Rouge Advocate Sunday Magazine*, 1 April 1984, pp. 7–8.

Interview.

D363

Angie Struck, "Delivery: Versatile Poet Mixes Humor with Readings," *College Heights Herald* [Western Kentucky University], 3 April 1984, p. 9.

Article; quotes Dickey.

D364

Barry Bearak, "Some Verse, Some Worse," *Los Angeles Times,* 16 April 1984, pp. 1, 8, 9.

Article; quotes Dickey.

D365

Charles Israel, "S.C.'s Poet Laureate," *The State Magazine,* 23 September 1984, pp. 8–10.

Article; quotes Dickey on Ennis Rees.

D366

Jane Oppy, "James Dickey Headlines Writers at Brookstone Fair," *Columbus [Ga.] Ledger and Enquirer,* 23 September 1984.

Article; quotes Dickey.

D367

William Page, "River City Interview with James Dickey," *Memphis State Review,* 5 (Fall 1984), 30–39.

Collected in *The Voiced Connections of James Dickey.*

D368

Steve Crowley, "A Day with Dickey: Special Deliverance," *Cougar Courier* [Brookstone School, Columbus, Ga.], 3 October 1984, p. 1.

Interview.

D369

Jane Oppy, "Author James Dickey Delights Audience with His Readings," *Columbus [Ga.] Enquirer,* 5 October 1984, p. A10.

Article; quotes Dickey.

D370

Paul Marks, "Dickey Charms 'em Here: Scatters Humor But Makes Point," *Rome [Ga.] News-Tribune,* 17 January 1985, p. A1.

Article; quotes Dickey.

D371

Bob Basil, "Poet Shares Works, Insights," *Stanford [University] Daily,* 12 February 1985, pp. 1, 10.

Article; quotes Dickey.

D372

Steven Walburn, "An Afternooon of the Poet: James Dickey Writes the Mighty Line," *Goodlife,* March 1985, pp. 40–42.

Interview.

D373

Don O'Briant, "Dickey Comes Home to Draw New Strength," *Atlanta Constitution,* 16 May 1985, p. B1.

Article; quotes Dickey.

D374

Don O'Briant, "Writers Come Home to Roots," *Atlanta Constitution,* 20 May 1985, pp. B1, B4.

Article; quotes John Oliver Killens, Harry Crews, Olive Ann Burns, and Dickey.

D375

Sam Hodges, "Poet James Dickey Gets High Grades from His Students," *Tampa Tribune-Times,* 2 June 1985, pp. G1, G4.

Article; quotes Dickey. Syndicated by UPI. Also noted under various titles in *Raleigh [N.C.] News and Observer,* 2 June 1985; *Columbia Record,* 3 June 1985; *Christianburg [Va.] News Messenger,* 9 June 1985; and *International Herald Tribune,* 10 June 1985.

D376

"I Like . . . The Most Creative Zoo Anywhere . . . Columbia's," *B-106 Presents Columbia's Favorites,* Summer 1985, p. 4.

Survey; quotes Dickey.

D377

William W. Starr, "Summer Reading," *The State,* 28 July 1985, p. B5.

Article; quotes Dickey.

D 378

"Appalachia: Myth and Reality: A Panel Discussion," *James Dickey Newsletter*, 2 (Fall 1985), 11–16.

Panel discussion among Boyd Lewis, Paul Hemphill, Terry Kay, Floyd C. Watkins, and Dickey.

D 379

Hank Nuwer, "James Dickey: Limitations and Infinities," *Rendezvous*, 21 (Fall 1985), 43–54.

Interview. Collected in *The Voiced Connections of James Dickey*.

D 380

Andy Duncan, "James Dickey Previews New Book for Audience of Students, Faculty," *The Gamecock*, 2 October 1985, p. 8.

Article; quotes Dickey.

D 381

Jason Karlawish, "Interview: James Dickey," *Northwestern [University] Review*, 11 October 1985, pp. 1, 6, 9.

D 382

William W. Starr, "Dickey's New Novel in Editors' Hands," *The State*, 13 October 1985, p. F7.

Article; quotes Dickey.

D 383

"Disaster in Space," excerpt from *CBS News Special Report* (25 January 1986). Single sheet, xerographic copy.

Includes Dan Rather's "paraphrase" of Dickey's statement on the *Challenger* explosion.

D 384

"A Writer's Desk," *Saturday Review*, 12 (January/February 1986), 69.

Article; quotes Dickey.

D385

Don O'Briant, "The Poet as Older Visionary," *Atlanta Constitution,* 28 February 1986, pp. C1, C2.

Article; quotes Dickey.

D386

David Gillespie and Tom Landess, "Dickey on the South," *Southern Partisan,* 6 (Spring 1986), 23–29.

Interview.

D387

Georgia Dullea, "Having a Good Read: There's No Place like Home," *New York Times,* 10 April 1986, pp. C1, C6.

Article; quotes Dickey. Also noted under different title in *Columbia Record* (21 April 1986).

D388

John Branston, "James Dickey: On 'Deliverance,' Burt Reynolds, Tennis and . . . ," *Memphis Commercial Appeal Mid-South Magazine,* 13 April 1986, pp. 14–15.

Interview.

D389

Abby Ellis, "Dickey Probes and Explores the Depth of Imagination," *Rocky Mountain News* [Evening Edition], 16 April 1986, p. 19.

Interview.

D390

Bill Husted, "Prolific Poet Sees Craft as Highest Form," *Rocky Mountain News,* 18 April 1986, p. 96.

Interview.

D390a

Gracie Chapman, "Time Loves Ben Greer," *The State Magazine,* 20 April 1986, pp. 8–10.

Article; quotes Dickey.

D391

Alan Katz, "Humor Abounds in Violent Evening," *Denver Post,* 23 April 1986, p. C1.

Article; quotes Dickey.

D392

Margaret Carlin, "Poet Dickey Lures Listeners with Mood, Dialect," *Rocky Mountain News,* 23 April 1986, p. 54.

Article; quotes Dickey.

D393

Alan Katz, "James Dickey Tells Poets They Must Take Risks: This Hulk of a Man Isn't a Bit Hesitant to Embellish His Rough-and-Ready Image," *Denver Post,* 27 April 1986, p. 22.

Interview.

D394

Chris Handal, "Talking with James Dickey: A Man of Perpetual Possibilities," *Rock Hill Herald,* 18 May 1986, p. B9.

Interview.

D395

Anne E. Hartung, "Authors Academy Hails S.C. Writers," *Anderson [S.C.] Independent-Mail,* 18 June 1986, p. B1.

Article; quotes Dickey.

D396

"Poet to Be First Living Author Honored by Writer's Academy," *Columbia Record,* 19 June 1986, p. A15.

Article; quotes Dickey.

D397

Anne E. Hartung, "Dickey Plays 'Metaphysical Scrabble Game,'" *Anderson Independent-Mail,* 29 June 1986, pp. A1, A2.

Interview.

D 398

"Dickey's Out of Hospital, 'Doing Well,' " *Columbia Record,* 8 July 1986, p. B7.

Article; quotes Dickey.

D 399

Dannye Romine, "Summer Reading: Area Novelists Try It All," *Charlotte Observer,* 3 August 1986, pp. F1, F13.

Article; reports choices of Dickey and 12 other writers. Dickey's list includes *A Journal of the Plague Year* by Daniel Defoe; *The White Devil* and *The Duchess of Malfi* by John Webster; letters and diaries of Virginia Woolf; and poetry by Betty Adcock.

D 400

Pat Dickey, "Poetry: The Love and Work of James Dickey," *Creative Loafing* [Atlanta], 23 August 1986, pp. B5, B7.

Article; quotes Dickey.

D 401

Keith Graham, "James Dickey and His Muse Are Back in Form," *Atlanta Constitution,* 26 August 1986, pp. D1, D19.

Article; quotes Dickey.

D 402

Anne Kennedy, "Images: Writer-Poet James Dickey Spreads His Words and Ideas in Roswell," *Roswell [Ga.] Neighbor,* 27 August 1986, p. B1.

Article; quotes Dickey.

D 403

Kathryn Jeffries, "USC Professor Autographs New Book," *The Gamecock,* 24 September 1986, p. 6.

Article; quotes Dickey.

D 404

Mike Shepard, "Dickey Took Difficult Path to Writing Fame," *Albany [Ga.] Herald,* 21 October 1986, p. A5.

Interview. Slightly revised as "Poetry Dickey's Favorite Form of Writing," *Albany Herald,* 22 October 1986.

D405

[Roger Bryant], "The Road Back," *Columbia Record,* 1 October 1986, pp. C1, C3.

Interview. Syndicated by AP. Also noted under various titles and credited or uncredited to Bryant in *The State,* 5 October 1986; *Charleston News and Courier/Charleston Evening Post,* 5 October 1986; *Athens [Ga.] Banner-Herald/Daily News,* 5 October 1986; *Dallas Morning News,* 26 October 1986; and *San Diego Union,* 15 December 1986.

D406

William W. Starr, "USC Symposium on Writer Jarrell Quite Successful," *The State,* 12 October 1986, p. F6.

Article; quotes Dickey.

D407

Leslie Bennetts, "Old Names, Young Readers," *New York Times Book Review,* 14 December 1986, p. 28.

Article; quotes Dickey.

D408

Susan Steck, "Famous Writers," *Insignia* [Spring Valley High School, Columbia, S.C.], 1 (1987), 19.

Interview.

D409

"Pages '87," *People,* 27 (5 January 1987), 60.

Column item; quotes Dickey.

D410

Mark Dolan, "Poet, Novelist James Dickey Puts Final Touches on 36-Year Project," *Florida Times-Union/Jacksonville Journal,* 25 January 1987, pp. E1, E5.

Interview.

D411

Gordon Van Ness, "A Different Kind of Deliverance," *The State Magazine,* 25 January 1987, pp. 8–11.

Interview.

D412

Beth Hill, "Teaching Beth to Write a Novel," *Carolinian* [University of South Carolina], March 1987, p. 4.

Article; quotes Dickey.

D413

Nan Robertson, "Parnassus-on-Potomac: Poets Change a Capital," *New York Times* [late edition], 31 March 1987, p. C13.

Article; quotes Dickey.

D414

Gordon Van Ness, "Living Beyond Recall: An Interview with James Dickey," *James Dickey Newsletter,* 3 (Spring 1987), 17–26.

Collected in *The Voiced Connections of James Dickey.*

D415

Michael Hirsley, "On Wings of Words," *Chicago Tribune Sunday,* 10 May 1987, pp. 9–10, 12–15, 29.

Interview.

D416

William W. Starr, "Alnilam: James Dickey's Novel Explores Father and Son Relationships," *The State,* 17 May 1987, pp. F1, F10.

Article; quotes Dickey. Collected in *The Voiced Connections of James Dickey.*

D417

Charles Trueheart, "James Dickey's Celestial Navigations," *Washington Post,* 24 May 1987, pp. F1, F6, F7.

Interview. Also noted under different title in *Detroit News,* 28 June 1987.

D418

Sam Staggs, "*PW* Interviews: James Dickey," *Publishers Weekly,* 231 (29 May 1987), 62–63.

Interview.

D419

Charles E. Claffey, "James Dickey: Writing, Risking, Soaring," *Boston Globe,* 16 June 1987, pp. 69–70.

Interview; first part.

D420

Charles E. Claffey, "The Poet in Control," *Boston Globe,* 17 June 1987, pp. 77, 79.

Interview; second part.

D421

R. Z. Sheppard, "Into the Wild, Mystical Yonder," *Time,* 129 (29 June 1987), 71.

Review of *Alnilam;* quotes Dickey.

D422

Charlotte Buak and Gwen Thomas, "Literary Poker," *Pencil Press Quarterly,* 1 (Summer 1987), 4, 6–7.

Interview.

D423

James Wolcott, "Big Daddy," *Vanity Fair,* 50 (July 1987), 24, 26.

Interview.

D424

Katherine Stephen, "17 Years After 'Deliverance,' Dickey Reaches to the Stars," *Los Angeles Times,* 9 July 1987, sec. 5, pp. 1, 15.

Interview.

D425

Bob Gingher, "James Dickey Talks About Story Behind 'Alnilam,' " *Greensboro [N.C.] News & Record,* 19 July 1987, p. E5.

Interview. Collected in *The Voiced Connections of James Dickey.*

D426

"In the South, We Know All of Our Cousins," *USA Today,* 28 August 1987, p. A9.

Interview.

D 426a

Dannye Romine, "James Dickey Shares His 'Creative Variety,'" *Charlotte Observer*, 25 October 1987, p. B4.

Article; quotes Dickey.

D 427

Dottie Ashley, "Dickey Honored: USC's Poet-in-Residence Elected to Academy of Arts and Letters," *The State*, 4 December 1987, p. A16.

Article; quotes Dickey.

D 428

"James Dickey: Named to Elite Arts Academy," *Columbia Record*, 18 December 1987, p. A20.

Editorial; quotes Dickey.

D 429

Susan Buchanan, "Poet-in-Residence Gets WIS-TV Award," *The Gamecock*, 10 February 1988, pp. 1, 2.

Article; quotes Dickey.

D 430

Ken Autrey, "James Dickey's American Poetry Course: A Recollection," *James Dickey Newsletter*, 4 (Spring 1988), 2–8.

Article; quotes Dickey.

D 431

Dorothy Sutton, "On the Trail of the 'Real' James Dickey," *James Dickey Newsletter*, 4 (Spring 1988), 21–24.

Article; quotes Dickey.

D 432

W. Stevens Ricks, "James Dickey to Share His Insights on Writer Flannery O'Connor," *Atlanta Journal and Constitution* (24 April 1988), p. H2.

Interview.

D433

Wayne Holmes, Joseph Costello, Mark Greenberg, and Randy McConnell, "James Dickey at Drury College," *James Dickey Newsletter,* 5 (Fall 1988), 16–25.

Interview. Collected in *The Voiced Connections of James Dickey.*

D434

"Poet James Dickey Inducted into Academy of Arts and Letters," *Carolinian,* September 1988, p. 15.

Article; quotes Dickey.

D435

William D. Starr, "Writers Connected at Charleston Meet," *The State,* 18 September 1988, p. F5.

Article; quotes Dickey.

D436

"Renaissance of Southern Literature Topic of Carolina Writers' Meeting," *The Gamecock,* 19 September 1988, p. 3.

Article; quotes Dickey. Syndicated by AP.

UNLOCATED CLIPPINGS

D437

"Poet Dickey's Insight," a Milwaukee newspaper (c. 1964).

Article; quotes Dickey.

D438

Carolyn Fisher, "Poet's Gift Is Evident," *Atlanta Times Magazine Sunday South* (c. Summer 1964), p. 10.

Article; quotes Dickey.

D439

Walker Lundy, "Prize-Winning Poet Didn't Believe News," probably an Atlanta newspaper (c. March 1966).

Article; quotes Dickey.

D 440

Susan Ross, "National Book Award Winner Dickey Holds Residence Position at Carolina," *The Gamecock* (c. January 1969).

Article; quotes Dickey.

D 441

Adger Brown, "Phrases Don't 'Make' Novels: Dickey, USC's Poet-In-Residence, Submits Draft of First Novel," *The State* (c. January 1970).

Interview.

D 442

Bill C. Little, "Man About . . . One Man's View," *Peoria Journal Star* (c. August 1972).

Column item; quotes Dickey's response to a letter from Little.

D 443

Phil Pruitt, "Reading Caps Cultural Coup at University," *Columbia Record* (c. 1973), pp. A1, A10.

Article; quotes Dickey.

D 444

"Storm King Names Four to Board of Visitors," Cornwall-on-Hudson, N.Y., newspaper, 10 January 1973.

Article; quotes Dickey.

D 445

Helen C. Smith, " 'Fought War' to Prevent This," probably an Atlanta newspaper (c. November 1973).

Article; quotes Dickey.

D 446

Robert Hefner, " 'Buckhead Boy' Will Return with Words for Tasting Wine," *North Side News* [Atlanta] (c. Summer 1974).

Interview.

D 447

" 'The Zodiac' on Sale," *The State* (c. mid-November 1976).

Column item; quotes Dickey.

D448

John Roberts, "South Pays Price for Its Success," *Greensboro [N.C.] Record* (c. 19 November 1976), pp. B1, B2.

Article; quotes Dickey.

D449

Perry Flippin, "Once Nearly Seized as Obscene, Movie Packs 'em In," *Sherman Democrat* (c. 28 November 1978).

Article; quotes Dickey.

D450

Cathy Lint, "James Dickey Visits Campus, Reads from His Best Work," probably William & Mary student newspaper (c. 19 September 1978).

Article; quotes Dickey.

D451

William Childress, "The Bard of Lake Katherine" (May 1982).

Interview.

D452

Dave White, "Gritty, Witty Poet Brags on His South," *Birmingham [Ala.] News* (c. 1983).

Interview.

D453

Molly Read, "James Dickey: 'Invent Is the Magic Word,' " probably an Atlanta newspaper (c. 1984).

Article; quotes Dickey.

D454

Ginger Lundy, "Dickey: 'Poetry Center of Everything,' " *Spartanburg Herald-Journal* (c. October 1986), pp. B6–B7.

Interview.

E. Later Collections of Poems

All of the poems in these volumes appeared in previous Dickey collections.

E 1 THE ACHIEVEMENT OF JAMES DICKEY
1968

THE ACHIEVEMENT OF JAMES DICKEY | A COMPREHENSIVE SELEC-
TION OF HIS POEMS WITH A CRITICAL INTRODUCTION | LAURENCE
LIEBERMAN | University of Illinois | SCOTT, FORESMAN AND COMPANY

1968. Wrappers. P. 86: '1 . . . 68'.

  24 poems: "The Heaven of Animals," "The String," "The Jewel," "The Performance," "The Lifeguard," "In the Tree House at Night," "The Hospital Window," "The Dusk of Horses," "Springer Mountain," "Cherrylog Road," "In the
Marble Quarry," "The Ice Skin," "Bums, On Waking," "Drinking from a Helmet," "The Firebombing," "The Shark's Parlor," "Pursuit from Under," "The
Fiend," "The Sheep Child," "Sun," "Power and Light," "Encounter in the Cage
Country," "False Youth: Winter," "Falling." All previously published.

E 2 POEMS
1968

James | Dickey | POEMS

Melbourne, Australia: Sun Books, 1968. Wrappers.

  17 poems: "The Performance," "Walking on Water," "Into the Stone," "The
Salt Marsh," "In the Mountain Tent," "Cherrylog Road," "The Scarred Girl,"
"The Poisoned Man," "The Ice Skin," "Approaching Prayer," "Slave Quarters,"
"The Sheep Child," "Snakebite," "A Letter," "Deer Among Cattle," "The Leap,"
"Falling." All previously published. Locations: JRB; MJB; ScU.

E 3 THE EARLY MOTION
1981

[all within frame of decorations and double rules] THE | EARLY | MOTION |
Drowning with Others | and | *Helmets* | James Dickey | *Wesleyan University
Press* | MIDDLETOWN, CONNECTICUT

373

1981. Cloth and wrappers. Copyright page: 'First edition'.

Previously unpublished "Preface" by Dickey, pp. vii–ix.

60 poems. Reprints entire contents of *Drowning With Others* and *Helmets*.

E 4 FALLING . . .
1981

JAMES DICKEY | FALLING, | MAY DAY | SERMON, | and | Other | Poems | [shield] WESLEYAN UNIVERSITY PRESS | *Middletown, Connecticut*

1981. Cloth and wrappers. Copyright page: 'First edition'.

Previously unpublished "Preface" by Dickey, pp. vii–viii.

25 poems previously published in *Poems 1957–1967*: "Falling," "The Sheep Child," "Reincarnation (II)," "Sun," "Power and Light," "The Flash," "Adultery," "Hedge Life," "Snakebite," "Bread," "Sustainment," "A Letter," "The Head-Aim," "Dark Ones," "Encounter in the Cage Country," "For the Last Wolverine," "The Bee," "Mary Sheffield," "Deer Among Cattle," "The Leap," "Coming Back to America," "The Birthday Dream," "False Youth: Two Seasons" ("False Youth: Summer," "False Youth: Winter"), "May Day Sermon to the Women of Gilmer County, Georgia, by a Woman Preacher Leaving the Baptist Church."

E 5 THE CENTRAL MOTION
1983

The | Central | Motion | POEMS, | 1968–1979 | James Dickey | [shield] Wesleyan University Press | Middletown, Connecticut

1983. Cloth and wrappers. Copyright page: 'First Edition, Wesleyan Poetry | First Wesleyan Paperback Edition, Wesleyan Poetry'.

Previously unpublished "Preface" by Dickey, pp. vi–vii.

46 poems. Reprints entire contents of *The Eye-Beaters* . . . , *The Zodiac*, and *The Strength of Fields*.

E 6 INTERVISIONS
1983

[medium brown script] Intervisions | Poems and Photographs | James Dickey and Sharon Anglin Kuhne | [medium brown roman] Foreword by Betty Adcock | [decoration] | VISUALTERNATIVES | PENLAND, NORTH CAROLINA

1983. 3,000 copies.

10 poems: "Walking on Water," "The Being," "Awaiting the Swimmer," "Springer Mountain," "The Flash," "Dust," "The Ice Skin," "False Youth: Two Seasons (Winter)," "The Underground Stream," "Dark Ones." All previously published.

Note: A poster (24″ × 18″) distributed to advertise this book reprints "The Underground Stream."

Appendices / Index

Appendix 1

Compilers' Notes

1. An unidentified clipping from an Atlanta magazine has a childhood photo of Dickey with his brief Christmas memories.

2. A xerographic transcription of the 1983 National Public Radio *Sunday Show* interview with Dickey by Connie Goldman was privately circulated. See C 319.

3. A xerographic letter by Dickey commending a Columbia, S.C., production of Marsha Norman's *'night Mother* was distributed to the University of South Carolina Department of English, 28 August 1985.

4. During 1956–1961 Dickey was employed by the following advertising agencies: McCann-Erickson, 1956–1958, senior writer (Coca-Cola account); Liller, Neal, Battle, and Lindsay, 1958–1960, copy chief (Armour Fertilizer and Lay's Potato Chips accounts); Burke Dowling Adams, 1961, creative director (C&S Bank and Delta Airlines accounts).

5. Proof for "The Greatest American Poet": 10½" × 13". 10 leaves printed on rectos only. Probably intended for prepublication circulation. Location: ScU.

6. *The Biblical Etchings of Marvin Hayes. A Catalog of the Exhibition* (Birmingham, Ala.: Oxmoor House, [1976]). Includes foreword by Dickey. Wrappers. Not seen.

Appendix 2

Major Works About Dickey

Ashley, Franklin B. *James Dickey: A Checklist*. Columbia, S.C., & Detroit: Bruccoli Clark/Gale Research, 1972. Primary.

Baughman, Ronald. "James Dickey," *Contemporary Authors Bibliographical Series, Volume 2: American Poets,* ed. Baughman (Detroit: Gale Research/ Bruccoli Clark, 1986), pp. 71–105. Primary and secondary bibliography, with essay describing and evaluating important secondary sources.

————. *Understanding James Dickey*. Columbia: University of South Carolina Press, 1985.

Bowers, Neal. *James Dickey: The Poet as Pitchman*. Columbia: University of Missouri Press, 1985.

Calhoun, Richard J., and Robert W. Hill. *James Dickey*. Boston: Twayne, 1983.

Calhoun, Richard J., ed. *James Dickey: The Expansive Imagination: A Collection of Critical Essays*. De Land, Fla.: Everett/Edwards, 1973.

De La Fuente, Patricia, ed. *James Dickey: Splintered Sunlight: Interview, Essays, and Bibliography*. Living Author Series no. 2. Edinburg, Tex.: Pan American University, 1979.

Elledge, Jim. *James Dickey: A Bibliography, 1947–1974*. Metuchen, N.J., & London: Scarecrow Press, 1979. Primary and secondary.

————. "James Dickey: A Supplementary Bibliography, 1975–1980: Part I," *Bulletin of Bibliography*, 38 (April–June 1981), 92–100, 104. Primary and secondary.

————. "James Dickey: A Supplementary Bibliography, 1975–1980: Part II," *Bulletin of Bibliography,* 38 (July–September 1981), 150–155. Secondary.

Glancy, Eileen K. *James Dickey: The Critic as Poet: An Annotated Bibliography with an Introductory Essay*. Troy, N.Y.: Whitston, 1971. Primary and secondary.

James Dickey Newsletter, ed. Joyce M. Pair. Dunwoody, Ga.: DeKalb College, Fall 1984–   . Includes a continuing primary and secondary bibliography by Robert C. Covel.

Kirschten, Robert. *James Dickey and the Gentle Ecstasy of Earth*. Baton Rouge: Louisiana State University Press, 1988.

Lieberman, Laurence. *The Achievement of James Dickey: A Comprehensive Selection of His Poems with a Critical Introduction*. Glenview, Ill.: Scott, Foresman, 1968.

South Carolina Review, 10 (April 1978). Dickey issue.

Weigl, Bruce, and T. R. Hummer, eds. *The Imagination as Glory: The Poetry of James Dickey*. Urbana & Chicago: University of Illinois Press, 1984. Critical essays.

Wright, Stuart T. *James Dickey: A Bibliography of His Books, Pamphlets, and Broadsides*. Dallas, Tex.: Pressworks, 1982. Primary.

Index

383

Pittsburgh Series in Bibliography